AFTER WE DIE, WHAT THEN?

This book forever *rends the veil* between Earth and what has been called heaven or paradise, by *opening the door* on the development of what may be man's *ultimate electronic communication system.*

It is far from being fantasy or science fiction. Actually, its report of findings from sixteen years of world-wide interdisciplinary research into the basic nature of man correlates with the emerging projections of *quantum physics.* And it provides, *as no other book has ever done,* confirmation that the *individual mind, memory banks, personality and soul* survive death and the disintegration of the physical body. It shows why the reader *cannot* die, *even by suicide or atomic holocaust.*

The original manuscript was submitted for critical review to a panel of twenty-two ministers, scientists, priests, physicians, rabbis, educators and psychiatrists from Winnipeg to Capetown and from Tokyo to Zurich. Their unqualified endorsements have been confirmed by many thousands of readers. Translations of the first edition have been well-received in Japan, South America and India.

Although confirming the validity of the world's great religions, it does not preach any new gospel, dogma, creed, religion or "ism." It is as scientifically accurate as is possible at this stage of man's evolution.

Perhaps its greatest contribution is to show why and how the life we live TODAY determines the *quality* of life we each will live AFTER we "die."

The book is written in simple and easy-to-understand language. It uses 42 pictures and diagrams to make it possible to treat this complex and mind-expanding subject in less than 200 pages.

Other Books by George W. Meek:

From Seance to Science, 1972

From Enigma to Science, 1973

Healers and the Healing Process, 1977

Collapse and Comeback, 1979

As We See It From Here, 1980

The Spiricom Technical Manual, 1982

The Magic of Living Forever, 1982

Books About George W. Meek:

The Ghost of 29 Megacycles, by John G. Fuller, 1985

This book does not attempt to preach any new gospel, dogma, creed, religion or "ism." It does not attempt to convert you to the concepts it discusses. If any portions ring true to your "still, small inner voice," fine. If not, reject them!

New Expanded Edition

AFTER WE DIE, WHAT THEN?

Evidence You Will Live Forever!

by George W. Meek

A METASCIENCE BOOK

ARIEL PRESS
Columbus, Ohio

TABLE OF CONTENTS

IV. Specific Questions and Specific Answers

V. The Certainty of Living Forever

Appendices

LIST OF ILLUSTRATIONS

ACKNOWLEDGEMENTS

It would not have been possible to assemble the information presented here without the cooperation of four of the outstanding telepathic channels I have discovered during a sixteen-year global search for such rare talent: Sarah Gran Heironymus, Shirley Shultz, Patricia Ann Faxon, and R.B., who asks to remain anonymous.

Each of the following, in his or her own way, has contributed to the sixteen years of research on which this book is based:

Gilbert Anderson
Hernani Andrade
Raymond Bayless
Itzhak Bentov
William and Maria Brown
Hana Bushbeck
Ken Carey
Willard Cerney
Trevor James Constable
Grace and Ivan Cooke
Robert Crookall
Joaquin Cunanan
Bruce Dapkey
Harry Edwards
Jule Eisenbud
David Ellis
Sarah Estep
Leslie Flint
JoAnn Floyd
Jerry Gross
Bertha Harris
Robert Jeffries
Anna Jeffries
David and Ann Jevons
Paul Jones
Friedrich Jurgensen
Shafica Karagulla
Robert Kesselring
Hans Otto Konig
Robert Laidlaw
Peter Leggett
Robert R. Leichtman, M.D.
Lawrence LeShan
Judy Luckwell
Henry and Mary Mandel

Marcus and Marika McCausland
Lucille McNames
Robert N. Miller
Dennis Milner
Pat Mitchell
Raymond Moody
Carl Munters
Henry and Diane Nagorka
Mary Alice O'Neil
Leslie Price
Constantine Raudive
Marilyn and John Rossner
Theodor Rudolph
Lillian Scott
Mary Scott
Franz Seidl
Sigrun Seutemann
Ernst Senkowski
Richard Sheargold
Harold and Martha Sherman
Donald Shultz
George Singer
Ted Smart
Alfred Stelter
Mary Swainson
Attila von Szalay
William Tiller
Paul Trovillo
Norbert Unger
Walter and Mary Jo Uphoff
Mary Van Meer
Robert Ward
William A. Welch
Ruth White
Olga and Amborse Worrall

(The individuals just listed may or may not agree with all opinions and concepts expressed in this book.)

The following persons in seven countries read the preliminary manuscript and made valuable suggestions and criticisms:

Margaret Hamilton Bach	Rev. Robert E. Miller
Joaquin Cunanan	Dr. Dennis Milner
Rabbi Simon Friedman	Dr. Hiroshi Motoyama
Glen Forrester Hamilton, M.D.	Hans Naegeli-Osjord, M.D.
Hans Heckmann	Father Neff
H.T.E. Hertzberg	Leslie Price
Dr. Robert Jeffries	Jeanne Rindge
Dr. D.M.A. Leggett	Don and Shirley Shultz
Robert R. Leichtman, M.D.	Sir Kelvin Spencer
M.C.F. Leisher	Rev. T.N. Tiemeyer
Albert Mevi	Hazel Topps

Special thanks are due John White for extensive editorial suggestions and to Jorge Rizzini for permission to use the materialization photographs in Chapter 11.

My research colleague William J. O'Neil deserves the primary credit for the historical breakthrough reported in Chapters 15 and 16. History may show his accomplishment has done as much to rend the veil between this life and the afterlife as any event in the last 2,000 years.

The many years of hard and frustrating work of Erland Babcock and Hans Heckmann are bringing us even closer to the goal of interference-free, two-way instrumental communication with dwellers on the mental-causal-celestial planes of consciousness.

And of course, this book would never have come into being without the 52 years of loving and capable collaboration of Jeannette D. Meek.

DEDICATION

This book is lovingly dedicated to
these *Earth-plane* dwellers:

prophets,
sages,
holy men,
mystics,
mediums,
telepathic channels,
electronic technicians,
scientists, and

all enlightened dwellers
on higher planes of consciousness

who collectively helped to construct the
composite picture of life-without-end
as presented in this book.

AFTER WE DIE, WHAT THEN?

What This Book Is About

All of us, regardless of education, race, sex, color, or creed, and regardless of wealth or social status, have three things in common:

We have survived the birth process;

We are now alive;

We will die.

Each of us is traveling a road which has a funeral at its end. We cannot help shying away from the very thought of what must come, if we are honest with ourselves. We must find satisfying answers to such questions as:

*Is death **really** the end?*

After doing my best to struggle through this life, am I blotted out forever, as materialists say?

Do I lose my personal identity and become some formless non-entity, absorbed in a great unconscious?

Can I believe the Biblical and accumulated religious lore about life after death?

Will I, and my body, lie in a cold dark grave until some far-off and uncertain judgment day?

Is there truth about purgatory, and about a hell with fire and brimstone?

Is all this talk about a loving and compassionate God just utter nonsense?

Why hasn't my minister, priest or rabbi answered these questions for me?

I was born with an inquiring mind and am a natural skeptic. I have spent more than half a century trying to resolve the enigma of life and afterlife. Quite frankly, most of what I read and what I was told was either conflicting or just didn't "make sense." It just didn't "add up."

So I took my quest to the far corners of the globe, making inquiry of the wisest ones I could find in any country to which I traveled. I pressed deeply into independent research, engaging the help of trained investigators. Finally I gave up a professional career to spend the remainder of my life, if need be, in the focused endeavor to find convincing answers and to put them into a comprehensive pattern which would resolve these uncertainties. I wanted answers to questions that have *plagued all thinking persons since man became the thinking creature he is.*

Sixteen years have been spent in self-financed, intensive travel to most parts of the globe. I sought and found kindred souls in twenty countries—medical doctors, psychiatrists, physicists, biochemists, psychologists, hypnotherapists, physiologists, psychics, healers, parapsychologists, ministers, priests and rabbis. And gradually, as the years slipped by, I *found* the answers I sought.

Fortunately, in just the last twenty-five years we have learned more about the life we will be living *after* we shed our physical bodies, than was known *in all of the earlier periods of recorded history!*

Our research resulted in the building of an instrumental system of communication which permitted more than twenty hours of conversation with persons who died and were buried but who are today *still alive and able to tell us fascinating details of life after death.*

This book is the first to provide details on developments which will have a profound effects on civilization as did the invention of the telegraph, telephone, radio, television, the first airplane or the project that launched mankind into outer space.

It is written in simple language. It makes use of a question-and-answer format and easily understood diagrams and photographs to convey its message.

George Meek

PART ONE

Am I Both Caterpillar and Butterfly?

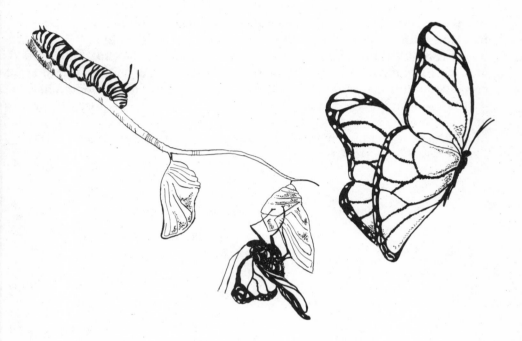

Does doubt within him rise and grow,
As he spins his cocoon?
Is this the end of all he knows?
Has darkness come too soon?
Does he cry out to God in fear
Of losing all he holds most dear?
"Lord, why must I become as dust,
and leave the world I love and trust?
Ah, my Creator, now I see:
It's this cocoon which sets me free!"
　　　　　—*Joyce M. Fox*

We are all familiar with the seeming magic depicted in the drawing on the previous page, where a wet, squishy caterpillar spins himself a burial robe and later emerges into a new world as a beautiful, colorful and vibrantly alive butterfly. This sounds like sheer magic, and is, but I assure you that in creating you, the Master Magician has perfected his "tricks" still more. In *your* case, you will shed your wet, squishy body and, eliminating the step shown here as the chrysalis, emerge *immediately* into a new world with your mind, your memory banks and your personality intact.

CHAPTER 1

Not Back to School

In writing this book, I have set for myself a most difficult task. I want to show you why it is not possible for you to die, even if you commit suicide or are a victim of an atomic holocaust.

I want to answer the dozens of questions you have about what happens *after* you leave your physical body—about what can be a glorious or a distressing experience.

I want to answer questions which are unanswered—and probably not even considered—by books you read in school or the reading you have done in the Bible, the Talmud, the Koran or other holy books.

In fact, I want to answer questions for which you would not find answers today in the best scientific libraries.

I want to share knowledge with you that will be the subject of more exhaustive treatment in books not yet written—books available ten to twenty years from now.

So it is obvious that this material could not be obtained by going *back* to school, nor—as present matters stand—by further study of the so-called hard sciences. In the pages which follow we are going far beyond the current restrictions of chemistry, physics, microbiology, neurophysiology, brain research, psychiatry and the findings of our best medical internists.

Skilled surgeons have been dissecting the body and brain for the last 150 years. No dissection has located the "spirit" or "soul." No surgeon has been able to isolate the *mind* from the brain, to throw light on the question of survival of the individual mind, personality and soul.

There *is* a vast contribution to be made by science—as you will see later in Part II—but it is still so new, so poorly understood and so narrowly recognized by scientists themselves that the majority cannot tell you what will be happening after you leave the caterpillar-like body. This does not mean that they won't get the answers eventually. Dr. Fred Hoyle, the eminent British cosmologist, has said: "When science begins the study of nonphysical phenomena, it will make more progress in one decade than in all the centuries of its experience."

Science, however, may not make quite as rapid progress as Dr. Hoyle predicts. Dr. Hiroshi Motoyama made an interesting observation when he, as one of the reviewers of the early draft of this manuscript, read Dr. Hoyle's statement. Dr. Motoyama, himself a scientist with an international reputation, is also a Shinto priest and psychic deeply schooled in spiritual matters. He is founder and president of The International Association for Religion and Parapsychology in Tokyo,

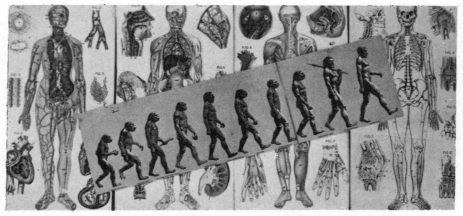

Fig. 1. Evolutionary development of man's physical systems

Japan. Dr. Motoyama remarked, "In one sense the research will be more difficult than Dr. Hoyle anticipates. Science has limited means for its contact with and search of spiritual things."

But we need not wait ten, twenty, or thirty years! The material assembled in this book will help give you many of the answers right now.

First, it is necessary to recognize the physical body for what it is: an *electro-biochemical mechanism* of truly magnificent conception and design. It has evolved (Fig. 1) over the many millions of years since life first came ashore from the primordial seas. Think of its many "systems": the skeleton, the blood circulation, the nerves, etc. Think also of its many important organs, such as the brain, heart, lungs, pancreas, kidneys, liver, genitals, large and small intestines, etc.; the two to three square yards of skin which make up the body's all-enclosing envelope; and the organs that provide our five senses. Individually, each of these is fantastically complex and perfected to an awesome degree. And, unlike any manmade mechanism or machine that must go into the repair shop for even a minor malfunction, the electro-biochemical mechanism that is the physical body is endowed by its Creator with a built-in capability to maintain and even repair itself.

Most of what we know about our surroundings is a result of the working of man's five senses—touch, taste, smell, sight, and hearing. In fact, almost everything we think we know about our world and the universe has come to us through one or more of these sense organs. We feel quite content in our belief that we can rely on these sense organs to give us a completely factual, dependable, and highly accurate picture of the universe in which we are each immersed. But this is a *false belief!*

Consider the sense of sight. Our eyes can see the merest fraction of what is going on all around us. They can detect only matter which reflects light in the very narrow band of wavelengths we call the visible spectrum. Laboratory research has shown that there is much going on all around us in wavelengths that our limited sense organs cannot detect.

8

Supersensible Sight

In our laboratory at Metascience Corporation, I can filter out all *visible* light so that as far as the eyes can tell, it is dark. But special photographic color films will record wavelengths of light from objects that the eyes cannot detect. Such color films record pictures of some very strange living forms that baffle my scientific friends. Fig. 2 is an example.

When Fig. 2 was taken, the room was dark except for certain wavelengths of light beyond the range of normal human vision. No flash was used. But when the film was developed, the unique object at the left was photographed in lovely shades of blue, pink, peach, red and violet. (This small black-and-white reproduction does not show the delicate inner workings or "organs" of this strange and normally invisible life form. They are much more apparent in the color enlargements.)

What is mind-bending is that such objects occupy space in our windowless laboratory and seemingly pass instantaneously through the "solid" brick walls. Such objects also pass through my body as if it were *transparent*—which, as a matter of fact, it is!

Fig. 2. Photo of a normally invisible life form and a transparent physical body

When the color negative of Fig. 2 was used to make color enlargements we were astonished to see that the film had recorded in good detail the *back, seat and front legs* of the chair on which I was sitting. It was even possible to see and count the upholstery tacks hidden behind my trouser-covered leg, as well as the chair back, which was concealed behind eight inches of flesh, blood and bone!

Well, naturally I was shocked. Such a thing cannot happen *in the world of our five senses.* I showed this photo to scientists and photo specialists* throughout the United States and abroad. They were at a loss to explain it. But there is a saying to the effect that "if you find even *one* white crow, that proves forever that not all crows are black."

Science, quite rightly, makes a fetish of "replication." By this, scientists mean that it is necessary to be able to *repeat* a phenomenon under controlled laboratory conditions. Hence, we persevered in our search for "white crow number two." Many months and more than 4,000 color photos later, we again succeeded in photographing the *transparency of the human body.* Those who are unfamiliar with the trials and tribulations of research may naturally wonder why it took more than 4,000 photos before the next white crow was captured. I will explain.

Thomas Alva Edison was one of the world's greatest inventive geniuses. For forty-four winter seasons he operated a research laboratory in Ft. Myers, Florida, where our laboratory was formerly located. When Edison was trying to perfect the filament for the electric light bulb, his assistants became very discouraged. One of them said, "Mr. Edison, in trying to find a filament which will be satisfactory, you have tried more than 9,000 different materials. It is obvious you're attempting the impossible." To which Mr. Edison is said to have replied, "Well, we now know 9,000 materials which will *not* work. Let's get busy and find the one which *will* work."

Pioneering on the edge of the unknown—whether it be to encapsulate light in a little glass bulb or capture spirit entities on film—is a slow and sometimes discouraging job. Nature does not give up her secrets easily. (This laboratory work is still progressing, but at a slow rate.)

---

* If you are scientifically or photographically oriented, it is almost a mathematical certainty that you already have not one but several ideas for "explaining" the strange effects in Fig. 2. But consider these three points. First, I am not a photographic novice. I acquired my first 35 mm camera 53 years ago, and in the following half-century, I have used practically every type of camera and am familiar with all stages of the photographic process. Second, *all* qualified critics who have examined the color photographic blowups have found no error upon the closest of examination. Third, as I pointed out on the opening page, this is a *nontechnical* book. Documentation of our research will be the subject of later releases.

Supersensible Hearing

A similar situation exists with respect to what our *ears* are able to tell us about what we call "reality." The most acute hearing in an adult covers only the range of 20 to 16,000 cycles per second. A dog has a wider range of auditory perception. We are familiar with the "silent" whistle for calling dogs, the one which emits sound waves at vibratory frequencies beyond the range of the human ear.

In the past few years, scientific research in our laboratory and that of a colleague has been aimed at exploring phenomena beyond the sensory ability of our auditory system to detect. Just as we are pioneering beyond the capability of our sense of sight, we are also exploring beyond our sense of hearing.

We were initially motivated to do this because of our research with healers. We became intrigued by the many healers encountered in our worldwide studies who said they "heard voices of departed spirits" who guided them in their healing work. As I explained in *Healers and the Healing Process,** this subject has been referred to for thousands of years in literature, both religious and secular.

We felt that the time had come to take a serious scientific look at the subject. After all, at least some souls have been today locked behind bars in mental hospitals all over the world because they committed the sin of "hearing voices" that no *sane* person could hear. Ipso facto, there are no such voices and the person is obviously quite crazy.

Well, Virginia, there *are* such voices, although few persons can hear them. Your auditory system can pick up the sound of your mother's voice as she asks you to help on some household chore. But that auditory system, marvel of perfection that it is, does not tell you that the room in which you are standing is filled with hundreds of voices being carried on the air waves of radio and television stations. Nor does it tell you that the room is also filled with the voices of spirit entities who once lived in physical bodies just like yours. Their voices are at wavelengths or frequencies much much higher than even the radio and television signals which you cannot hear.

Everything in our world, this universe and the Cosmos, results from **energy,** and **energy** manifests as vibration at some specific frequency.

The sound energy imparted to the molecules of air from a spoken word is at a very low frequency—from a few hundred to a few thousand per second. Our radios receive waves of energy which vibrate at *hundreds of thousands* of cycles per second. Our telephone conversations are carried across the country, across the oceans or to an astronaut in a spacecraft by energy with a vibrational frequency of *millions* of cycles per second. Light waves, with which we are able to

---

* Published in 1977 by Theosophical Publishing House, Wheaton, Illinois.

see, have a frequency of roughly 12,000,000,000,000 cycles per second. That's twelve *trillion!* Soft x-rays, hard x-rays, gamma rays, etc., vibrate at progressively higher frequencies.

Just as it was necessary to supplement our hearing capability by inventing the radio to send and receive energy at higher frequencies than airborne audio sounds, man must invent new devices that will allow him to "tune in" to the still higher frequencies of the voices of, say, the discarnate spirit doctors who are working with healers. Thus, Virginia, this is a parallel to our work in developing photographic "seeing" capability to go beyond the energy wavelengths our visual system can detect. *This means using magnetic tape to capture sounds (voices) we never knew existed and photographic film to see things that we never knew existed.*

All of this knowledge is teaching us that we know very little about important aspects of our body, mind and spirit. Our ignorance of what we know about the "solid," everyday, "material" world can be described in one word: *colossal.* As will be shown later, these normally invisible sights and unheard sounds have a most important bearing on the question of life after death.

A Wet, Squishy Body

Just as the caterpillar has a soft squishy body, so do you and I. Each of us is born in a sea of water (Fig. 3) and when we step on the scales, most of what we are weighing is water. As we see in Fig. 4, more than 60 percent of the young woman's weight is water. It would take at least

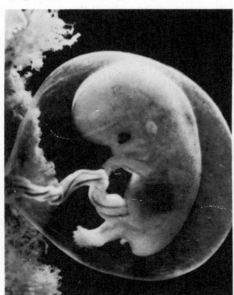 

Fig. 3. Human embryo suspended in sea of water   *Fig. 4. Water content of human body*

nine gallon jugs to hold an equivalent amount, and her brain is at least 80 percent water by weight.

Since we are embarked on a search to see what part of us survives the death of our physical bodies, it would seem we can narrow our search. Obviously the *water* will dry out *after* the person dies—it will evaporate. So whatever survives must be in the part which makes up less than 40 percent of the physical body.

A Body Filled With "Empty" Space

Furthermore, the soft, wet, plastic mass which we are talking about is found to be "empty"! By this I refer to the fact that our present-day insights into the nature of matter show us that most of the space taken up by the human body is 99⅓ percent void (leaving aside the possibility of the so-called ether or equivalent). Andrew Glazewski, the late scientist-priest of Britain, explains it thus:

"To illustrate this, imagine borrowing an atom from, for example, a hand. For the sake of convenience let us accept the Bohr model of the atom, magnified so that the nucleus is the size of an apple—where would the next atom be? Between 1,000 to 2,000 miles away! Looking upon our bodies on this scale we would see a vast universe containing many millions of trillions of atoms forming billions of galaxies. If the nuclei of those atoms were shining, as they are centres of energy, we would confront a vast, celestial, starry sky of unimaginable spaces. So you see, our body, of which we have only a statistical perception when using our senses, is actually a great "void" with little centres of energy in forms of atoms dispersed at enormous distances. One biological cell contains many millions of galaxies of atoms."

Now we can begin to understand why it was possible, as I reported a few pages earlier, for a camera to look right through the flesh, blood, organs and bones in my chest and record a picture of the chair's back. Like you, I am a wet, squishy mass largely filled with "empty" space.

How Much Does A Soul Weigh?

Since we would like to identify that portion of the individual person which survives death of the physical body, it would seem we can now narrow our search even further. Obviously the water portion will *evaporate* during the days, weeks and months after death. Yet as we will see later, there is rather solid proof that the essence—that is, the mind, personality and soul—depart the physical body within a period of *minutes* to a maximum of three days. Thus, although Biblical writings are replete with references to "the water and the spirit," it does not seem that water as such is the carrier for mind, personality and soul.

There have been a few serious attempts to measure the loss of weight that takes place at the instant of death. One piece of research stands out. While this work was done a long time ago, there has never been serious question of the methodology, the integrity of the scientist who did the research or the quality of the findings.* McDougall found the instantaneous weight loss at death varied between ½ and ¾ ounce.

The research of McDougall seems to have been replicated in the work of five physicians at a Massachusetts hospital.† These men built a large and very delicate balance. On one platform they would lay a person who was at the very point of death, while on the other platform they would place counterweights so as to bring the large pointer into a balanced condition. At the moment the heart stopped beating, the doctors said, "With startling suddeness the pointer moved, indicating a weight loss from the now dead patient's body. The amount of the weight loss which we encountered over such tests in a six-year period varied between one-half and one ounce."

Over the years, most of us familiar with these finding have found it difficult to believe that it could be possible to put the mind, personality and soul *into such a small package.* Recently, however, with the advances in solid state physics, we have had dramatic indication of how man himself is able to put a vast amount of information into a very small package. A small crystalline chip weighing less than 20 percent of the above-mentioned weight loss can store 100,000,000 "bits" of information. So it no longer seems so preposterous that our Creator has devised an infinitely more compact and efficient method of "packaging" the individual human mind, personality and soul.

Thus we have arrived at the point where we see that the body *and* the brain are largely made up of water and that, in reality, both are largely "void" of any "solid matter." Physicists have now come to the conclusion that even atoms are *not* solid at all, but are disturbances in some nonphysical continuum. Morever, there seems to be a possibility that the surviving mind, personality and soul may be "contained" in a very small and perhaps almost weightless "package."

These considerations have tremendous importance for us in trying to track down just what part of the caterpillar-like body it is that might have a chance to survive through eternity. But at this point it is only sensible for you to ask: How can anyone answer my questions about life after death in a scientific way when medical science has not even proven that man *has* a mind or spirit? Since medical science has not proven that the brain is anything more than a collection of perishable cells (which are 80 percent water), how can my mind possibly survive the death of my physical body?

---

* Carrington, H., *Dr. McDougall's Experiments*, Archives of the American Society for Psychic Research, Vol. 1, 1907. The later work of Crookall (see Bibliography) provided good correlation with the McDougall data.
† John Langone, *Vital Signs—The Way We Die in America*, 1974, Little Brown, New York.

Your Brain Is NOT Your Mind

Certainly one of the greatest blocks modern man has in understanding life after death stems from having been told that the brain and mind are synonymous. However, a different picture emerges for those serious researchers into the nature of man who can look beyond conventional notions. For such scientists it has become increasingly obvious that the brain and mind are *not* the same thing.

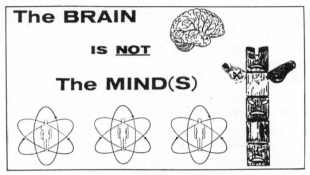

Fig. 5. The brain is not the mind(s)

One of the most conclusive pieces of evidence was provided by the research of the eminent Canadian neurosurgeon, Dr. Wilder Penfield. He was considerably surprised at how large a piece of the brain he could surgically remove with little or no effect on the ability of the patient to carry on living as usual. To use a now out-of-date analogy comparing the brain with a telephone switchboard, it was almost as though several of the "operators" went out for lunch, but as long as even one was still on duty, the calls could come in and go out much as usual.

In this same connection, it must be noted that neither Penfield nor any other brain surgeon has been able to identify any specific brain cells or regions of the brain as being what psychoanalysts refer to as the id, ego, and superego; neither could the psychologist identify the brain's site for conscious, subconscious, or superconscious states of mind. Yet concepts attributing three levels or aspects to the human mind existed hundreds of years before psychiatry and psychology came into existence.

For example, both the native peoples of the Pacific and American Plains Indians recognized *three levels* of mind and represented them in their tribal totem poles. The totem pole shown at the right of Fig. 5 and in Fig. 6 was carved by a Cherokee Indian. It shows wings adjacent to the topmost level of the Indian's self. Years ago, the Indian knew that the highest level of his mind and spirit would leave the physical body at death, and like a butterfly, fly on to a higher level of existence. Only today is the white man discerning a scientific basis for much of the knowledge of the "primitive."

In this age of the computer, we find another analogy for helping to

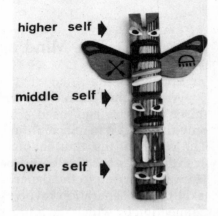

Fig. 6. American Indian and Polynesian concepts of the three levels of being

understand how the mind functions and can even operate as an entity distinct from the body and its brain. Like the computer programmer, the mind works *through* the brain but **is not** the brain.

We know that the brain controls all aspects of the body that it serves. We can say that the body, the "bio-electrical mechanism," is controlled by its computer, the brain. We can go further and say that the brain is infinitely more sophisticated than the most advanced computer yet built by man. But we also must say that the brain, like even the fanciest computer, is totally useless unless there is a *programmer*—some intelligence *separate and distinct from the computer itself.* It is only in the last three decades—a mere instant in humanity's long evolutionary climb—that science has given us a valuable tool which enables us to understand that the *mind* is the programmer, that it interpenetrates the "empty space" in our wet, squishy, physical body; and that it can control every single action of the more than 60,000,000,000,000 cells that make up the physical body.

What is this mysterious and magical tool?

CHAPTER 2

The Mind and the Jelly Mold

A wise old fellow who wrote about death in the Bible, perhaps thirty centuries ago, used a beautifully poetic description for which only the most recent scientific research gives basis for understanding. The writer of the 12th chapter of the book of Ecclesiastes said: "...or ever the silver cord be loosed (severed) or the golden bowl be broken..." He was referring to the departure of the mind and soul from the bowl (skull). The separation involves the severing or cutting of the tenuous connection by which the mind and soul have been attached to the brain while cradled in the bowl or skull. To understand more fully the role the silver cord plays in life after death, let us consider the following analogy.

Jelly Molds and Energy Fields
If a cook wants to mold gelatin into an attractive shape for a salad or dessert, he or she must resort to the use of a mold made of plastic, metal or paper. The cook looks at the mold and knows what shape the watery, jelly-like material will assume when it cools and hardens. If the mold is battered and bent, the molded product will be shaped accordingly. *Energy fields* behave like jelly molds.

In beginning physics courses, there is an experiment in which a magnet is placed beneath a piece of paper on which iron filings are randomly sprinkled. The invisible energy field of the magnet becomes visible as the filings are molded into the pattern of the lines of magnetic force. Thus the iron filings are *molded into a shape* by an invisible field of magnetic energy. You can see a jelly mold, but your limited eyesight cannot see an energy field. Yet the *invisible* energy field of the magnet is just as real as the metal or plastic jelly mold.

In Fig. 7, I show how a powerful magnet will send its energy field through the cells and bones of a hand, and still organize iron filings. Even after passing through the hand, the energy field is so strong that it can overcome gravity and hold thousands of small pieces of steel in a precise pattern.

In Fig. 8, I performed a more modern experiment and placed a bar magnet in front of a color television screen. In brilliant colors a fascinatingly complex picture of energy fields around the magnet became visible to the eye and was captured on color film.

The reader may be inclined to think, "Yes, these 'fields' may surround and penetrate magnets and other material objects, but what about living objects such as *plants* and *people*? Do these have energy fields?"

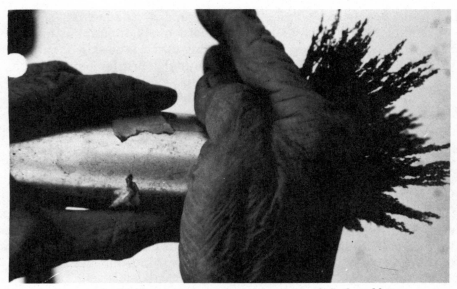

Fig. 7. Magnetic lines of force passing through blood, flesh and bones

Historically, the credit for answering this question goes to Dr. Harold Saxton Burr and F.S.C. Northrop, both of Yale University School of Medicine. In 1935 they published a paper, "The Electro-Dynamic Theory of Life." This pioneering work fully documented the existence of invisible but dynamic fields of energy interpenetrating and surrounding *all living matter*. This work went largely unnoticed for forty years because it just did not fit with *accepted* scientific attitudes about the nature of matter.

In the period between 1940 and 1960, the Kirlians, a husband and wife team of Russian scientists, refined an old technique of electro-

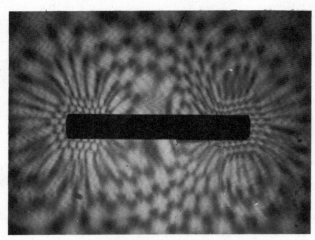

Fig. 8. Energy fields around a bar magnet

18

photography pioneered by Bardouc of France at the beginning of the 20th century. They were able to record on photographic film the otherwise invisible energy fields extending beyond the skin of men and animals. And in the late 1970's, a young British scientist, Rupert Sheldrake, had the temerity to hypothesize the existence of what he called *anthropomorphic fields* as a formative force in living bodies and tissues. His book, *A New Science of Life,* was held up to ridicule by the most prestigious British science magazine, *Nature.* The reviewer, probably frightened by the *far-reaching implications for many fields of science,* labeled it "a book fit for burning."

Also in the late 1970's, following the path pioneered by Burr, Northrop and the Kirlians (but with no knowledge of the work of Rupert Sheldrake), I may have been the first to capture on photographic film the beautifully-colored energy fields of *my own etheric body,* momentarily projected into the space at the right of my physical body as shown in Fig. 2 (page 9).

Simultaneously with the work of Sheldrake and Meek, two British scientists, Dennis Milner and Edward Smart, were doing pioneering work with electro-photography. The illustration in Fig. 9 shows the energy fields around a freshly plucked leaf and the magnetized needle from a compass. Notice that the energy field surrounding the leaf is attracted or drawn to the field which exists around the magnetic pole of the compass needle.

Thus, for the first time in the history of man, these various research projects have begun to provide insights suggesting that in some way man's energy fields might provide a clue for the understanding of the

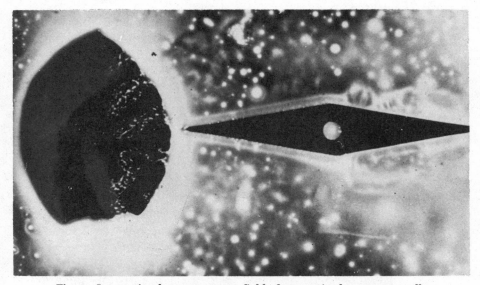

Fig. 9. Interaction between energy field of magnetized compass needle and freshly plucked plant leaf

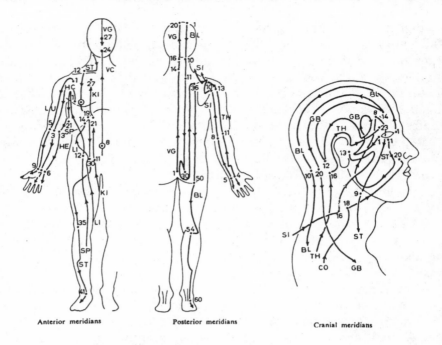

Anterior meridians   Posterior meridians   Cranial meridians

Fig. 10. Acupuncture meridians

nature of consciousness. To a "dreamer" such as the author, there comes a "hunch" that man's invisible energy fields might ultimately provide the key to solve the mystery of the survival of the human mind, memory banks, personality and soul. *The latter chapters of this book will report on the extent to which this hunch has been verified.*

When I talk about "energy fields," you naturally ask, "What kind of energy?" I will try to answer this question as nontechnically as possible. First, you should know that the physical body utilizes electricity. The cells have the ability to generate electricity, using as fuel the food we eat. Some of this electricity flows through a network of nerves just as the electricity in your house or apartment flows through the electrical wiring system. Second, there is a very subtle type of energy that the Chinese discovered more than 3,000 years ago. It seems to flow primarily on and near the surfaces of the body along what are called acupuncture meridians (Fig. 10). The Chinese made such drawings of these energies centuries before the time of Christ.

Shortly after writing the above paragraphs, I was traveling in The Peoples Republic of China. In the museum in Soochow I stood before a large bronze figure of a man—taller than my six-foot-three frame—and learned how *two hundred years ago* the medical students were trained to insert acupuncture needles at the proper locations. A very small hole had been drilled through the hollow bronze casting at the precise location of each acupuncture point. The bronze figure was then

20

covered with a thick wax and filled with water. A student instructed to insert a needle for a particular malady would know he had not hit the right place unless he was greeted by a spurt of water.

Traveling on to Nanking, I got dramatic proof of the efficacy of acupuncture when used as an anesthetic. A small group of which I was a member visited the Nanking General Hospital. The general administrator, after giving us a talk on their use of acupuncture, took us on a tour of the out-patient and recovery wards and four operating rooms. Wearing surgical gowns and face masks, we proceeded to watch four operations, all major, in which acupuncture was the *only* anesthetic. I will describe one of these to give you a better understanding of the reality of these energies which I am discussing and about which our modern science knows very little.

The patient, a 40-year-old man, was being operated on for an ulcerated stomach condition which had not responded to treatment. A few hours before the operation he was given orally a very mild tranquilizer to ease the perfectly normal fear of the dangers which might lie ahead once he was wheeled out of his room and into the operating room.

Upon arrival in the operating room, a nurse inserted three small needles into the periphery of the patient's left ear. Each needle had a small wire extending to a nearby instrument—about the size of a small tape recorder. This instrument supplied a six-volt direct current to each needle. These three needles provided the only anesthetizing effect.

Extending up from the patient's throat area was a cloth screen about one foot square which prevented the patient from observing the actions of the surgeons. However, we could see the patient's face as well as all the actions of the surgeons. With the hospital administrator serving as translator, we were able to converse with the patient at all stages of the operation.

The two surgeons, standing on each side of the operating table, made the incision. Gradually they progressed to the point where they took the patient's stomach and lifted it up so that they could carefully inspect it. The condition they found apparently warranted their decision that it was necessary to remove fully sixty percent of the stomach. This they did. Then they completed the many details and closed the incision. At no time did the patient experience discomfort. He apparently had no knowledge of what was going on.

One of our group was an American surgeon in his sixties. Knowing nothing about the subtle and invisible energy systems and related energy fields of the human body, he was totally mystified. I observed him standing aside and through his face mask mutter, "Incredible. Absolutely incredible! There is just no anatomical basis for this nonsense." How right he was! None of the present day medical texts on anatomy discusses the invisible—but very real—energy systems such as the acupuncture meridians.

In the post-operative ward, we talked to patients who had had major operations in the preceding days. Most of them—providing their digestive tracts had not been operated on—were able to enjoy a full meal a few hours after the operation. Within 24 hours most were able to get out of bed and walk. Few needed to stay more than two or three days.

Further evidence on the new vistas opened for medical treatment through a growing understanding of the invisible acupuncture meridians and the part they play in the functioning of our bodies was given when I stopped off in Tokyo to get up to date on the scientific research of Dr. Hiroshi Motoyama, the parapsychologist and Shinto priest I mentioned earlier. Dr. Motoyama has used his knowledge of acupuncture to devise an electronic system for making a medical diagnosis of a person in fifteen minutes that would otherwise take days of detailed and costly hospital tests. These diagnostic machines are now in daily use in 22 large hospitals in Japan.

While studying healers living in the rice fields of a northern part of the Philippines, we were fortunate enough to capture on film a red-orange stream of healing energy (Fig. 11). Josefina Sisson is just starting to treat the eye of a patient who has come from the out-back area of Australia. This momentary blast of healing energy was *invisible* to the members of the five-man team of specialists we had with us, but it was *detected* and recorded by the emulsions on the photographic film.

Ancient writings speak of still another type of energy as being

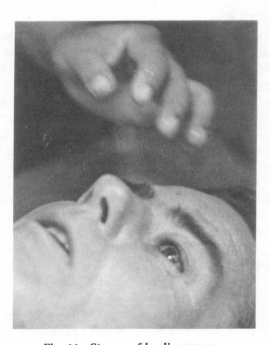

Fig. 11. *Stream of healing energy*

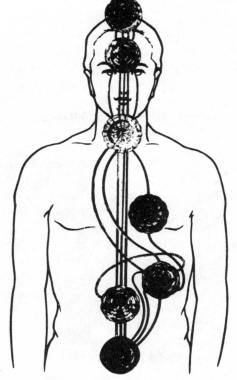

Fig. 12. Diagram of chakra energy centers

involved in human life and have called it by names such as prana, od, odic force, ki, baraka, etc. This subtle energy from the cosmos enters the body through whirling energy vortexes known as chakras, located roughly as indicated in Fig. 12. Only recently have an American scientist, Itzhak Bentov of Boston, Massachusetts, and the Japanese scientist, Dr. Motoyama, invented equipment which can prove that these normally invisible energy centers actually do exist.

I have revised this edition of the book to include the foregoing comments on acupuncture as they have a very direct bearing on our search for evidence of life after death. Since no surgeon has ever opened the body and found a soul, we have to assume that the soul is not of the same material as the physical body and, if it exists, it must be invisible. Since it is hard—almost impossible—for any of us to believe something unless we can see it, we can sympathize with my surgeon friend who could not even believe what he *saw* in the four operations, because in a lifetime of surgical practice no one had taught him about the reality of the *energy fields* of man.

As of now, no dependable means exists for photographing or instrumentally detecting the subtle cosmic energies that activate and flow through the chakra system—a very important part of your physical body. On rare occasions the energies present in a very gifted psychic person are so intense, so powerful, that they can affect the emulsion of photographic film, as they did in Fig. 13.

This photo is of an American scientist, who wishes to remain anonymous, and his small son. The father and son are *highly psychic*, as is his eight-year-old daughter, who snapped this *extremely rare* photo with a simple instamatic-type camera with a built-in flash. It shows the energy stream bursting upward from the crown chakra of the boy and blending with the energy shooting upward from the father's crown chakra.

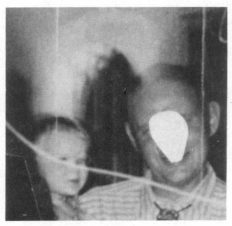

Fig. 13. Head chakra energies

I have introduced you to the subject of these normally invisible and hard-to-detect energy fields for a very important reason. Without such knowledge you could not understand how it is that the most significant parts of you—your mind, personality and soul—*must* survive the death of your physical body.

I said in the opening pages that I would "keep it simple" and present concepts largely through photos and diagrams. I feel sure that enough has been presented to make it clear that the brain is not the mind, that the mind(s) are energy fields, and that these normally invisible energy fields shape, control and animate all matter.*

Now we are ready to face up to a seemingly preposterous statement.

We Live on Seven Levels and in Two Worlds

We have examined at some length the fantastically wonderful and complicated *physical* body. We have discovered that it is largely empty

---

* For the technically-inclined reader, one of the most interesting scientific pieces of brain-mind research is the development of the holographic model by K. Pribram and D. Bohm. (See M. Ferguson, *Brain-Mind Bulletin*, July 4, 1977.) However, this new model does not recognize that the mind is something distinct from the brain and will survive and function normally long after the brain has returned to dust.

space. We have learned that energy fields can and do penetrate the physical body as though it were transparent and had little substance. We have learned that the brain is not the mind. We have learned that the body is electrically powered and that it also utilizes two other anciently-postulated energy systems of which twentieth-century science knows very little.

Hence it will not come as a great surprise that *interpenetrating* our physical body there is another "body" made up of a large number of energy fields, each of which collects and organizes cells into shapes or organs precisely the same way the magnet in Fig. 7 organizes the thousands of iron filings into a specific pattern.

In fact, there is *an energy field for every major organ and bone in the physical body*, and these control all of the individual cells. They provide what we might call the *intelligence* which builds the organ in the first place, provides it with the life force, keeps it running in harmony with the other parts of the body, and repairs and maintains the organ or bone.

For centuries occult literature has called this vast collection of energy fields the "etheric body." Western scientists have been very slow to investigate this body because up to now it has been invisible and could not be weighed. (Science is largely dependent on the ability to *observe* and *measure* whatever it is that is being studied. Moreover, most scientists have been conditioned to pay attention only to those things which they measure and weigh and observe which fit in with their expectations—i.e., within the framework of thought of *contemporary* science.) Russian scientists have been more ready than Western scientists to undertake research on the etheric body of man. They have become convinced of its reality and have coined their own name for it— the *bioplasmic* body.

The physical body operates primarily on electricity. The *bioplasmic body* utilizes the energy systems which are involved in acupuncture meridians and the chakras.

But once we have started to take man apart and have found that he is actually living on two levels of being, this is not the end of the matter. There are actually *five additional* levels of being!

How can we possibly picture in our minds *seven* levels of being? Well, we are certainly familiar with the physical body. Now that we have learned that it is largely empty space, we can even imagine there is another energy occupying the same space as the physical body. So, since we can think of "bodies," let us just *imagine* there are *five additional* bodies. After all, when we look at an onion, we have no trouble discerning that there are many layers making up that onion. Or let us recall an experience most of us have had when we were purchasing a new dress or a new suit of clothes. We put the garment on and then stood between mirrors arranged so we could see over our shoulder

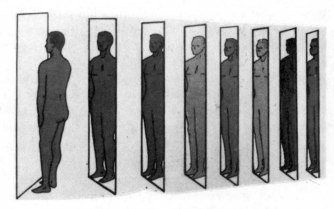

Fig. 14. Multiple image (body) concept

in order to check the fit of the back of the garment. At the same time, we could also see our image repeated several times, each image looking a bit smaller and farther away behind our back. Note the arrangement in Fig. 14—an extension of a common experience.

Our next step is to identify *these levels of being.*

We have already identified the physical body and its interpenetrating bioplasmic body. Then we come to the mind. From our earlier discussion of the mind, you will recall that long before the writings of Dr. Sigmund Freud of Vienna, Austria, the American Plains Indians and the Polynesians knew about and utilized their knowledge of the *three* levels of mind.

Now it is quite appropriate for us to think of these three minds as being three separate bodies. This is not as fanciful as it might seem. Only in the last few years, it has been discovered that most of the many millions of cells in the physical body have what the scientists call "communication capability." This means that the cells can receive and send messages. We are also learning that the cells go beyond this func-

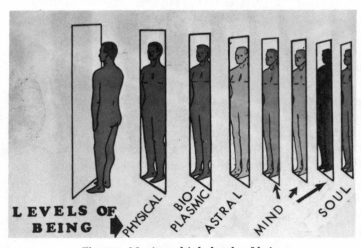

LEVELS OF BEING   PHYSICAL   BIO-PLASMIC   ASTRAL   MIND   SOUL

Fig. 15. Man's multiple levels of being

26

tion; it is almost as though each cell has a mind of its own. Now we can begin to understand that not only is "the brain not the mind," but that *the mind function extends throughout the entire body.*

Also it seems that since the beginnings of the human race almost all religions on all continents have taught that man has a soul. Since we need some means of creating a picture of the soul, let us use just one more invisible body to represent the invisible soul.

But—and this is extremely important, as we will see shortly—nature has put the soul and the levels of mind in a nice neat *package.* For the last few centuries occult and esoteric literature has called this "package" the "astral body." So now let us put it all together and arrive at Fig. 15.

As of now, our scientific instrumentation is such that we can detect and measure energy relating directly to *only the physical and the bioplasmic bodies.* The other so-called bodies or energy fields are "invisible," as indicated in Fig. 16. That is, we do not have instruments that will measure them. Actually, this is not the serious barrier it might appear to be. Modern physics includes many concepts that even today are not confirmed by anything more solid than informed speculation.

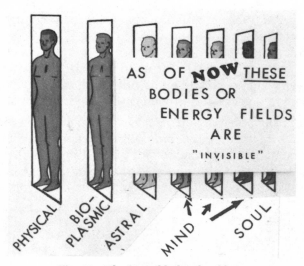

AS OF **NOW** THESE
BODIES OR
ENERGY FIELDS
ARE
"INVISIBLE"

PHYSICAL   BIO-PLASMIC   ASTRAL   MIND   SOUL

Fig. 16. The invisible levels of being

Please note that in some of the diagrams I use the word "spirit" and in some I use the word "soul." I do this because for most readers the terms are interchangeable. Properly speaking, however, the word "spirit" distinguishes the nonphysical portions of our being from the physical body, whereas "soul" relates to that *individualized portion of* the Creator which resides in each of us. Indeed, the soul might be defined as that individualized spark or portion of spirit energy which

27

originated in and emanated from what man has called The Creator, God, The Godhead, Cosmic Consciousness, Universal Mind, etc., and which manifested downward into the denser realms of spirit, where it is involved in working, learning, loving and growing back to the Divine source from which it came. The soul already resides in and will always continue to reside in what I will later refer to as "the worlds of spirit."

This concept of multiple bodies gives us a method of visualizing how parts of the individual person—the real, the everlasting "I"—*might survive death*. This is portrayed in Fig. 17.

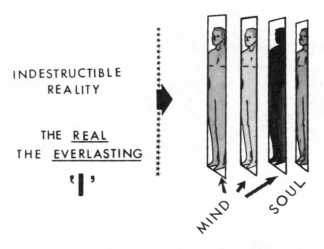

INDESTRUCTIBLE
REALITY

THE <u>REAL</u>
THE <u>EVERLASTING</u>

'I'

MIND   SOUL

Fig. 17. The real, the everlasting "I"

If the minds and spirit or soul of the individual person are *nonphysical*, it is not such a strain on the imagination to conceive of this portion surviving the death of the physical body. Recalling the brain-computer analogy, the computer may be damaged or even destroyed, but the intelligence that acted as programmer for the computer is still very much alive.

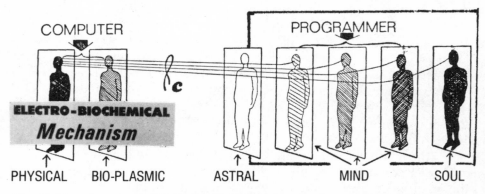

COMPUTER   PROGRAMMER

ELECTRO-BIOCHEMICAL
Mechanism

PHYSICAL   BIO-PLASMIC   ASTRAL   MIND   SOUL

Fig. 18. The programmer of the electro-biochemical mechanism we call the physical body

In Fig. 18, I have separated the two sets of bodies to help you further visualize this process. This begins to suggest the mechanism by which a good clairvoyant sees what, since Biblical times, has been called "the silver cord" (marked by the letter "c" in the diagram). Literature is full of accounts of how a good clairvoyant observes the gradual loosening and then the separating of the silvery energy cord as a person is dying.

This multiple body analogy also begins to help parapsychologists visualize how it is that while the physical body of a sensitive is relaxing and lying peacefully in bed, his consciousness can travel far and describe scenes en route. In other words, this helps you to understand the mechanism of the out-of-body experience, or OBE, to use parapsychological terminology. This is what has been known for thousands of years in occult literature as astral travel. Notice particularly that term "astral travel." It is a marvelous clue to the reality of life after death.

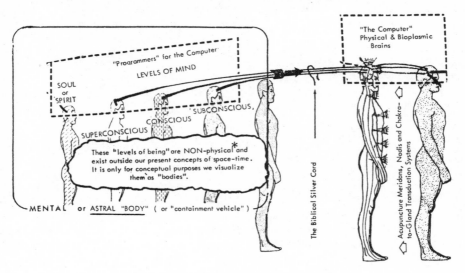

Fig. 19. Figure 18 presented in a different form

Fig. 19 sums up these ideas in a slightly different way. Just as the skin covers all of the internal organs and skeleton of our physical body, the astral body functions as a skin or covering for the three levels of mind and soul. It contains them and makes a unit of them. This package or bundle is *the real you*. It contains the more enduring parts of your memory banks, your emotional patterns, your personality and your soul.

This is the "programmer," of which I wrote earlier.

It is connected to and works through your physical brain—that quart or so of water which is your personal computer.

It is still "material," but not in the sense of matter as you know it. It is of such a fine, rapidly vibrating energy that it is similar to what you think of as light rays.

Normally it stays well within the confines of the physical and bio-plasmic bodies. But at night when you are in deep sleep, it can *leave* your body and travel. During life in the physical body, it always remains connected to your physical body by an invisible elastic web-like "wiring harness" that is attached to the brain—the so-called silver cord.

Now, just as we have *bodies* interpenetrating each other, some scientists tell us that we can have interpenetrating *worlds*. (The term they prefer is "space-time systems.") But for our purposes in discussing life after death, let's just say there is an astral world that occupies the same space as our physical world. And—wonder of wonders—our physical body lives in the physical world while our astral body lives and functions in the interpenetrating *astral world*.

In Part III, you will see how this knowledge of the astral world makes it very easy to explore the mystery of life after death.

CHAPTER 3

All Packed and Ready To Fly!

Perhaps your mind is still reeling from all the theories about seven bodies and the statement that you live in two worlds at the same time. With so many problems and so much strife, all of us frequently feel like the person who called out, "Stop the world, I want to get off." But it really isn't so complicated as it might first seem. We now have progressed to the point where we can think in terms of:

| the physical body | } | (plus) | the bioplasmic body | } | (plus) | the astral body | } | (containing) | the levels of mind and soul |

Perhaps it will help to recall how as a child you took scissors, folded a sheet of paper back and forth on itself three times and then cut out a paper doll. Now that you are older and a bit more creative, it is no problem for you to cut out dolls and label them as I've done in Fig. 20.

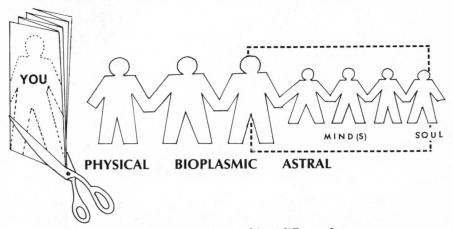

YOU

PHYSICAL   BIOPLASMIC   ASTRAL   MIND(S)   SOUL

Fig. 20. Figure 18 presented in a different form

When we are born, we are all "folded" into one nice neat package. As we progress through life we continue to stay largely within the confines of the physical body, the package which also contains our bioplasmic and astral bodies. But every man, woman and child on the planet shares the same fate. *At some time the package breaks open.* At some time, sooner or later, the physical body reaches the end of its usefulness. From illness, violent accident, suicide, homicide, death in war, or just plain old age, our physical body becomes inoperative. It dies.

What happens to the bioplasmic body when the physical body dies? Well, that body also dies. But usually it stays around for just a little while, sometimes only for a few hours. In the majority of cases, it will have disintegrated completely within three days. It is reabsorbed into the great cosmic supply of the energies, normally invisible to people, which activated the acupuncture and chakra systems. The etheric body has served its purpose of molding matter into the many organs used to form the physical body and served to channel the cosmic energies which were required to keep the body operational.

And what happens to the *astral* body? Aha! This is the crucial question. *It is completely alive and functional* after the death of both the physical body and the etheric body. It continues to live in the same "second world" in which it has always lived—the astral world which completely interpenetrates and occupies the same space that the physical world does. This is symbolically portrayed in Fig. 21.

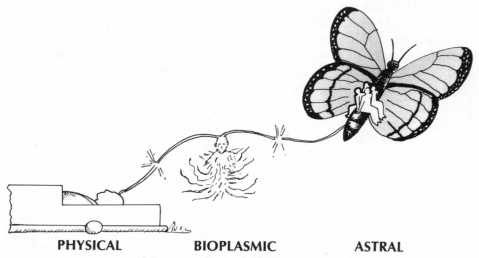

PHYSICAL   **BIOPLASMIC**   **ASTRAL**

Fig. 21. Symbolic survival of bodily death

This individual astral body contains all of the memory banks, emotional patterns, personality and soul that it had before it departed from the physical body. These are all neatly contained in one "package." When you someday find yourself without your physical body, you will find that your personal baggage is all neatly packed and that you—like the butterfly—are ready to *fly*. You have left behind your caterpillar-like body. Unlike the caterpillar, you need not waste time spinning a cocoon. There is no need for you to spend a season or two before you can split your cocoon and emerge as a beautiful creature ready to enter on flights of exploration. In making man, our Creator surpassed even His handiwork in making the caterpillar and butterfly.

You are all packed and ready to fly!

Summary of Part I

If this were the conventional "how to" book, this space would contain a list of the 10 most important points brought out in these three short chapters. Actually, these chapters are so short that you can review and summarize them by glancing at the subheadings in each.

I will merely point out that we have faced up to and suggested possible answers to these two questions:

How can anyone answer my questions about life after death when medical science has not even proved that man has a mind or spirit?

Since medical science has not proved that the brain is anything more than a collection of perishable cells (which are 80 percent water), how can my mind possibly survive death of my physical body?

As a welcome change from all of the serious and semi-technical jargon in these three chapters—and with a promise that I will not return to such investigations in the remainder of this book—consider the poem on the following page. It provides a whimsical summary in poetic language.

A Butterfly

by G. Eustace Owen

A butterfly rested upon a flower,
  Gay was he and light as a flake.
And there he met a caterpillar
  Sobbing as though his heart would break;
It hurt the happy butterfly
  To see a caterpillar cry.

Said he, "Whatever is the matter?"
  And may I help in any way?"
"I've lost my brother," wept the other,
  "He's been unwell for many a day;
Now I discover, sad to tell,
  He's only a dead and empty shell."

"Unhappy grub, be done with weeping,
  Your sickly brother is not dead;
His body's stronger and no longer
  Crawls like a worm, but flies instead.
He dances through the sunny hours
  And drinks sweet nectar from the flowers."

"Away, away deceitful villain.
  Go to the winds where you belong.
I won't be grieving at your leaving,
  So take away your lying tongue.
Am I a foolish slug or snail,
  To swallow such a fairy tale?"

"I'll prove my words, you unbeliever.
  Now listen well, and look at me.
I am none other than your brother,
  Alive and well and fancy free.
Soon you'll be with me in the skies
  Among the flirting butterflies."

"Ah!" cried the mournful caterpillar.
  "'Tis clear I must be seeing things.
You're only a spectre sipping nectar,
  Flicking your ornamental wings,
And talking nonsense by the yard.
  I will not hear another word."

The butterfly gave up the struggle.
  "I have," he said, "no more to say."
He spread his splendid wings and ascended
  Into the air and flew away.
And while he fluttered far and wide,
  The caterpillar sat and cried.

BAH!! YOU'LL NEVER GET ME UP IN ONE OF THOSE THINGS.

PART TWO

What Evidence of Survival Is There?

Foreword

For the past 6,000 years, most religions have promulgated the conventional belief in immortality. However, their leaders have done very little to convert faith and belief into actual knowledge of the certainty of life after death.

Now, for the *first time in human evolution*, the picture begins to take full and comprehensive shape, for as man approaches the end of the twentieth century, pieces of the puzzle suddenly begin to fall into place. In Part II, we will identify and examine eleven of the most fascinating types of evidence.

We have considered the wonder of the caterpillar which becomes a gorgeous butterfly. Easily we regard the human being as an even more fantastically marvelous creature which may be designed by our Creator to survive death, decay and dissolution of its purely temporary physical body.

Reports of rapidly emerging knowledge about the multidimensional nature of man further strengthened the basis for belief in life after death. But one may still ask, "Is there factual *evidence* that we will be alive after shedding the caterpillar body?"

Were you to undertake your own search for actual proof, the obvious approach would be to determine what has already been written on the subject. You would soon discover that there are many books about it. Very good collections are in England, where you could find 10,000 to 30,000 volumes in each of five libraries. In the United States, three psychical research libraries list more than 100,000 books related to the subject.

Some of the most meaningful material, however, is found only in technical journals of many branches of science—particularly physics, microbiology, the neurophysiology of the brain, paraphysics, and parapsychology. Unfortunately, many of the authors of these do not have a broad enough knowledge in other scientific fields, or in religion and metaphysical and occult lore, to understand fully the significance of their own findings as they might relate to survival.

To make it still more complicated, some of the most interesting research work being done is not yet in print.

In this section we assemble *factual evidence* from these wide-ranging sources.

CHAPTER 4

Historical and Religious Writings

Survival Evidence—Area 1 of 11

"Bury—bury me just where you please if you can only catch me. Have I not often told you and the wise men that this body is not Socrates?"

We begin with what has already been written. Carl Wickland, M.D., in the monumental research work reported in his book, *Thirty Years Among the Dead*, provides a good summation:

"Fiske, the historian, says: 'Among all races of men, as far as can now be determined, ancestor worship (contact with the spirits of the departed) was the earliest form of worship,...prevailing in Africa, China, Japan, among the Aryans of Europe and the American Indian tribes.'

"Allen, in his *History of Civilization*, writes: 'Rude tribes the world over are found to have ideas of a human soul, a spirit world, and generally a belief in immortality. Savages consider the next life simply a continuation of this; they also recognize another self which has mysterious powers. Death is the abandoning of the body by this mysterious other self, which is conceived of as still existing in the near neighborhood. The loves and hates of this world are transferred to the spirit world.'

"Confucius said: 'Bemoan not the departed with excessive grief. The dead are devoted and faithful friends; they are ever associated with us.'

"The writers of classic times—Socrates, Herodotus, Sophocles, Euripides, Plato, Aristotle, Horace, Virgil, Plutarch, Josephus, Maximus of Tyre—repeatedly refer to spirit existence as a well-known fact. Cicero wrote: 'Is not almost all heaven filled with the human? Those very gods themselves had their origin here below, and ascended from hence into heaven.'

"Early Christianity's recognition of spirits is too well authenticated in the writings of St. Anthony, Tertullian, Origen and their contemporaries to require emphasis.

"The Bible is replete with references to spirit existence. 'We also are compassed about with so great a cloud of witnesses.' Heb. 12:1. 'Beloved, believe not every spirit, but try the spirits, whether they are of God.' 1 John 4:1. 'The spirits of just men made perfect.' Heb. 12:23. 'There is a natural body and there is a spiritual body...First that which is natural, and afterward that which is spiritual.' 1 Cor. 15:44, 46. Many other similar Biblical citations might be given.

"Swedenborg contributed volumes on this subject. Dr. Samuel Johnson said: 'I do not believe in spirits—I have seen too many of them.'

"Shakespeare, Milton, Wordsworth, Tennyson, Longfellow, and many other poets write with profound understanding of the continued existence of man.

"We are all familiar with the convincing results of the psychical research work of modern scientists, philosophers, ministers, physicians, psychologists and other investigators—Prof. Crookes, Alfred Wallace, Sir Oliver Lodge, Sir Arthur Conan Doyle, Rev. R.J. Campbell, Archdeacon Colley, Rev. Newton, Rev. Savage, W.T. Stead, Camille Flammarion, Dr. Baraduc, Dr. Janet, Prof. Richet, Cesare Lombroso, Dr. Hodgson, Dr. I.K. Funk, Prof. James, Prof. Hyslop, Dr. Carrington and many others.

"Dr. Thomas J. Hudson, author of *The Law of Psychic Phenomena*, wrote: 'The man who denies the phenomena of spiritualism today is not entitled to be called a skeptic; he is simply ignorant.'

"The Rev. Dr. George M. Searle, rector of the Catholic Church of St. Paul the Apostle, New York City, said: 'The reality of the existence of spirits in modern spiritism is no longer an open question, even among scientific men who have examined the subject. Anyone who considers the manifestation of them as mere humbug, trickery or delusion is simply not up to date.'

" 'In our times no one denies the real existence of spiritualistic facts, except a few who live with their feet on the earth and their brains in the moon,' wrote G.G. Franco, S.J., in *Civilta Cattolica*. 'Spiritualistic phenomena are external facts which fall within the range of the senses and can easily be observed by all, and then such facts are attested by so many well informed and credible witnesses, it is useless, as well as foolish and ridiculous, to fight against proved evidence. The facts remain assured, even for reasonable men.' "

However, even if I gave page after page of such historical and Biblical quotations, it would not *prove* survival. All I endeavor to show in this chapter is that for thousands of years there has been, around the globe, a common thread of belief in both *spirits* and an *afterlife*. It would be prudent to assume that where there is so much smoke there may also be fire.

CHAPTER 5

Deathbed, Near-Death, and Out-of-Body Experiences

Survival Evidence—Area 2 of 11

Much of the search for evidence that one's mind, personality and soul survive death of the physical body is to be found in death-bed, near-death and out-of-body experiences.

The past few years have seen books on these subjects become overnight bestsellers. *On Death and Dying*, by Elisabeth Kübler-Ross, M.D., and *Life After Life*, by Raymond Moody, M.D., have each sold more than 3,000,000 copies and have each been translated into more than 25 languages, while subsequent books by these and other authors have also received acceptance throughout the world. Their popularity testifies to a thirst for knowledge that reassures there *is* a life after death.

One might think that the above activities represent a completely new' area for research, but this is not the case. The references in the Appendix show that writing on these subjects started more than 100 years ago. During this past century, many persons labored to add to the great body of knowledge which now fully supports and substantiates the work set forth in the above-mentioned bestsellers. In fact, it is most significant that Dr. Moody and Dr. Kübler-Ross had very little knowledge of the work of prior researchers. The fact that their work dovetails so precisely with the findings of Cobb, Crookall, Savage, Hyslop, Richet and others serves to add great significance to this area of survival research.

By comparison, the purpose of *this* book is to supply the reader with new knowledge of *what actually happens* in life after death.

Because of the ready availability of books on deathbed and near-death experiences, I will not make an *in-depth* report on them. I will, however, briefly review the subject. Then I will do something that has been widely overlooked. I will relate these experiences, particularly near-death ones, to the rapidly-increasing findings of researchers working with out-of-body experiences.

First, let's define our terms.

Deathbed Cases: Observations by medical people and psychical researchers of what a dying person reports in the moments before death of the physical body. Often these reports include visions of deceased loved ones, religious figures and afterlife scenes.

Near-Death Cases: The subjective reports of persons who, through illness or accident, nearly died or who clinically died and were revived.

Out-of-Body Experiences: Experiences in which the consciousness of a person seems to get *outside* that person's physical body. This consciousness then reports what it sees, hears, and does, and where it travels during the time when it is seemingly displaced from its physical body.

The Deathbed Experience

One of the most extensive pieces of research yet done on the deathbed "visions" was published in 1961 by Dr. Karlis Osis—a lengthy monograph, *Deathbed Observations by Physicians and Nurses.* Dr. Osis sought the experiences of 10,000 American physicians and nurses. An analysis was made of the detailed reports of 640 respondents. A high proportion of these had witnessed their patients' reactions to and reports of unseen deathbed visitors. Dr. Osis drew these major conclusions:

1. The dying often go into inexplicable exaltation before death.

2. They see visions of apparitions to a much greater extent than persons who are not approaching death.

3. Usually, these apparitions are of persons who have died. However, visions of living or religious personages are occasionally seen.

4. Drugs or other aspects of illness seemingly do not account for these visions.

5. Many of the dying persons intuitively realize that these apparitions are coming to take them into death and a continued existence.

In 1977, Dr. Osis and a colleague, Dr. Erlendur Haraldsson, published *At the Hour of Death.* This book extended the above studies and included reports of experiences of more than 1,000 additional doctors and nurses. Significantly, this work was based on the experiences of persons dying in India as well as in the United States. The deathbed visions were very similar in spite of racial, cultural and religious differences.

These scholarly and scientific studies in turn have been found to correlate very well with the pioneering work done over a period of 30 years and reported in the several works of Dr. Robert Crookall of England.

Near-Death Experiences

Please recall that in Fig. 19 in Part I, the *nonphysical* part of a person was shown separately, outside of the physical body but attached diagrammatically with a tenuous connection known since early Biblical days as the silver cord.

This ability of the mind, personality and soul to detach itself from the physical body should be kept in mind in reading through this short selection of excerpts of near-death cases reported by Dr. Moody in *Life After Life:*

"A woman recalls, 'About a year ago, I was admitted to the hospital with heart trouble, and the next morning, lying in the hospital bed, I began to have a very severe pain in my chest. I pushed the button beside the bed to call for the nurses, and they came in and started working on me. I was quite uncomfortable lying on my back so I turned over, and as I did I quit breathing and my heart stopped beating. Just then, I heard the nurses shout, "Code pink! Code pink!" As they were saying this, I could feel myself moving out of my body and sliding down between the mattress and the rail on the side of the bed—actually it seemed as if I went *through* the rail—on down to the floor. Then, I started rising upward, slowly. On my way up, I saw more nurses come running into the room—there must have been a dozen of them. My doctor happened to be making his rounds in the hospital so they called him and I saw him come in, too. I thought, "I wonder what he's doing here." I drifted on up past the light fixture—I saw it from the side and very distinctly—and then I stopped, floating right below the ceiling, looking down. I felt almost as though I were a piece of paper that someone had blown up to the ceiling.

" 'I watched them reviving me from up there! My body was lying down there stretched out on the bed, in plain view, and they were all standing around it. I heard one nurse say, "Oh, my God! She's gone," while another one leaned down to give me mouth-to-mouth resuscitation. I was looking at the *back* of her head while she did this. I'll never forget the way her hair looked; it was cut kind of short. Just then, I saw them roll this machine in there, and they put the shocks on my chest. When they did, I saw my whole body just jump right up off the bed, and I heard every bone in my body crack and pop. It was the most awful thing!

" 'As I saw them below beating on my chest and rubbing my arms and legs, I thought, "Why are they going to so much trouble? I'm just fine now." '

" 'Boy, I sure didn't realize that I looked like that! You know, I'm only used to seeing myself in pictures or from the front in a mirror, and both of those look *flat*. But all of a sudden, there I—or my body—was, and I could see it. I could definitely see it, full view, from about five feet away. It took me a few moments to recognize myself.'

" 'I could see my own body all tangled up in the car amongst all the people who had gathered around, but, you know, I had no feelings for it whatsoever. It was like it was a completely different human, or maybe even just an object....I knew it was my body but I had no feelings for it.'

" 'After it was all over, the doctor told me that I had a really bad time, and I said, "Yeah, I know." He said, "Well, how do you know?"

and I said, "I can tell you everything that happened." He didn't believe me, so I told him the whole story, from the time I stopped breathing until the time I was kind of coming around. He was really shocked to know that I knew everything that had happened. He didn't know quite what to say, but he came in several times to ask me different things about it.'

" 'This is sort of funny, I know, but in nursing school they had tried to drill it into us that we ought to donate our bodies to science. Well, all through this, as I watched them trying to start my breathing again, I kept thinking, "I don't want them to use that body as a cadaver." ' "

Out-of-Body Travel

In the foregoing paragraphs we have been considering out-of-body awareness only in relation to the experiences of persons who have come close to dying but recovered sufficiently to be able to describe their short out-of-body sojourns. Even better evidence of the ability of the mind, personality and soul to leave its physical cloak or overcoat has been given in recent years by persons who develop the ability to leave their bodies *whenever they so desire.*

One of the most accomplished out-of-body "travelers" is Robert Monroe, a former radio and television broadcasting executive and electronic engineer. In his book *Journeys Out of the Body,* he tells how he developed the ability, and of his actual experiences with out-of-body travel over a 20-year period.

Monroe is now teaching this ability to small groups of people throughout the United States. Several years ago, I spent ten days at a lovely ranch in Montana where Monroe conducted training sessions, during which he acquainted fifty people with the basics of the technique. In the year following this indoctrination workshop, approximately twenty percent of the people learned to leave their bodies at will. To show the reality of this activity, consider this example from Monroe's personal experiences:

One Saturday in 1963 when Bob Monroe was 55 years old, he decided to see if he could contact a woman friend of the family who had gone someplace on vacation—but he did not know where. He lay down, relaxed, and left his body. He traveled until he found himself in the kitchen of a beach cottage where his friend was sitting, talking with two teenage girls. He tried to "communicate" with her but had no success. He decided to give her a pinch on her right leg. She suddenly jumped up in surprise. A week later when they met, he asked her if she had felt anything at the time the incident took place. She exclaimed in surprise, pulled her dress just above the knee and showed a discolored spot and said, "Don't you ever try that trick again without giving me warning!" The description of the kitchen, the teenage girls and many other details which he had written down upon returning to his body agreed precisely with what the woman was able to report.

The parapsychology literature is now full of reports of scientific research dealing with this new awareness of the mind's ability to leave temporarily its physical habitat. No distance limitation on such travel has yet been observed. Subjects at Stanford Research Institute report back from their travels around the state of California. The Russians are reported to have developed these *remote viewing* abilities for purposes of military surveillance. Experimenters have even "traveled" to the back side of the moon and recorded their observations, which were later confirmed by American and Russian astronauts who made investigations.

It should be obvious that if the mind, personality and soul can take leave of the physical body and function in space adjacent to or far away from the body without losing consciousness, then it can remain outside of the body when the body decays in death, since it is obviously independent of the body.

CHAPTER 6

Apparitions, Hauntings and Ghosts

Since the beginning of recorded history, people in all parts of the world have reported apparitions, hauntings and ghosts. To what extent, if any, does this throw light on the survival question?

There is considerable overlapping of these terms in many people's minds, so I will clarify them here. Webster's *Third New International Dictionary* defines *apparition* as "the unexpected or supernormal appearance of someone living or dead." It is obviously unnecessary to consider living apparitions; those of the dead will be included in my references to ghosts.

The term *haunting* is defined as "an act of frequenting, especially by a *disembodied spirit.*" Here we come a bit closer to the survival question. Centuries of reports of hauntings establish two essential elements in the phenomenon: an old house or dwelling place of some kind, and the restlessness of a human spirit. The first represents an unbroken link with the past life of a former occupant. The second is believed to be caused by various factors. These include the person's remorse over an evil life, his shock at a violent death, important unfinished business in the physical world, excessive attachment to material life, or the failure to realize that he has "died" and is now living in another realm.

Such hauntings provide many types of activity. Strange noises are heard, objects are displaced, lights are seen where none exist, existing lights are turned on and off, and objects are moved about. An actual temperature drop may be felt in the atmosphere. Sometimes an unbearable stench is detected, and often people on the premises experience a feeling of discomfort or even horror. They sometimes report seeing insubstantial shapes, phantoms, apparitions or *ghosts.*

What are ghosts? Webster's dictionary tells us that a ghost is "a disembodied soul; the soul of a dead person believed to be the inhabitant of the unseen world, or to appear to be living in bodily likeness." A disembodied soul, inhabiting an unseen world. Yes, these certainly relate to the question of survival. At least this gives us indication that perhaps *there is a soul* and perhaps it can *leave the physical body at death.* So that brings us face to face with ghosts. Are ghosts real?

There is ample—and increasing—evidence that they are. The evidence falls into two basic categories—what might be called "solid ghosts" and "vaporous, shadowy, indistinct or even invisible ghosts."

The materialized forms of clothed human bodies that I will discuss in Chapter 11 are actually examples of solid ghosts. One of the finest pieces of research in the field is the seven years of work presented in *Ghosts in Solid Form* by Gambier Bolton. This small book summarizes the official records of three research societies in London early in this century. It reports on the questions and answers exchanged with the solid ghosts. Here is an example of such verbal exchanges:

"**Dr. A.C.:** From your appearance, and the firmness of your arms, hands, and bust, I assume that you are at this moment fully materialized. Please show us your lower limbs, so as to convince us of this fact.

"**Ghost:** No, Doctor, I cannot do that now, but if you will give me time to return to 'Florrie' (the sensitive) for two minutes, I will get more power, and will then gladly do so.

"She returned to the spot where the sensitive was seated on her chair in a state of deep trance; and in less than two minutes she once again walked into our midst, and, lifting up her white draperies, showed us her legs bared from the knees downwards. She then placed one of her feet upon Dr. A.C.'s knee, and permitted him to touch both her leg and foot, in order to prove to him and to us that she was fully materialized in every respect.

"**Dr. A.C.:** How is that you had no lower limbs three minutes ago, and were obliged to return to the sensitive before you could obtain them?

"**Ghost:** Doctor, when we come to you people on earth in this way, our great desire is that we may be recognized first by *our voices*, then by *our faces.* That is why so many of us materialize only the head, throat, arms, and hands, and the upper portion of our bodies. That is quite enough for you to identify us by, as a rule, and in doing this we are able to save "the power" for the use of other entities who may wish to materialize as soon as we have finished. Tonight there is any amount of "power" here, as you seven men are all in such good health; and as only two of us intend to use it, I am able to show myself to you fully materialized from head to foot, just as my predecessor "Katie" used to do, through this very sensitive, to Sir William Crookes. But you may take it from me as a fact that *full-form* materializations in this country are rare, for the reason which I have stated; the vast majority being *partial* manifestations only."

More recently, the owner of a rented house in Huntsville, Alabama, was growing frustrated because his tenants were so disturbed by "unseen" visitors that after a month or two of such unnerving experiences, they would decide to move. After the third tenant vacated the property, the owner enlisted the help of Joe Gambill, a local man who was reported to be able to talk with ghosts and persuade them to cease activities such as opening and closing doors, causing items to fall from the shelves, making strange noises and giving the feel of chill air at the moment the ghost passed one's person.

45

Joe, who held a very responsible position in a U.S. government research activity, had a highly developed psychic sensitivity in which his clairaudient ability permitted him to *hear* the words spoken by a ghost. However, he did not have sufficient clairvoyant ability to *see* the ghost. Hence he expended a great deal of photographic film trying to capture with the camera what he was unable to see. After wasting much film, he decided to use his highly-sensitive dowsing ability to help him locate the ghost so that he could point his camera toward the area in the room where the ghost was located.

Late one evening, he went to the now-vacated house and quickly got into conversation with the ghost. The ghost readily explained that he had been killed in a fire that destroyed a house that had stood on this site some 30 years previous to the erection of the present one. He was now completely lost and frustrated. At this point, Joe used his dowsing rods and located the position of the ghost. He dropped his dowsing rods, raised his camera, pointed it in the direction indicated, and snapped the shutter. The resulting photograph is shown in Fig. 22. Joe then explained to the ghost about his present situation and gave instructions as to the steps he should take to "move into the light" and get on with the many opportunities which his new life in the world of spirit could provide.

Fig. 22. Photograph of a live ghost

While to the uninitiated, the ghost may look like just an oddly shaped white cloud of steam or vapor, it correlates well with our scientific studies: the two floppy and folded appendages are the two streams of energy that project cyclically from the mind, and the white spike at the top relates to the emanations from the crown chakra at the top of the energy field that makes up the mind, memory banks and soul.

Even from this very short review of the subject, it is obvious that *apparitions, hauntings and ghosts* make a valuable contribution to the research findings relating to the continuity of individual life.

CHAPTER 7

Obsession and Spirits

Survival Evidence—Area 4 of 11

This is one of the areas that provides some of the best evidence of survival. Literature for thousands of years has clearly reported the existence of obsession and possession.

To assure that we are all in accord with the usage of these terms, let's refer to Webster's *Third New International Dictionary*. I have emphasized parts of the definitions:

Obsession: 1. Siege; 2. The *act of a devil or spirit in besetting a person, or impelling him to actions from without.*

Possession: The *condition of being dominated by something* (as an extraneous personality, demon, passion, idea), a psychological state in which one's normal personality is replaced by another.

Thus, by commonly accepted definition, a spirit can *obsess* a living person. The person is then in the condition of being *possessed.*

As we saw in Part I, the departure of one's mind and soul from the body at death on some occasions occurs so naturally and smoothly that it is quite common for a person at first to be unaware of what has just transpired. Many persons, particularly those *having no knowledge whatever of spiritual life,* are totally unconscious of having passed into another state of being. However, no longer having the physical sense organs, they find their eyesight is "turned off." Lacking any comprehension of the nature and purpose of their existence, they are *spiritually blind.* The Bible calls this zone the "outer darkness." They actually are in a realm—a very real world of spirit—which we today refer to as the *astral.*

The astral realm, as we will discuss in much greater detail later, is made up of various levels. Upon shedding the *physical* body, a person will normally awaken *within three days* on that astral level *for which his recent earth life has qualified him.*

The lowest of these astral levels, zones, or planes interpenetrates the earth and occupies the same region in which we live! Recall that in Part I we learned that modern science has shown that our senses have fooled us as to how "hard" and "solid" this world is. Actually, even our physical bodies were found to be 99.99999 plus percent **empty** space. So just lay aside for the moment your unbelief that a departed spirit can occupy the same space you occupy. In fact, you can now well understand how *many* departed spirits can occupy the body of just one living person!

It has been observed that death does not make a saint of a sinner, nor a sage of a fool. The individual carries over all of the old beliefs, the old habits, the old desires and all of his faulty teachings and religious dogmas. Those who believe that there is no afterlife are not at all prepared for what they find. (Later I will discuss in detail what happens to those who find themselves arriving on the *higher* astral planes. Here in this examination of obsession and possession, we are concerned *only* with those who because of their deeds—and misdeeds—have arrived on the lowest astral plane.)

Those departing souls who arrive on the *lowest* of the astral planes find that they lack physical bodies and are bewildered by the almost total darkness that seems to surround them. Some may be attracted by the "magnetic" energy field that emanates from nearby mortals and is seen clairvoyantly as "light." (These mortals might even be the friends and relatives attending the funeral of the deceased!) Consciously or unconsciously, a few of these attach themselves to the "magnetic" auras of those still in the flesh, thereby finding an avenue of expression by obsessing human beings. In such cases they will influence the possessed person with their own thoughts, imparting their own emotions and weakening the will power of the possessed person. In some cases, this "takeover" can be so complete that they will actually control the possessed person's actions and often produce great distress, mental confusion and suffering.

This is a fact of life almost totally unrecognized by present-day psychiatry. These *earthbound* souls are the supposed "devils" of all recorded history. They are of *human* origin—the direct result of lives filled with human selfishness, lives warped by false teachings and ignorance, and lives thrust blindly into a very real type of "hell" or "purgatory," in bondage to ignorance. We can also be possessed by nonhuman devils—by elementary spirits or so-called elementals and by devilish thought-forms—but these phenomena are somewhat different.

For some, references to obsession and possession must have an air of *unreality.* Therefore, let's go back over recorded history so that it can be understood that I am not trying to introduce some new and untested ideas in this search for evidence of survival. Here are just a few items to be found on the pages of history over the last 2,000 years:

Homer referred repeatedly to demons and said: "A sick man pining away is one upon whom an evil spirit has gazed." Plato held that demons obsessed mortals. Socrates speaks directly of demons influencing the possessed (the insane). Plutarch wrote: "Certain tyrannical demons require for their enjoyment some soul still incarnate; being unable to satisfy their passions in any other way, incite to sedition, lust, wars of conquest, and thus get what they lust for." Josephus says: "Demons are the spirits of wicked men."

Obsessing or possessing spirits are frequently mentioned both in the Old and New Testaments. In I Samuel 16:23, we read: "David took an harp, and played with his hand: so Saul was refreshed, and was well, and the evil spirit departed from him."

So common was knowledge of spirits and spirit obsession in the time of the apostles that the ability to cast out evil spirits was considered one of the most important signs of genuine discipleship, and it must be admitted that a considerable portion of the work accredited to Jesus was the casting out of demons.

A few quotations from the New Testament will suffice. "Jesus gave his twelve disciples power against unclean spirits, to cast them out." Matt. 10:1. "Jesus preached...and cast out devils." Mark 1:39. "A certain man which had devils a long time...Jesus had commanded the unclean spirit to come out of the man...He that was possessed of the devils was healed." Luke 8:27, 29, 36. "Vexed with unclean spirits." Luke 6:18. "The evil spirits went out of them." Acts 19:12.

"Master, I have brought unto thee my son, which hath a dumb spirit....And He asked his father: How long is it ago since this came unto him? And he said, Of a child....Jesus rebuked the foul spirit, saying unto him, Thou deaf and dumb spirit, I charge thee, come out of him, and enter no more into him. And the spirit cried, and rent him sore, and came out of him: and he was as one dead; insomuch that many said, He is dead. But Jesus took him by the hand, and lifted him up; and he arose." Mark 9:17, 21, 25-27. Similar occurrences, labeled "psychopathological," are not at all uncommon in psychiatric research.

Tertullian with authority challenged the heathen to a trial of superiority in the matter of casting out demons. Minucius Felix, a Roman, wrote in *Octavius*: "There are some insincere and vagrant spirits, degraded from their heavenly vigor...who cease not, now that they are ruined themselves, to ruin others."

More recently, Dr. Godfrey Raupert of London, who was especially delegated by Pope Pius X to lecture on spiritism to Catholic audiences in America, said in substance: "It is no longer possible to put the subject of psychic phenomena aside. The scientific men all over the world have recognized spiritism as a definite and real power, and to shelve it is a dangerous policy. Consequently the Pope has asked me to tell Catholics the attitude to take toward the subject....The Church admits the reality of these spiritistic phenomena and their external intelligences, in fact, it has always admitted their reality. The problem at present is to discover the nature of the intelligence. We are now on the borderland of new discoveries which may revolutionize the world. It is not the time yet for an explanation of all the phenomena. We must suspend our judgment until the subject is better known. The study of spiritism is a new one and therefore dangerous....A partial knowledge of the subject may cause grave dangers (resulting in obsession or possession)."

Julian Hawthorne wrote in one of the leading American news-papers: "Thousands of evil-minded and evil-acting men and women die every day. What becomes of their souls or spirits? They want to get back here....The increasing boldness and frequency with which they take advantage of their opportunities is illustrated in many ways....Two acts of defense are open to us. We may stop the source of supply of these undesirable visitors and we may close the doors."

Surely any reasonable person will find that the foregoing historical review documents the reality of obsession and possession. But most of us like to go from the general to the specific. Let us consider first one of Dr. Wickland's cases which he reported in *Thirty Years Among the Dead,* and then a case in which I was personally involved.

Mrs. Wickland was a superb deep trance medium. Dr. Wickland would place a mentally disturbed patient in a chair beside his wife. Mrs. Wickland would go into trance, making her vocal cords available for use by the obsessing entity. Dr. Wickland would then carry on a conversation with the invader, gradually enlightening it as to where it was and convincing it to depart—usually in the company of some helpful spirits summoned for that purpose.

If this procedure seems strange and hard to believe, let me report my personal contact with the Wickland work, although I never met them personally. When Mrs. Wickland died, Dr. Wickland could not find another medium in the United States who could function in the same way. He went to England in 1932 to see if he could locate such a medium there. He found that Mrs. Bertha Harris could function just as efficiently as had Mrs. Wickland. Dr. Wickland and Mrs. Harris spent five days working with mental patients in one of London's hospitals. A large percentage of these patients were promptly enabled to leave the hospital. I personally conducted research for many months into Mrs. Harris' psychic abilities. I reported on a portion of this work in the last half of my book, *From Seance to Science.*

The following case history provided by Dr. Wickland demonstrates several of the issues of dying we have been discussing, including possession:

"Mrs. Wickland became entranced and fell to the floor, the spirit clutching at her throat and crying: 'Take the rope away! I am in the dark. Why did I do it? Oh, why did I do it?'

"When the excited spirit had been somewhat quieted, she told that her name was Minnie Harmening, that she was a young girl and had lived on a farm near Palatine. As she was speaking brokenly, between sobs, it was difficult to distinguish her words, and I understood her to say that she came from "Palestine," which seemed rather strange.

"The spirit was in great grief because she had hung herself, and thought the body of the psychic was her own, and that the rope was still about her neck.

"She said that on October 5th, without any cause or premeditation, she had been overpowered by a desire to take her life, and when alone had gone to the barn and hung herself.

" 'A big man with a black beard made me do it. He [a possessing entity] met me in the barnyard and hypnotized me, and made me hang myself to a rafter, but I don't know why I did it.

" 'My brother John found me and cut me down, and my parents were almost beside themselves. But I am not dead. I am at home all the time and I talk to my mother and father. I try to comfort them and make them know that I am not dead, but they do not notice me and do not answer me. My folks all sit around the table crying, and there is my empty chair, but no one answers me. Why don't they answer me?'

"We could not at first convince her that she was expressing herself through the body of another, but after a lengthy conversation, she was somewhat enlightened and comforted, and left with spirit friends.

"Previous to this incident, neither Mrs. Wickland nor I had heard of the Harmening suicide mystery and we did not know that such a girl had ever existed.

"Several days later, a reporter from one of the Chicago dailies came to interview us regarding our research work, and I related our recent experience with the Harmening girl.

"In great surprise he said that he himself had been the reporter on the Harmening case and that the girl had lived in Palatine, Cook County, Illinois. The dead body of the girl had been found hanging in her father's barn, but no one knew of any cause for suicide, although the girl had always been peculiar."

Fourteen years after the above session, the spirit Minnie Harmening put in another appearance, coming through the medium, Mrs. Wickland:

" 'I want to thank you for all the help you have given me.

" 'When I committed the act which took my life I was only a young girl of sixteen. I had so much suffering afterwards and was very, very miserable. I could see my father and mother sitting at the table crying and I could not help them.

" 'When the time came for my body to be buried the minister would not take it into the church, and would not bury it, because, he said, I had committed a sin in taking my own life. He also said that I could not be buried in the graveyard because of my act, and he would not even look at the funeral as it passed by.

" 'I did not do the deed myself. I was obsessed. It was very hard for my father and mother and sisters. The minister would not even come into the room where my body lay, but spoke from another room; he was too holy to be where the body was. This made it harder for my parents.

" 'Do not think that by taking your own life you can bury yourself in the hereafter. I was obsessed when I took my life and did not know

52

what I was doing, but I am suffering because my father and mother are still mourning for me. Very often I go to see my poor old mother, and she is very old now.

" 'I am the girl who lived at Palatine. You remember me, don't you?

" 'The neighbors made it still harder for my folks because they told mother what a disgrace it was for the family. I feel very badly about the matter.

" 'I want to thank you for the help I received here. It was through you that I received light and understanding. I am happy in a way, but not real happy, because I feel the grief my father and mother have.

" 'When I lived, I did not understand obsession. After I had hung myself, I saw a man beside me, staring at me. Just when the rope was around my neck, I came to; I tried my best to get it off my neck, but I had kicked the box from under myself and my whole weight was on the rope and I could do nothing. I scratched my body in an effort to free myself, but it was no use.

" 'If one take his own life he goes through a bitter experience, and suffers greatly—yes, suffers greatly.

" 'I thank you very much for the light and understanding I have received, for it has been a great help to me.' "

I consider myself fortunate that my personal knowledge of the *reality* of obsession and possession is not limited to what can be found in books. Let me share just one interesting case with you.

In February 1974, I was awakened at 3:15 a.m. by the ringing of the telephone. An acquaintance, Bill, was calling me in great distress. Before he had uttered more than a few words, a strange voice cut in and cursed me with such gusto and vocabulary as I have seldom heard. Bill would try to get in a few more words to explain what was going on but would be interrupted constantly by the strange voice uttering more curses and insisting that I stay out of their affairs (the word "their" referring to the fact that *two* entities had obsessed Bill).

Finally, I got the picture into focus and told Bill that I could not handle this case personally but that he should carefully put the phone back on the hook and I would try to have someone call him.

I dressed hurriedly, walked to my nearby office and laboratory, and looked up the telephone number of my friend Henry Mandel. Mandel, then 78 years old and living in St. Petersburg, Florida, was one of the best healers I had encountered in my worldwide studies of healers.*

I got Henry out of bed at 3:30 a.m. and explained the situation. I gave him Bill's number and asked him to phone immediately. At 4:45 a.m., Henry phoned me back and reported the mission accomplished.

---

* His work is reported on pages 28-30 and in Appendix B of *Healers and the Healing Process*. He died in 1978.

But news of equal importance was that Henry had had the presence of mind to turn on the telephone-attached tape recorder just a few minutes after making contact with Bill and his "visitors." The copy of that tape is one of my prized possessions. The conversation between Henry, Bill, the two entities and a friendly helper in the spirit world just has to be the strangest telephone "conversation" I have ever encountered!

After this episode, I undertook to help Bill learn how to prevent any further invasion by such low level spirits and to open himself to contact only from higher level spirits. Bill then developed into a good medium with specialized powers of clairvoyance and clairaudience. With these talents, he became a very effective healer through the aid of a medical doctor in the middle astral planes. We will return to this subject of "Spirit Doctors" in Chapter 8.

The reference just made to Bill's mediumship brings to mind that many well-known figures were mediums without the matter being made public. A case in point is Mary Baker Eddy, founder of Christian Science. In her early life, she was an accomplished medium and gave public sittings. Her natural sensitivity later made her receptive to teachings from higher levels of the worlds of spirit as well as from Dr. P.B. Quimby—teachings that have done and are daily doing tremendous good in the lives of countless persons all over the globe. (And if you want some really interesting reading you should see what *she* has said through mediums in the past 20 years! There are a few parts of *Science and Key to the Scriptures* she would like to re-edit.)

It would be worthwhile to put together a well-documented book on obsession and possession. Such is long overdue, if we are ever to stop the practice of sending thousands of wonderful human beings to the mental hospitals just because the psychiatric profession as a whole has refused to look beyond the tips of the noses of Freud and some of his successors.

Surely enough has been said to indicate that any research studies on survival must consider very carefully 2,000 years of authenticated experiences with obsession and possession.

CHAPTER 8

Spirit Doctors

During my intensive full-time research into the nature of man these past sixteen years, one of the key areas of study was investigation of the people known as healers. As I met and traveled with medical doctors, psychiatrists, scientists, and parapsychologists in many countries, we continually encountered the controversial question of "spirit doctors."

Almost none of the healers we met in Brazil, England, the United States, the Soviet Union, Mexico, Scotland, South Africa, or the Philippines had any medical knowledge. Relatively few had an education beyond high school—and most of the healers in the Philippines and South Africa had either no education or only one or two years of grade school. When asked, "How do you know what is wrong with the patient," the answer usually was, "My guide (or "my protector" or "my spirit doctor") tells me what the trouble is and what should be done about it." This was very hard for the members of our various research teams to accept. Since we all knew about the capability of the human mind to put on a series of spectacular and often bizarre dreams each night—even in full color, with musical accompaniment and striking scenery—it was easy to smile deprecatingly and assure ourselves that here was merely a figment of the healer's imagination. But after encountering Arigó and his "Dr. Fritz," we were no longer so sure of our deductions.

You may have read in *Time* or *The Reader's Digest* about the Brazilian healer José P. de Freitas, popularly known as Arigó. Two paragraphs in the *Time* story of October 16, 1972 give the overall picture:

"Even before he died last year in an automobile accident at the age of 49, the peasant known as Arigó had become a legend in his native Brazil. Claiming to be guided by the wise voice of a long-dead physician whom he had never known personally, the uneducated healer saw as many as 300 patients a day, diagnosing and treating them in minutes ....He treated almost every known ailment, and most of his patients not only survived but actually improved or recovered.

"A few years ago, reports on the exploits of such miracle workers would have drawn little more than derision from the scientifically-trained. Now, however, many medical researchers are showing new open-mindedness toward so-called psychic healing and other methods not taught in medical schools."

As a boy, Arigó had no education except for two years at a parochial school from which he was dismissed because, in his own words, he was too stupid to continue. His subsequent career involved hard labor, either in the fields or mines, and later, a clerical job in a social security office. Nobody ever saw Arigó read a book, or even attempt to read one, as was discovered in an extensive sociological study of his background. For all practical purposes, Arigó could be considered an illiterate. Thus, it was necessary to consider very seriously the hypothesis that there indeed may have been a voice presenting itself in his head. The important question is: What was its source?

Arigó the healer was able to make a complete diagnosis by merely looking at a patient. A team of medical doctors and scientists from the United States took 3,000 pounds of medical diagnostic equipment with them to Brazil for the Arigó research. Andrija Puharich, M.D., the team leader, arranged to have a diagnosis made of each of about 450 patients, taken at random from the lines that formed daily to obtain Arigó's services. When comparing the team diagnoses with the instantaneous ones Arigó called out in Portuguese in the time it took patients to walk the few steps from the head of the line to stand before him, it was concluded that there was good agreement in 92 percent of the cases. Puharich later confided in me, "George, we will probably never find out, but there exists the sneaking suspicion in my mind that Arigó may have been right in the other 8 percent!"

Equally beyond medical comprehension was the fact that Arigó was one of the few healers who prescribed every known modern molecular medicine. In two cases, he dictated a prescription for medicine that had just been put on the market in Europe but which had not yet been imported into Brazil.

Arigó often treated a few hundred patients a day—patients who seemingly suffered the full range of human ailments. Usually Arigó would complete his handling of the patients in one to four minutes each.

How could this be? Arigó said all the credit was due to "Dr. Fritz," who spoke into his right ear. Since we were not able to come forth with any alternative explanation that fit the facts as they were gradually assembled from the study of Arigó's many abilities, we decided to investigate the question in depth. Our research continues.* I will share with you just one case I have been following carefully over the years.

In Chapter 7, I told of my friend Bill, who had become possessed by two entities. I mentioned that we had helped him learn how to ward off further attacks by low level spirits and to open himself to contact with more evolved spirits.

---

* Some results of this research are presented in *Healers and the Healing Process*.

Later Bill did perceive, clairaudiently and clairvoyantly, a much more evolved intelligence. This spirit said he was a former medical doctor and wanted to help Bill become a healer. Bill was naturally quite mystified by the whole procedure. Under our close monitoring, he developed into a very capable healer. All of his diagnoses and treatment instructions came from an entity who called himself "Doc Nick." Bill, knowing nothing about the practice of medicine, was continually struggling with the words Doc Nick would speak into his right ear. On his 59th birthday, we gave Bill a medical dictionary so that he could look up the spelling and meaning of the medical terms he was hearing clairaudiently!

This is just another in the great and growing number of cases where former medical doctors on the middle and upper astral planes *are able to continue doing what they are most interested in—helping suffering humanity.*

Robert R. Leichtman, M.D., an internist with highly developed clairaudient and clairvoyant capabilities, made an important point about help from Spirit Doctors when he read the first draft of the manuscript for this book. He said, "Dramatic as it is to observe a Dr. Fritz working through an Arigó or a Doc Nick working through Bill, we should point out that most of the help from Spirit Doctors is *not* of this variety. By far the greatest benefit comes from the Spirit Doctors working through both the patients and the medical professionals by influencing their thinking while they are in the waking or dream state—by ordinary telepathy."

We are far from knowing as much about this situation as we want to know. Research is being pursued avidly. With every additional bit of research into the questions surrounding Spirit Doctors, there is mounting evidence of survival.

CHAPTER 9

Spirit Photographs

Survival Evidence—Area 6 of 11

If you have never heard of "spirit photographs," the material in the following paragraphs may tax both your imagination and your credulity. However, after researching this subject over the past decade, I feel it is an area that certainly must be considered in any serious study of survival.

Perhaps a good way to get an introduction to this subject is to share with you some material I recorded in the home of Mrs. Bertha Harris of Golders Green, a suburb of London. Mrs. Harris has for more than 60 years been one of the finest mediums of this century. Her abilities, and her crusty and unvarnished habit of telling the truth as she sees it, resulted in her being a trusted friend of King George VI, Sir Winston Churchill and Charles de Gaulle. After two years of personal study of Mrs. Harris' psychic abilities in the areas of psychometry, clairaudience, clairvoyance and precognition, I reported my findings in Part II of *From Seance to Science*. In a taped interview in 1972, Mrs. Harris provided this enlightening first-hand account of what "spirit photography is all about.

"Spirit photography occurs when a photograph, taken under any condition, shows an 'extra' when developed. Usually an extra face appears in addition to the one being photographed. These extras do not appear as frequently today as they did in the days of my youth when I learned the technique of psychic photography.

"My father supplemented his income with photography. Regularly, as a child, I saw him emerge from the dark room in our house where he used the wet plates which were later to be superseded by films. He made his own sensitive paper, chemicals from his own formulas, enlargements, and so on. At the age of sixteen, I was taught to retouch the negatives to make the people look more attractive. As a matter of fact, I went through the whole process of professional photography.

"To my father's astonishment, he used to get what he called 'ghosts' on his film. This was rather a nuisance, for he often had to travel twenty miles to photograph a subject, only to return home and find there was an intruder in the picture. Some of these 'damned ghosts,' as he irately called them, were extraordinarily exciting to me.

"Near our home, for example, lived Lady Yates, the owner of many high-stepping and temperamental hunters. One of them, named Becky

Sharp, would be groomed only when the groom's little boy sat on her back, for the two were greatly attached to each other. At the age of four, the child fell ill and died not long afterwards, but during his convalescence he would be carried out to the stable to pet the horse. A few weeks after the boy died, my father was asked to photograph Becky Sharp in order that her picture could appear in an exhibition. When the negative came back from the dark room, it showed the dead boy sitting on the horse's back.

"Even more staggering was the occasion when we went to photograph a bridal couple in a country church. The bride looked radiant on the arm of a handsome young solider, and the photographs seemed likely to turn out well. When they were developed, however, the soldier was not there. Instead, a sailor stood in his place. Needless to say, this was very distressing to the bride's mother, who was especially worried about the groom. 'What are we going to do with this?' my father asked her.

" 'Oh,' she exclaimed, 'It will kill him if he knows. A couple of years ago my daughter secretly married that sailor, and then he was killed.'

"It appeared the sailor had come to the wedding and superimposed himself on the photograph. Not surprisingly, the bride's mother begged us to destroy the negative. Later my father said to the groom, 'I'm very sorry, sir, but that photograph was a failure.'

"That was one photographic assignment which could not be repeated, but tremendous problems of embarrassment and expense were caused when ordinary portraits had to be repeated. The fact is that my father was a spirit photographer even though he knew nothing about Spiritualism or psychic photography. No wonder he was angered by the intrusion of these extras. 'These ghosts are haunting me,' he would cry. Then one day, I did not assist him in the dark room as usual, and no spirits appeared on the film. Suddenly we realized that my presence somehow caused the appearance of the extras, though we did not understand why. The spoiling of film by these uninvited spirits was very costly, and I was henceforth barred from the dark room!

"Some years later, after I had entered Spiritualism and was working as a medium, I went sometimes to the Crewe Church, about fifteen miles from my home in Chester. En route to Crewe on the train one time, I found myself in conversation with the woman who shared my compartment. It turned out that the woman was Lady Conan Doyle, and she was on her way to Crewe Church to see Billy Hope who, at that time, was one of the world's leading spirit photographers. Lady Conan Doyle invited me to accompany her and I accepted, though the evening did not unfold as anticipated.

"Before the evening service, Billy Hope came to the church and lamented, 'There are no spirit photographs for you. They just aren't coming any more. Ever since Mrs. Buxton, my assistant, went into the hospital, the spirits haven't appeared.'

" 'Do you think,' I asked him, 'that possibly you and Mrs. Buxton have some kind of power which causes the extras when you are together but fails when you are apart?' Then I told him of my father's experience with me.

" 'I am the same,' he said.

"Thus it happened that while Mrs. Buxton was in the hospital for several months, Billy Hope came to Chester to take his photographs in my presence. Wonderful extras appeared. If I took the photographs without Hope, however, no spirits were revealed in the developed picture. It was apparent that the power to produce the extras had to be drawn from two cooperating persons. This theory was confirmed by my spirit guide, whom Billy questioned one day when I was in trance. Rather surprisingly, though, when Billy asked my guide about the mechanical process of receiving the extras, he was told that the lens played no part. The picture of the spirit was printed directly on the plate.

" 'In that case,' Billy asked, 'How do you always manage to get them right side up?'

" 'Oh, don't worry about that,' my guide said obligingly. 'We'll give you some upside down!' And they did.

Fig. 23. Typical early 19th century spirit photography

Fig. 24. Sir Arthur Conan Doyle shortly before his death

Fig. 25. Photo of Doyle produced at his request two months after his death

" 'They've pulled a fast one on us this morning,' Billy would remark on such occasions."

Over the years while working with Billy Hope and others, Mrs. Harris collected a large album of photographs which had faces and figures of people who had died. Unfortunately for science, this album was destroyed in the same bomb attack in World War II that broke Mrs. Harris' back. From the few photographs that survived from this period, four are shown in Fig. 23.

Sir Arthur Conan Doyle, medical doctor and author of the Sherlock Holmes stories, spent the last eleven years of his earth life traveling the world speaking on behalf of the cause of Spiritualism. Two years after his death he made arrangements to "come back" in a series of 22 sittings with medium Grace Cooke of London. Doyle desired to tell how he found things in the new worlds he was inhabiting, and in particular he wanted to correct some of the erroneous ideas he had presented in his lectures on Spiritualism. For example, he, along with other Spiritualists of his day, had said there was no reality to the concept of reincarnation. He wanted to testify to the fact that reincarnation *is* a reality.

At the end of the series of talks, Doyle himself made the arrangements from his level of existence to provide evidence of his survival of bodily death. Ivan Cooke, the medium's husband, in his book *Thy Kingdom Come* (the revised edition was entitled *The Return of Arthur*

Conan Doyle) tells how Doyle said, "I am endeavoring to give you a proof on a photographic plate." He then described the steps by which such a photograph actually was produced within the next 24 hours. It is reproduced in Fig. 25, next to a photograph of Sir Arthur while alive (Fig. 24).

Another piece of research on spirit photography will be of interest. One day while working in our laboratory we utilized the spiritually sensitive abilities of a trusted psychic to garner some information on spirit photography. We asked a friendly soul who travels at will throughout the world of spirit to locate for us for the following day a person who had participated in spirit photography and materialization research while in the flesh. When we met we were told that a person had been selected who would share experiences encountered both in the flesh and in the world of spirit.

During the process of "testing the spirits," we learned that we were talking to Rev. Sophia Bush; that she had led her own Spiritualist Church in Miami for many years; and that she had been involved in spirit photography and materialization for 30 years. In an aside she observed, "This was more in my early years in Spiritualism. Once one learns the *reality* of these phenomena, one becomes far more interested in *spiritual development* than playing around with psychic phenomena."

In addition to talking about conventional spirit photography such as is shown in Figures 23 and 25, she told us about other types as well. "We took photographic paper and each person present placed the sheet over the forehead or the heart. We sat in darkness thinking intently of a particular dear one who had gone on ahead. After fifteen or twenty minutes, we washed the photographic paper in the developing fluid and dried it under red light. Often we were surprised at the pictures, which were very recognizable. Incidentally, this is an old process which has even been done with very thin silk cloth and no photographic emulsion."*

A parapsychologist reading these remarks by Rev. Bush might say that the latter account is an example of *thought* rather than *spirit* photography. As of now we do not know enough about the process to agree or disagree. We can only observe that the recording of a person's *thoughts* on photographic emulsion—and often without using the lens of the camera—is as *far outside the capability of today's science to explain* as is the modification of a photographic emulsion by the imprinting of *faces* of persons long since dead and totally unknown to the researchers.

With our rapidly expanding scientific knowledge of light and other energy forces, it is likely that in the decades ahead, photography of persons on the higher planes of being will become commonplace.†

---

* Is it possible that the *matter-energy exchange* involved here is related in any way to the image scientists have recently scrutinized so thoroughly on the cloth *shroud of Turin*?
† For those interested in reading more, the definitive book on spirit photography is *Beyond the Spectrum* by Cyril Permutt, published in 1983 in England.

CHAPTER 10

Materialization

Survival Evidence—Area 7 of 11

If it is difficult to accept the reality of spirit photography, it is even more difficult to accept the reality of *materialization*.

By the term "materialization," I refer to the fact that all or a portion of a person who has died and been buried or cremated can reappear in a three-dimensional form. This reappearance can have such a high degree of likeness to the deceased physical body that it is instantly recognized. Preposterous as it may seem, research in many countries has shown the reality of this extremely rare phenomenon. In Chapter 6 we gave an example of such research dealing with *ghosts in solid form*.

In past centuries such experiences were surrounded by mystery. Materializations recorded in the Bible have been considered miraculous, mythical or allegorical. In Exodus 3:2-22, the materialized figure of an angel is reported as appearing to Moses. In Matthew 17:1-3, it is reported that the materialized figures of the long-dead Moses and Elijah appeared to Jesus, Peter, James and John. And according to Luke 24:13-31, the form of Jesus appeared and spoke to two disciples as they walked on the road to Emmaus. Then some hours later, the *fully materialized* figure of Jesus appeared to the assembled disciples (Luke 24:33-51). The disciples were terrified and thought they were seeing a ghost. Jesus spoke to them and called attention particularly to His hands and feet. He suggested that they verify that these hands and feet were not some vaporous spook or a figment of their imaginations.

Is all of the above just scriptural nonsense?

It is only natural that we may be skeptical of the survival evidence written down 2,000 years ago about a religious figure. Let us move forward to this century.

In the past 100 years, occasional small groups of serious-minded people have carried on research that resulted in materializations no less dramatic than those recorded in the Bible. Sir William Crookes in England, Schrenck-Notzing in Germany, Pavlowski and Kluski in Poland, Carlos Mirabelli in Brazil, and Harry Edwards in his work in England and South Africa have succeeded in producing materializations. These materializations have been no less dramatic and real than those of Moses and Elijah, and that of Jesus appearing to and speaking with the apostles on two occasions after His burial. Some readers may find these modern examples more credible than the Biblical references.

Carlos Mirabelli of Brazil must be credited with some of the most fully-documented cases of materialization. The 1927 publication of the *Zeitschrift fuer Parapsycholgie* reports on pages 450 to 462 on a series of materialization experiments that collectively were observed by 557 persons:

"This seance which took place at nine o'clock in the morning was attended by many people of note. The room in which the test was conducted was situated on the ground floor and was eleven meters long by ten meters wide. The windows opening upon the street were faced with iron bars; the floor was composed of narrow strips of wood which had been examined one by one to make sure that they could not be manipulated surreptitiously. Everything was found to be in order, and it was definitely established that the only way of forcing an entrance into the room would be to break through its thick walls or its doors framed in stone.

"Mirabelli, seated in a chair, turned pale, indicating the approach of a deep trance. His eyes bulged and twisted about as though someone were trying to strangle him, while beads of sweat stood out all over his body. Suddenly three sharp raps sounded on the table which stood in the room, and a child's voice called out: "Papa." Dr. Ganymed de Souza who was present declared with great emotion that he recognized the voice of his little daughter who had died of the grippe in the capital. Everyone sat in tense expectation, and presently the shape of a girl appeared beside the medium. Almost beside himself, her father stepped out of the circle, spoke to his child, went close to her and folded her in his arms. Amid convulsive sobs he assured the others again and again that it was his own daughter whom he was holding, and that the dress worn by the apparition was the same as that in which she had been buried.

"All the while, Mirabelli lay as though in death-agony, cowered in his chair, his complexion waxen, his muscles completely relaxed, his breathing weak and wheezy, his pulse barely perceptible.

"Colonel Octavio Viana now rose to convince himself of the reality of the apparition. He also took the child in his arms, felt her pulse, looked into her deep fathomless eyes, and asked her several questions, which she answered rationally, although in sad monotones. Viana also was able to confirm that the vision was tangible. Dr. de Souza then recalled several childhood incidents in his daughter's life to the apparition, receiving replies which showed that his remarks were understood. *The apparition was photographed*, a copy of the picture being appended to the investigating committee's report.

"After the picture had been taken, the child began to soar about the room, rising into the air and plunging about like a fish in its native element. The spectators had risen to their feet and followed the vision, which remained at a height within easy arm's reach. The medium meanwhile continued to imitate the child's motions with his forearms. She floated about in the air a few seconds longer, and disappeared all of a sudden, after having shown herself for thirty-six minutes by daylight and under unexceptionable conditions to a gathering of educated men, who testify that they saw before them a perfectly formed human being.

"Dr. Ganymed de Souza thus lost his daughter for the second time, so deeply was he moved by what he had seen. *The statement which sets out this occurrence is attested by the signatures of ten men holding the degree of Doctor of Science.*"

The best documented case in recent years that I have uncovered in my study of this phenomenon occurred in 1963 in São Paulo, Brazil. A group of 15 medical doctors, psychiatrists and lay people undertook to conduct an "iron-clad" experiment. They built a cage made of iron bars, one side of the cage serving as a door. Inside on a simple chair, they placed a woman medium who had previously participated in successful materializations. (Only a very special medium is of use. The materialized figure is made up of energy substance taken from the medium's physical body, as well as from the bodies of those present.) The medium was secured by leather straps and padlocks to the chair and the iron cage, as indicated in Fig. 26.

Some minutes after the medium was in deep trance, her head fell over her shoulder. Then it was noted that white material was issuing from her nostrils and her left ear, as seen in Fig. 27. At this point, the

Fig. 26. *Medium securely fastened in enclosure before trance*

Fig. 27. *Medium in trance with ecto-plasmic formations issuing from left ear*

research leader pulled the thin black cloth curtains mounted inside the iron bars of the cage in order to decrease the intensity of the light in the area where the spirit entities were utilizing the ectoplasmic material being drawn from the body of the medium as well as from the bodies of the research team members standing outside the iron cage. (*White light*, both from the sun and electric lights, inhibits and may even prevent the materialization process. This scientific fact, not generally understood, has in years past resulted in critics charging fraud, because the majority of materializing mediums would only consent to work inside a *totally darkened* room or "cabinet.")

With the passage of time, the white material increased in volume and built up into a fully-formed five-foot-high figure of a Catholic nun clad in full vestment. At this stage, two of the researchers handed an open Bible to the figure, whose hands were starting to extend between the iron bars, as indicated in Fig. 28.

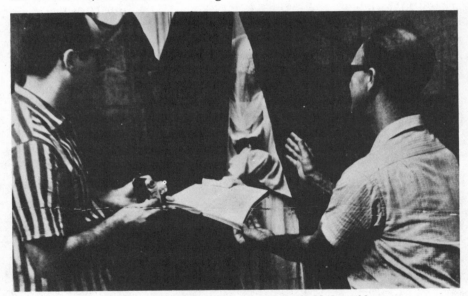

Fig. 28. Materialized figure ready to hold the Bible

The figure took the Bible and held same in its hands, as can be seen in Fig. 29. In this remarkable photograph, note the two arrows pointing to the iron bars which pierce the robed figure. The figure is just starting to move out of the iron cage *by moving through the bars just as though they were not there.* (Recall that in Part I, Chapter 1, Fig. 2, the chair on which I was sitting seemingly had moved forward *through* my body and was photographed in detail.)

The materialized figure moved forward through the steel bars and out of the cage until it was fully exposed, as is seen in Fig. 30. Note that the upper arrow points to an assembly of white pearl-like beads making

Fig. 29. *Materialized figure holding the Bible and starting to pass through the steel bars*

up an ornament on the forehead level. Now look at the very first material to issue from the medium's nostrils in Fig. 27. It will be seen that this decoration was among the first material to be formed.

In Fig. 30 note that the bottom arrow calls attention to the lacework structure of the outer shawl, which partially covers the fully materialized crucifix. In the original negative, this material shows the warp and woof of the delicate white threads.

Fig. 30. Close-up of fully materialized figure showing cloth-like nature of veil, beaded head ornament and crucifix

At this point, it was possible for the members of the research team to recognize the face of the materialized figure. It was that of the medium's sister, a Catholic nun who had died two months previously.

The materialized figure gradually dissolved and disappeared. The researchers lost the opportunity to use the warm wax and cold water in the two buckets shown in Fig. 26. These were on hand to take fingerprints of the materialized fingers. Such wax impressions of the fingertips of a materialized form were obtained in Poland in research with the medium Kluski and in Boston with the medium Crandon.

In Chapter 9, I reported comments made by Rev. Sophia Bush, a Spiritualist minister who had lived in Miami before her death. After we discussed her experiences with spirit photography from the viewpoint of her work before and after death of her physical body, we turned to the subject of materialization of human beings. Two of Rev. Bush's remarks relate directly to the materialization case just presented.

"Now the type of person desiring to manifest is usually a spirit who wishes to reassure his grieving loved ones that he or she is *still among those present*. Some mediums are so proficient in helping to produce the materialized figure that it is difficult for those present to distinguish the ectoplasmic form from the physial form known to the loved ones. But sooner or later, the life force begins to leave the figure and it crumbles or dissolves. The energy of the manifesting spirit returns to the bodies of the sitter and those present."

This certainly relates to the materialization case we have just presented. The materialized figure was that of the medium's recently deceased sister. The nun's figure dissolved before the researchers could take the wax impressions of the hands and finger tips. The energy-matter exchange caused a collective weight loss of 27 pounds by the 15 physicians, psychologists and others who made up the research team. In this case, there was no means of measuring the weight loss of the medium. In other cases reported in the literature, however, the medium has been found to suffer a weight loss of from 15 to 40 pounds at the height of the materialization.

Realizing the importance of materialization to the survival question, I organized and led a small team of American and English scientists to Brazil in 1972. In our short stay we encountered a few persons who were reported to be materializing mediums. Our efforts to capture such phenomena on video tape, still cameras and movie cameras were unsuccessful. However, our camera techniques did allow us to detect a *fraudulent* effort on the part of one of the mediums who had agreed to work with our research team. The medium, locked in the iron cage, had his young son appear, garbed in white cloth from head to foot and standing outside the cage. He was not a very convincing "spook." Our infrared film had penetrated the totally dark room and recorded all of the important details. One photo of this fraud is included as Fig. 31.

Now, fourteen years later, having studied this subject in more detail, we realize that we ourselves contributed to the lack of success with the *sincere* mediums with whom we came in contact. For one thing, we now understand more fully why such materializations *cannot take place without the full approval and active collaboration of intelligences in the worlds of spirit.* These are specialists in the manipulations of the subtle energies of the human being. Man is only dimly beginning to grasp the realities of these energies, which seem to lie outside of our knowledge of the electromagnetic spectrum.

It has been 2,000 years since the aspostles examined the materialized hands and feet of their Master. With our now rapidly expanding knowledge of materialization, we can speculate that the next one or two decades will see this aspect of survival substantiated in a way that will cause the "material" sciences to add some new chapters to their textbooks.

But is the materialization phenomenon itself convincing *proof* of survival? Dramatic as it is, and even though it apparently was *convincing* to Jesus' disciples, we do not feel it is the proof demanded by today's scientists. And interestingly enough, those persons dwelling in the spirit world share the same opinion, as indicated in the next incident!

During the aforementioned 1972 trip to Brazil to study materializa-

Fig. 31. Fake materialized figure captured in total darkness with infrared film

70

tions, our team had the rare privilege of using the superb telepathic channeling services of Shirley Shultz to have a three-and-a-half hour question-and-answer session with a British medical doctor, "Joseph," who said that he had died approximately 100 years earlier. As a fitting conclusion to this chapter, note carefully the following exchange:

A Team Member: This team of scientists from the U.S. and England believe that if they can photograph a bona fide materialization of a person who has died, they will then have *solid scientific proof* of survival. Do you, yourself a dweller in the spirit world, agree?

Joseph: No. Even if you find and photograph some legitimate materializations, you would still not have your *proof* of entities from our side...that we exist...proof that we exist. And I will tell you why you would not. First, you would find many on your sphere who would not accept it. But even eventually it would not be proof. For eventually your scientists will understand that materializations involve a physical substance called ectoplasm. While it is partially manipulated by the spiritual entities themselves, it is also partially manipulated by the medium. So you will still not have *complete proof* of survival. The only way you will have complete proof is by *observing us as we are.* And for this you need to have a shield or screen for seeing us, and you will need to have an instrument for *hearing* us. Most importantly, you need to have an instrument which will *change our thoughts to sound*—or something which we ourselves can manipulate and use so that you will *hear our spoken words.* Now this is the only way you are going to have 100 percent proof that life exists after transition from the material body.

In Chapters 18 and 19, we share with you the results of our sixteen years of efforts to create equipment that does just that—change spirit thoughts to sound so that we can hear the spoken words of persons who have left their physical bodies.

CHAPTER 11

Reincarnation

Survival Evidence—Area 8 of 11

Is reincarnation a present-day fact or a centuries-old fiction? Nothing is more relevant to survival than the answer to this question.

In its simplest form, reincarnation is a belief that:

    a. Each person has a soul.

    b. The soul survives the death of the physical body.

    c. The soul then spends time in other realms of existence.

    d. Next the soul is reborn into a new physical body—human, not animal—for the purpose of further mental and spiritual growth.

    e. This cycle is repeated until the soul reaches a high state of development and reunites in full consciousness with God.

Although reincarnation is accepted by more than half of the population of the world, it is strongly resisted in Christendom. Most Christians believe in a, b, and c above, but relatively few believe in d and e—even though Jesus makes an oblique reference to reincarnation when He asks if the disciples think He is the reincarnation of Elisha. Research has also shown that the Essenes, the group in which Jesus seems to have lived as a young man, may have embraced the concept of reincarnation—as did most of the peoples who then lived to the east of Israel.

If you care to do serious research into the twin questions of communication with departed spirits and reincarnation, you will find that the earliest Biblical writings contained many references to each. The former was the obvious reason for the author of 1 John feeling the need to caution his flock to be careful, to test and make certain that the spirits to whom they were talking were "of God"—that is, to be sure the spirits were highly-evolved spirit teachers and not low-level or earth-bound spirits. There is some evidence that between 300 to 600 A.D., ecclesiastical actions resulted in reducing the number of references in the Bible to both spirits and reincarnation.

Regardless of the beliefs of contemporary Christians concerning spirits and reincarnation, both concepts have been a part of humanity's beliefs in many parts of the world since the beginnings of recorded history. This book is not the place for a scholarly presentation or historical review of the subject of former lives. *What is of importance is that present-day scientific research has turned its attention to the subject.* Few areas will have much more bearing on the survival question than what may now come from this new research into reincarnation.

Indicative of the interest of this subject to science is the scholarly and painstaking research being done by Dr. Ian Stevenson at the University of Virginia Medical School; Drs. Arthur Guirdham and Denys Kelsey, British psychiatrists; Dr. Hernani Andrade, Brazilian physicist; Dr. Hiroshi Motoyama, physiologist and Shinto priest in Japan; Dr. Raynor Johnson, Australian physicist; Robert Crookall of England with doctorates in science and philosophy; and Dr. Karlis Osis, formerly the director of research for the American Society for Psychical Research. With scientific investigators of this caliber devoting their time, we can only conclude that reincarnation is indeed a worthy subject for research. To provide you with just a short sampling of the kinds of cases that are under study, I will present two highly-abbreviated cases of persons who seemed to remember past lives. The first case is from Dr. Ian Stevenson's essay, *The Evidence of Survival of Claimed Memories of Former Incarnations:*

"**Case of Robert.** A six-year-old Belgian boy insisted that a portrait of his Uncle Albert (who had been killed in the First World War in 1915) was a portrait of himself. This boy was especially devoted to his paternal grandmother in contrast to her other grandchildren, who largely ignored her. He was happy and healthy when with her, sullen and disobedient when with his own parents. Albert, the boy's uncle and claimed previous incarnation, had been the marked favorite of the grandmother and had meant far more to her than her other son, the father of Robert. When Robert was three and first saw a swimming pool, he ran along the diving board and dived in. Albert had been a fine diver. When a visitor pointed a moving picture camera at Robert and turned the handle with a clicking noise, he protested, saying, 'Don't! Don't! They killed me that way the last time!' Albert had been killed by machine gun fire while trying to destroy a German emplacement. Robert, his grandmother reported, had used for her pet names Albert had used, and told her of likes and dislikes which Albert and she had privately shared."

For the second example of modern scientific research in this field, I have greatly condensed this case from Arthur Guirdham's *The Cathars and Reincarnation.* He opens by telling the background of his patient:

"She had been suffering for years from dreadful dreams of murder and massacre....I examined the woman for neuroses. She had none, but as the dreams had occurred with such regularity since the age of 12, she was worried about them. She was a perfectly sane, ordinary housewife. There was certainly nothing wrong with her mental faculties.

"After a few months, she told me that when she was a girl...she had written the dreams down. She had also written things that came into her mind, things she couldn't understand about people and names she had never heard of. She gave me the papers and I started to examine them.

[What first amazed him, Dr. Guirdham says, was the verses of songs she had written as a schoolgirl. They were in medieval French, a subject she had never taken at school, as he later checked.]

"I sent a report of her story to Professor Pere Nellie of Toulouse University and asked his opinion. He wrote back immediately that this was an accurate account of the Cathars, or Cathari, a group of people of Puritan philosophy in Toulouse in the 13th century.

"She also told me of the massacre of the Cathars. She told in horrid detail of being burned at the stake....I was astounded. I had never thought of reincarnation, never believed in it or disbelieved....She also said that in her previous life she was kept prisoner in a certain church crypt. Experts said it had never been used for this purpose. Then further research showed that so many religious prisoners were taken on one occasion that there was no room for all of them in regular prisons. Some had been kept in that very crypt....

"In 1967 I decided to visit the south of France and investigate. I read the manuscripts of the 13th century. Those old manuscripts— available only to scholars who have special permission—showed she was accurate. She gave me names and descriptions of people, places and events, all of which turned out to be accurate to the last detail. There was no way she could have known about them. Even of the songs she wrote as a child, we found four in the archives. They were correct word for word....

"I started this as a clinical exercise, and I have proved that what a 20th-century woman told me about a 13th-century religion—without any knowledge of it—was correct in every detail."

In 1875, a Unitarian minister, James Freeman Clarke, looked into the future and observed: "It would be curious if we should find science and philosophy taking up again the old theory of reincarnation, remodeling it to suit our present modes of religious and scientific thought, and launching it again on the wide ocean of human belief. But stranger things have happened in the history of human opinion."

Yes, the fact that more than one hundred years later our scientists are taking up the study of reincarnation is a "curious" and exciting development in man's search for proof of survival.

CHAPTER 12

Space-Time Relationships

Survival Evidence—Area 9 of 11

From the intense activities of scientists in the past two decades we have another finding that relates to our search for survival evidence. It deals with what they call "space-time relationships."

As far as you and I are concerned, we live and move and have our being in a well-ordered *three-dimensional* world: up-and-down, fore-and-aft, and sideways.

Not so, says the scientist.

He says we live in a *four*-dimensional world, and perhaps a world of five or more dimensions. First, he says, as a minimum, we must add a *time* dimension, if we are to comprehend the nature of reality. In fact, if we are to follow the present theorizing of physicists we would have to add two or even three types of time and get involved in a four-dimensional, five-dimensional, etc., "space-time" system.

This is far too complex for us nonphysicists, but in all of this new scientific explosion of human understanding, there is one crucially important nugget that can be stated simply. You and I live by the clock. Our lives are measured by seconds, minutes, hours, days, weeks, months and years. Our every action is related to time. We are born, live a certain number of years, and we die. Few of us indeed reach the century mark. There can be no argument with the clock or calendar. *We last only so many years.* Almost every person alive accepts this as the truth. But is it the truth, the whole truth, and nothing but the truth?

Not on your life!

Science is only bringing to light a very exciting fact about time. While it is true that our lives are measured by time, it is true **only insofar as it relates to the physical body.** Yes, our physical body is chained to the three-dimensional sequential space-time system. But the mind, personality and soul—actually at this very moment—*already exist* in an interpenetrating space-time system. And while it is almost beyond comprehension, watches, clocks and calendars don't even exist in the space-time system in which we will be spending **all** of our time after we cast off that old, worn-out overcoat of a body.

In recent decades, the science of physics has been making discoveries that will soon give us a *solid, scientific basis* for understanding how our nonphysical mind(s), memory bank(s), personality and soul temporarily inhabit the physical body and then depart that material

75

mass when it is cremated or buried in the ground. This revolution in scientific thought started with the discovery of a "particle" which seemed to be *massless* and capable of passing easily through thick concrete walls and heavy sheets of steel. Physicists called this particle, this packet of energy, a "neutrino." And in the last twenty years, they have discovered and named more than 100 *massless* particles. The study of these particles has led to the establishment of a whole new branch of physics known as quantum mechanics.

Michael Roll, a lecturer in subatomic phenomena in Bristol, England, succintly comments: "In a nutshell, our physicists have discovered other dimensions of existence with people in them who are exactly the same as we are. Some really good mediums are able to bridge the gap between these different dimensions of existence. They are speaking to people whose surroundings are as solid and as natural to them as ours are to us. They exist in our space, but as their subatomic particles—building blocks—are moving at such staggering speeds, they are out of range of our physical senses. A good example is to be found in radio and television. All the channels are operating in the same space, but at different frequencies—subatomic vibrations. *The supernatural and paranormal are natural and normal after all.*"

The true significance of this scientific revolution lies in the fact that the science establishment itself can begin to conceive of *worlds within worlds.* Science can now begin to be comfortable with the knowledge that there does seem, after all, to be an interpenetrating world or realm of existence, as has been taught by spiritual leaders for thousands of years.

Michael Scott, astrophysicist of Edinburgh University, Scotland, says, "I can now completely agree with the arguments about the reality of psychic phenomena and the existence of a normally unseen world. I am sure the explanation of these phenomena can be found in quantum mechanics, as applied at the subatomic level. *Here we will find the key to the unseen world.*"

The great significance of quantum mechanics is that at last science is creating a key that will enable mankind to comprehend scientifically what 2,000 years ago Jesus of Nazareth referred to as "the many mansions in my Father's house." This was His way of describing, in poetic terms, the realms in which we will be living when we depart our physical bodies. (See the large color chart inserted at the back of this book.)

If Jesus were speaking to an Earth audience today, He would perhaps substitute the phrase "higher levels of consciousness" for His phrase "many mansions." This would be completely compatible with the work of the quantum physicists and the transpersonal psychologists. It is of great significance for the field of survival research that the world's "First *International* Symposium on Mind/Matter Interface"

(Brazil, July 1985) and the first *national* "Conference on Survival and Consciousness" (Washington, D.C., October 1985) each had quantum physicists of world renown as speakers.

The findings of quantum mechanics are beginning to provide a basis for comprehending how another complete world can interpenetrate our material world and yet not be detected by our five senses. No wonder someone facetiously suggested that physics laboratories put a sign on their doors reading, "Closed For Repairs."

So present-day science has given us not one but two marvelously enlightening tools that add proof to the centuries-old preachments on survival we considered in Chapter 4. First, it confirms that our personality, mind and soul cannot "cease to exist" and "forever disappear" out of the cosmos. Second, it gives us a basis for throwing off the clock-and-calendar concept. It makes it far easier to understand that *we* do not die at the "time" our body dies.

CHAPTER 13

Conservation of Matter and Energy

Survival Evidence—Area 10 of 11

Late twentieth-century physics has been adding knowledge at such an unprecedented pace that it is difficult even to keep abreast of the month-by-month developments. Our whole concept of the nature of matter is undergoing drastic revision.

Scientists have long since discarded the concept in the university texts of my day that matter is made up of very small solid particles that could be thought of in terms of minuscule billiard balls. Later teachings involved picturing matter in terms of energy existing only in wave-like forms. Then it was concluded that sometimes the billiard ball concept was useful but that in other cases the wave theory was more helpful. Now the thinking of the physicists has become so complex—with talk about black holes and white holes, etc.—and it is so mathematically-oriented that there is scant possibility that we ordinary mortals can comprehend what it is they are saying about the nature of matter.

However, there *are* two findings to which we *can* relate. First, it is now concluded that the *mind* of the experimenter can in some cases *influence matter*. The second finding is that matter-energy can neither *be created nor destroyed*. All matter is energy and as the energy is changed or modified, the "matter" is merely energy at a different level of "existence."

A crude example of this is a liquid composed of hydrogen and oxygen. These elements, normally gases, combine to make a fluid substance we call water. If the translational rate of the molecules in water is slowed, by extracting heat, the fluid becomes a solid which we call ice. If the vibrational frequency of the molecules is speeded up, by adding heat, the fluid becomes a gas we call steam. If the steam is heated and the vibrational frequency speeded up to levels not commonly found in nature, it goes into a state for which the scientists have coined the word *plasma*. So now we have not three states for water but four—solid, liquid, gas and plasma.*

The significant thing is that for all practical purposes science is now telling us that *matter cannot be destroyed*. It can only be changed

---

* This is the source of the term devised by Russian scientists—"bioplasmic body"—to replace the older term, "etheric body."

from one form to another—that is, from one vibrational frequency to another.* This means that the law of conservation of energy applies to the energies of life as well as to material things.

This has definite significance in our search for evidence that the mind, personality and soul survive the death of the physical body. The *real* you, your mind, personality and soul, is in a very real sense energy—a "finer" energy at a very high rate of vibration which is un-detectable by our very limited five senses. And this energy does not suddenly cease to exist just because the physical body that it has been wearing changes into water vapor and dust.

Dr. Werhner von Braun, as many readers will recall, was a scientist who helped create Germany's World War II rockets and missiles and then later contributed greatly to the United States space program. Shortly before his death, he provided a succinct summary of the thoughts presented in the foregoing paragraphs: "Science has found that nothing can disappear without a trace. Nature does not know extinction. All it knows is transformation!...Think about that for a moment. Once you do, your thoughts about life will never be the same. ...If God applied this fundamental principle to the most minute and in-significant parts of His universe, doesn't it make sense to assume that He applies it also to the Masterpiece of His creation—the human soul? I think it does. And everything science has taught me—and continues to teach me—strengthens my belief in the continuity of our spiritual exis-tence after death. Nothing disappears without a trace."

So we can conclude that we are indeed fortunate to be living in a day when science itself has done so much to provide another piece of evidence testifying to the certainty of our survival in some form or other in some part of the universe.

---

* We hasten to explain to the scientific reader that little is known about the subtle energies involved in thoughts, emotions, the human aura and the soul. There is now a sufficient accumulation of research data to show that the energies that make up an individual person's thoughts, emotions, personality, memory banks and soul continue in existence after death and decay of the physical body. See "Realization of Holistic Health and its Sci-ence," by Dr. Hiroshi Motoyama, *Journal of Religion and Parapsychology*, June 1979, Tokyo.

CHAPTER 14

Communications Through Mediums
And Telepathic Channels

Survival Evidence—Area 11 of 11

The Christian Bible as well as most religious writings are replete with stories of people who "heard" voices, "saw" visions and foretold the future. In ages past, these rare people were called prophets, sages, seers and mystics.

In the early days of the American colonies, people with such abilities were sometimes called "witches" and were, in some cases, tortured and even burned at the stake. Even in this century in England, such people were ostracized and even imprisoned until the repeal of the Witchcraft Act in 1951.

Only within the last 140 years has serious research into the abilities of such people been conducted. Even up to *the present moment* such researchers are looked at askance by their peers. Hence, there are only a few intrepid souls in England, the United States, the Soviet Union, and Brazil who are today seriously engaged in conducting research in the area of communications from spirits.

Since we do not yet have an electronic means for direct communication with inhabitants now occupying the worlds of spirit, our present research is limited to the use of mediums. Because this is such a crucial area of research into life after death, I will take time to clarify what I mean by the term "medium"—our present terminology for a person who in centuries past was called a sage, seer, prophet or even a witch. I prefer to use the definition of mediumship given by Robert R. Leichtman, M.D., an internist who is himself one of the most accomplished mediums I have encountered in my worldwide search for such talents. The definition is from his book, *Edgar Cayce Returns:*

"Mediumship: The phenomenon of a nonphysical intelligence, usually a discarnate human, assuming some degree of control of a physical body in order to communicate something useful and meaningful. Mediumship is usually used for the transmission of information or inspired guidance, but can also be used to transmit varieties of healing energies. There are varying degrees of trance associated with mediumship and differing qualities of information communicated, depending on the quality of medium and the quality of the spirit using the process. Mediumship is distinguished from the phenomenon of possession in that it occurs only with the deliberate cooperation of the medium and produces a constructive result."

Take special note that Dr. Leichtman says that the *quality* of the information transmitted is dependent on the quality of *both* the medium and the spirit communicator. It is precisely because of this crucial qualification that *a very high percent of all communications through mediums fall into one or more of the categories of inconsequential, garbled, useless, mischievous, and even false and harmful.*

Today we realize that the merest handful of people throughout the world *have demonstrated* that they possess the capability to reach very far up in the worlds of spirit to contact high levels of intelligence while still very much immersed in the nitty-gritty, materialistic world of everyday living. It is precisely this factor that has caused all of the disbelief and scandal associated with mediumship and messages from the world of spirit. It is this—combined with the use of mediumship to make money—that has brought British and American Spiritualism to its present unenviable state. As soon as a medium sets himself or herself up as a paid channel for bringing through "messages" to bereaved family members, the trouble starts. Not being able to have uniformly good contact day after day with the communicators in spirit—but being expected to deliver a satisfactory message to the paying customer—the faking and deception starts. (This statement applies equally to much of the nonsense currently being brought through under the heading of "hypnotic reading of past lives.")

But just because some medical doctors are quacks, it does not follow that **all** doctors are quacks. Precisely the same is true of mediums. A Moses or an Elijah in olden times and a handful of mediums in the world today stand out as effective servants of their fellow men.

During the past 16 years, my fellow researchers and I have searched the world over to locate and work quietly with *deep* trance mediums who are *not* in "the business of mediumship." These people never advertise their abilities. In fact, some of our most useful and highest-level contacts with the world of spirit came into our laboratory through a 60-year-old man who had gone into trance once each month for twenty years in the presence of only his two closest friends.

If the reader is interested in studying this area in depth, I can say that some books listed in the bibliography resulted for the most part from communications through reasonably good *mediums.* But only in a few cases were the *communicators* in spirit currently living on some of the "higher levels"—which will be discussed in Part III.

In the case of my laboratory research, my prime objective has been and still is to check—with *very high levels of intelligence—that picture of the detailed workings of the worlds of spirit which I had been painstakingly assembling over the years.* **Therefore, let is be clearly understood that the material which I present in Parts III and IV are not just fan-**

ciful ideas brought forth by my fellow researchers and me. The concepts set forth in Part III, "A Blueprint of Immortality," have been confirmed by intelligences in the worlds of spirit that can be reached by only a very small percent of the people who consider themselves mediums.

So this book in itself is a living testimony to the reality of *high level* communications with spirits through mediums.

In one of our laboratory sessions with a thoroughly tested trance medium, a spirit entity introduced himself as Prof. Silas Roberts. He gave a very learned discourse on studies currently being conducted in the spirit world for the purpose of eventually helping man to solve the energy crisis, by developing a solid form of hydrogen for use as a fuel in cars and trucks. At one point, he reminisced about his work as a professor of chemistry in a small (unknown to us) college. He mentioned that a small bronze plaque had been put on the door of his laboratory by his former students after his death many years ago. I made it my business to visit this small college in Demorest, Georgia. Sure enough, on the chemistry lab door was the plaque with the date 1947 and words of esteem by the former students. In the years which have passed since the visit to the laboratory of Prof. Roberts, much additional evidence has accumulated to show that he is, in fact, who he says he is.

In this connection, I should cite the admonition of John. In the early days of Christianity—before the Bible was rewritten in parts to tone down the references to dwellers in the worlds of spirit—mediumship was common. But the tricky problems outlined above prevailed even then, and in his first epistle, John admonished his fellow Christians, "Try [test] the spirits [to see] whether they are of God."

Telepathic Channeling

The foregoing discussion of mediumship must be supplemented by a consideration of what is today termed *telepathic channeling*. This advanced level of communication with the spirit worlds, while relatively rare in past centuries, has today become more common. In our own research in the past sixteen years, we have encountered six superb telepathic channels. How does this form of channeling differ from the aforementioned mediumistic activities?

Physical state of the channel—The telepathic channel is usually very much awake and completely aware of surroundings, the opposite of being in trance. The presence of extremely bright lights may necessitate the use of dark glasses or an eye shade, but otherwise the channel is very much aware of the surrounding physical conditions. There is no need for a trance state, light or deep.

Method of delivery—The thoughts of the spirit communicator can be delivered by speaking, writing long-hand or use of the typewriter or word processor.

Level from which information can be obtained—While the majority of *mediums* can contact dwellers only on the upper portion of the lower astral or the middle astral planes, a superb *telepathic channel* can easily reach the *mental or causal planes* and occasionally contact residents on the celestial planes of consciousness. Naturally, the informational content from these higher levels of consciousness is of much greater value than that from the astral plane.

Accuracy of transmission—The accuracy of transmissions by many mediumistic persons is usually very low, perhaps less than 25 percent. By comparison, one superb telepathic channel who serves in our research sessions has been congratulated by the spirit communicator from the mental-causal plane who stated that, in his opinion, the channel brought through as much as *90 percent of the intended content.*

Need for little editing—Mediumistic communications often involve contorted or incomplete sentences, with the material sometimes coming out in a disorganized fashion requiring much time-consuming editing. By comparison, the flow through a good telepathic channel requires a surprisingly small amount.

We have not studied telepathic channeling just out of idle curiosity. Our objective was to be able to establish solid two-way communication *with dwellers on the mental-causal planes of consciousness.* We sought men and women who in their recent lifetimes *were* outstanding scientists and who now have a deep desire to join hands with us in *a particular collaborative venture.* This venture has as its objective the *creation of an instrumental system of communicating* with them and other dwellers on the higher planes of consciousness. *Only by the use of outstanding telepathic channels can this objective be achieved.* Here is one example of this type (further comment on their significance will be given in Chapter 15).

As I look at the bookshelf beside my desk, I see 30 large three-ring binders filled with hundreds of transmissions that have come through *one superb telepathic channel* in the last 22 months. One of these was a transmission volunteered on the occasion of my 75th birthday, when Sir Winston Churchill dictated through the channel (via the keyboard of the word processor) a message of commiseration and encouragement! He described in detail *his own personal feelings* as he himself had moved through his 70's and then into his 80's. The contents of this communication would convince all but the most hard-headed skeptic that the communicator was indeed who he said he was. Aside from the helpful insights in Sir Winston's discourse, there was solid information to *confirm* the continuity of life. He gave me permission to reproduce this personal letter in a quarterly issue of the newsletter of the Metascience Foundation. It brought unsolicited responses from numerous readers who expressed their deep appreciation for the highly relevant insights provided by Sir Winston.

Any serious researcher in the field of communication from the higher planes knows the crucial importance of screening out "imposters," usually friendly but mischievous spirits who are masquerading as famous persons. Having relentlessly followed the Apostle John's admonition about testing the spirits in my own sixteen years of such research, I was, of course, immediately on my guard when this communicator *said* he was Sir Winston Churchill. So I devised a test.

Since I lived in London for seven months during World War II, where I functioned as a technical advisor to several top-level boards directed by U.S. Ambassador W. Averell Harriman, the test I devised involved information known, in part, *to only five people*—Sir Winston Churchill, General Charles de Gaulle, King George VI, a highly respected and beloved English Spiritualist medium, Mrs. Bertha Harris, and myself. I asked the "purported" Sir Winston Churchill certain crucial questions, the answers to which could have been *known only to the five of us.*

Of the five persons involved, I was the only one still in a physical body in May 1985. To my knowledge, I was the only person in the world in May 1985 possessing the background knowledge on which my questions were based. The spirit intelligence with whom I was communicating promptly replied to my questions, giving answers that could be supplied only from the *presently existing memory banks of Sir Winston Churchill.*

It would be easy to expand the material in this chapter to several volumes, but our purpose is merely to indicate that *mediumistic and telepathic channeling* make up one of the eleven areas that should be considered if one is to embark on a serious study of the question of survival. And in Chapter 19, you will observe the crucially important role that *telepathic channeling* is playing in the *scientific research efforts* to establish the *certainty* of your living forever!

Summary of Part II

While there is not yet absolutely ironclad **proof** that you will survive death of your **physical** body, there is certainly *strong evidence* found in these eleven different areas:

1. *Historical and Religious Writings.* Since the beginning of recorded history, in all parts of the world, and in most of mankind's religions, there has been a common thread that *indicates survival.*

2. *Deathbed, Near-Death and Out-of-Body Experiences.* Careful research has clearly established that people in various cultures and with totally different religious backgrounds "see" loved ones and/or helpers coming to help them make the transition from their dying physical body into their new state of existence. Research has also clearly documented that the real you *can* leave the body and *travel*; and that this same "spirit body" (referred to by the Apostle Paul 2,000 years ago) carries you into your next state of existence.

3. *Apparitions, Hauntings and Ghosts.* Encounters with ghosts over 4,000 years in all parts of the world indicate that *something* survives death of the physical body.

4. *Obsessing spirits.* "Obsessing spirits" (the "demons" of the Bible) are still a reality today. They may be elementals, thought forms or spirits or souls of people who have departed their physical bodies and who, due to their baser habits of thought and behavior, are very much confused and in darkness. Still being attracted to the earth plane from which they have only recently departed, they attach themselves to the magnetic auras of living persons. They actually affect the thoughts, emotions and actions of the obsessed person.

5. *Spirit Doctors.* Very careful research by medical doctors, psychiatrists, psychical researchers and others suggests that healers in various parts of the world do, in fact, get help from dedicated medical doctors who themselves now live in the worlds of spirit. These doctors desire to continue their ministrations to ailing humanity. From their present vantage point, they know far more about cause and cure of physical and mental illness than they ever did when occupying their physical bodies.

6. *Spirit Photographs.* Dozens of photographers in many countires, using many kinds of cameras and film, with many types of lighting conditions (including total darkness) have obtained photographs of persons known to have died and whose bodies were buried or cremated. While this phenomenon is easy to duplicate by fraudulent means, there are fully-documented cases of the genuine thing.

7. *Materialization.* From Biblical times down to the present, competent witnesses have observed, touched, examined and even weighed bodies of persons and animals known to have died and been buried or cremated. Our present-day studies of the phenomenon and the rapid expansion in our knowledge regarding the physical universe and its interpenetrating nonphysical universe at last makes it possible to begin to understand the natural laws behind this "miracle."

8. Reincarnation. The beliefs of more than half of the world's five billion people, together with current scientific research, suggest that the individual soul survives the death of the physical body and may, under certain circumstances, inhabit a new human physical body.

9. Space-Time Relationships. The mind, personality and soul *already* exist in a separate and interpenetrating space-time system. This same interpenetrating space-time system is where we *continue* to live when we cast off our physical body.

10. Conservation of Matter and Energy. We have seen that science now accepts as one of its basic tenets that matter-energy can neither be created nor destroyed. The higher, finer matter that is our spiritual body continues to exist after the grosser physical body decays and returns to nature as gas, water vapor and particulate matter ("dust").

11. Communications from mediums and telepathic channels. From the earliest Bible days down to the present moment, there have been and are persons who have the ability to "live in two worlds at the same time," and thereby bring communications from persons who have passed into the world of spirit.

The vast accumulation of experiences summarized in these eleven areas of study *strongly suggest* that your mind, memory banks and soul will still be very much alive and active when *your* day arrives to lay aside your physical body. But we are not yet at a point where we can talk about the **certainty** of your living forever.

So now let us go at the survival question from a totally different approach. We are now in a position *to start on a mind-stretching journey.*

PART III

A Blueprint of Immortality

Foreword

For two thousand years people have speculated about the meaning of the phrase, "In My Father's house there are many mansions." Unfortunately, passing centuries have provided little understanding of this.

Suddenly, as never before in history, interpretations of the accumulated pronouncements of seers, sages and prophets; new revelations of the world's great religions; the findings of late twentieth-century science (particularly physics, neurophysiology and parapsychology); and current laboratory research on the borderlands of science at last enable us to see with understanding eyes. What we see is a *blueprint* showing the relative positions of the mansions. Moreover, it shows many activities carried on in some of these mansions—the very ones in which *we will someday be living—and in fact are already living.*

CHAPTER 15

A Tour of Many Mansions

Millions of spiritual creatures walk the Earth
Unseen, both when we wake, and when we sleep.

What if earth and heaven be to each other like
More than on earth is thought?

—John Milton

Putting It All Together

In Part I, we learned that there is a firm basis for saying:

• We are far more than our *physical* body.

• Our mind(s) and soul are *nonphysical.*

• These nonphysical portions contain our memory banks, our soul, and our own very individual personality.

• These memory banks, soul and personality can and do *survive* death of the physical body.

• Even during the first instant after death of the physical body, these minds, memory banks, personality and soul are just as vibrantly alive (although they may initially be at rest or sleeping) as they were during the years when we *temporarily* wore that physical body given to us by our parents and ancestors.

Then we took a brief look back over the centuries to see what types of *evidence* had accumulated to support the belief that the individual man and woman do survive death of the physical body. We examined eleven different areas and concluded that, *taken as a whole,* there is a strong indication of survival—much stronger than any materialistic counter-argument against survival.

But it is likely that at this moment there are still questions about what actually *happens* when the day comes—as it does for each of us—to leave behind the physical body we are temporarily wearing. You ask, "What happens then? Where do I go?"

We need a blueprint, a diagram that can help to locate and identify the "many mansions" the Nazarene said "are in my Father's house."

The blueprint of immortality which I now present is based upon:

• The experiences of many saints, sages, seers, prophets and mystics over the ages;

• The experiences and reports of certain enlightened persons who in the last 100 years have reached levels of cosmic consciousness;

• Similar experiences of some of my close personal friends and fellow researchers; and

• Research currently underway in several countries.

If you are as skeptical as I was, you probably are already questioning, "Just how accurate, how dependable, and how specific is this blueprint you propose to show me?" While the years ahead doubtlessly will provide additional details, most of the basic information presented has been authenticated by **present occupants** of the "mansions," brought through by mediums and telepathic channels of proven reliability.

Does one have to be an architect, engineer or college graduate to read this blueprint? No. If you will *follow carefully* just three simple steps, you will have a good basis for comprehending what Jesus himself had in mind when He spoke about the many mansions in His Father's house.

Packing for the Trip

Let us recall the essence of the concept which we considered in Fig. 17, reproduced here for easy reference. This simple diagram helps us to understand that the multiple levels of our minds and our soul constitute the indestructible portions of our being which the Apostle Paul 2,000 years ago termed the *spiritual body*. Now with the knowledge you gained in Chapter 2, you know that the various levels of the mind and soul are **nonphysical,** and still more important, that they are composed of invisible energy which is **indestructible.**

You also found in the chapters in Part II that over the centuries there have been eleven categories of evidence, as reported in thousands of books, that the invisible "spiritual" or "astral" body survives death of the physical body. But, you ask, "Where does this surviving body go? What happens to it? Where does it travel to?"

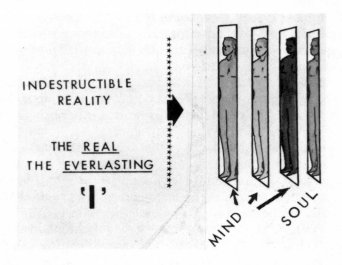

Fig. 17. The real, the everlasting "I"

90

Using A Road Map

Our most earnest research led us to believe that the best clues to answering these questions were given in the Nazarene's statement of 2,000 years ago—"In our Father's House there are many mansions."

This may not seem very specific, but recall that His listeners were not scientifically informed to the degree that we are. His listeners had never heard of *energy fields* (nor did anyone else for the next 1900 years). Jesus was forced to use poetic language to create a picture in the minds of His listeners. Fortunately, now at the close of the 20th century, we can *locate* the "mansions"—and we have learned enough in our 16 years of research to provide a rather accurate road map. Fig. 32 on page 92 charts the general territory to a degree never before possible. And it can be presented now only because of hundreds of hours of recorded conversations (via superb telepathic channels) *with persons who are today actually dwelling in the various mansions!*

Strange and unbelievable as it may seem, the Nazarene was telling the literal truth when He said, "The kingdom of heaven is *within* you!" He was not speaking in parables. The only problem is that during almost all of the past 2,000 years man and his "science" have not known enough about the nature of his own existence and the so-called material world to be able to comprehend His teaching.

No, there is no need to picture these mansions, planes, levels, or resting places as being in some faraway heaven, on some planet or far out space above the earth. *Most of these levels are surrounding and interpenetrating us now.* Recall the disclosure in Part I which introduced you to the knowledge that a) *our bodies and all of the material world are more than 99 percent empty space,* and b) *we live in two worlds at the same time.*

However, it does strain the imagination less if we simply picture these levels, planes, "mansions" or resting places *stacked one above the other,* with the lowest plane starting just above the earth's atmosphere. The simple sketch in Fig. 32 provides us with a good *preliminary* blueprint or roadmap.

Do not be concerned about the *names* of the planes or levels. There is not yet an agreed terminology.* The important fact is that *there are* these basic levels, regions, zones, planes, mansions, resting places—call them what you will.

---

* Any serious student of the accumulated mystical, occult, esoteric and religious lore will recognize that we have greatly oversimplified both our discussion and our diagrammatic representations of the planes (in *both* the lower and higher worlds of spirit). For instance, each of the three planes we have designated as astral will be found to contain within themselves many (from 7 to 49?) different vibratory levels. The same is true of the *still* higher planes. Recently a "teacher" on one of these higher planes expressed it this way: "There are many, many planes of life. We may be on a plane beyond yours; but believe me, my friend, there are planes beyond ours, far, far beyond ours, of which we know very little."

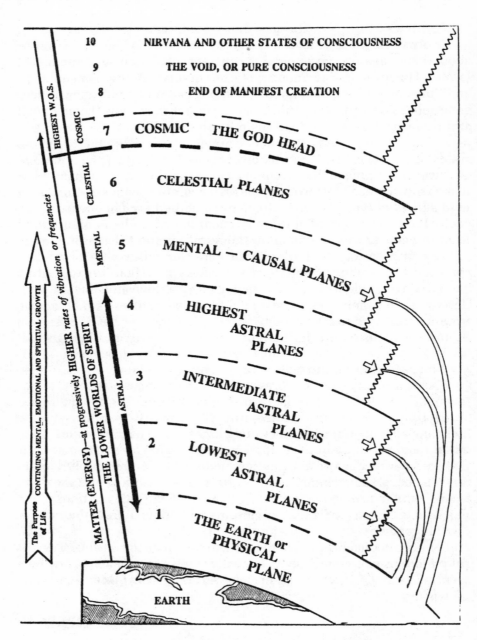

Fig. 32 — *Interpenetrating levels of life and consciousness*

"IN OUR FATHER'S HOUSE, THERE ARE MANY MANSIONS"

In speaking 2,000 years ago, the Man of Galilee used words like those above which the people of that day could understand. *Today,* He might entitle the above chart "Interpenetrating Levels of Life and Consciousness." We could understand these terms because late 20th century science has taught us that everything in the cosmos, including man, consists of various types of energy at different vibratory rates or frequencies.

Needless to say, we can only dimly comprehend the nature of the levels *above* the cosmic level. We know they exist as we know a little about them—again from some of the current inhabitants of these higher levels. However, rather than trying to contemplate the possibility of additional reality systems (9, 10 or 11), it is better to develop a deep comprehension of planes 1 through 6, so that they may become goals and promises for us when we leave Earth's dwelling.

Finding Lodging

Now that we have the excellent road map provided in Fig. 32, let us make inquiries as to just *who* dwells on the various planes of consciousness and *what type of daily activities* are offered for the occupants on each. We will treat each of these levels or mansions in a paragraph by itself, numbered to correspond to the numbers and titles in Fig. 32.

In a first reading of the six paragraphs that follow, it is best not to stop and try to understand all of the words in detail, nor to be concerned if some of the ideas are new, "far out," questionable, or even upsetting. In some cases you may not have been exposed to these ideas by your minister, priest, or rabbi simply because *he himself* has never been exposed to such information! Just read slowly and thoughtfully each of these paragraphs, *holding your questions in abeyance until you have finished reading them all.*

1. The Earth or Physical Plane

Here, on the surface of the earth, you now live in your **physical** body and also in your *interpenetrating* **etheric** and **astral** "bodies." The etheric and astral bodies are **non**physical.* They are a finer form of matter involving vibrating energy fields. They *interpenetrate* the physical body just as hundreds of radio and television waves are doing *at this instant.*

Your soul, personality and emotions, memory banks and mental or causal body are all contained in your **astral** body. When your physical and etheric bodies die (here called the *first* death), the "real you" is still **fully alive** in your astral body. Usually within minutes to a few days you find yourself functioning on that particular **astral plane** *to which the quality of your life on the earth has entitled you.*

---

* As stated at the outset, this is a nontechnical book. Therefore, this explanation is offered to the technical or scientific reader: we use the term *non*physical to refer to a finer and higher type of "matter-energy" undetectable by our present instrumentation. According to Motoyama, the "bodies" and "minds" of the physical, etheric or bioplasmic and astral levels of being exist simultaneously and independently, are closely related and are connected with one another—making up one human being. See his article on "The Realization of Holistic Health and Its Science" in *Journal of Religion and Parapsychology*, Number 20, June 1979, Tokyo, Japan.

93

2. Lowest Astral Plane

This dark, dismal, dangerous and often frightening world, which the Bible describes as "outer darkness, weeping, wailing and the gnashing of teeth," is the habitat of greedy, self-centered, unloving, resentful persons. Often they have fierce bodily desires and lusts. Here too may be drug addicts, sex perverts, alcoholics, murderers or suicides. It is also the abode of the less desirable "creatures" of nonhuman lines of evolution.

This level is traditionally referred to as **hell, hades** or **purgatory.** It is the human and nonhuman astral bodies from this plane that attach themselves to the magnetic auras or astral bodies of persons living on the earth plane (an act of "obsession"). Such a "possessed' person may act abnormally, be judged insane and institutionalized, or commit suicide.

3. Intermediate Astral Planes

Here, the person "awakes" minutes, days or weeks after departing the **physical body,** or months, years or centuries after arrival on the lowest **astral** plane.

This is primarily a *rest and rehabilitation region,* complete with hospitals and their staffs and institutions of learning and teachers. Help is given to dis-eased souls; persons who had traumatic experiences and/or sudden death; and persons with inflexible or erroneous mental, emotional or religious beliefs. The body is still "material" but of finer substance at a higher vibratory rate. Its appearance accommodates each individual's personal preference—usually the prime of earth life.

Here communication is by both thought and spoken word. Each person is encouraged to continue mental and spiritual growth. By such growth one progresses to the *higher* astral and mental planes, or from this level decides to re-embody for further learning and personal growth on the earth plane.

4. Highest Astral Planes

This wonderful realm of existence is what the Christian generally calls "heaven." Another appropriate term is "the summerland." There is no pain or suffering. There are happy meetings with those for whom a bond of *love* is felt, or groups formed of like-minded persons. There are unlimited opportunities and encouragement for each soul to grow in mental and spiritual consciousness. Interest in activities on planet Earth decreases. There are encounters with angels—lovely and helpful beings of nonhuman evolution.

Wider perspectives, greater vistas, magnificent panoramas! But eventually the soul must decide whether to return to the earth plane for more experience or to accept the **second** death. In the latter case, the *mind* and *soul* may shed its *astral* body or containment vehicle and be

94

reborn onto the **causal** or **mental** level for which it has become qualified. When reborn, the soul will function in its mental or causal body.

5-6. Mental and Causal Planes

These levels offer unlimited scope for the further development of the individual **mind** and **soul.** There is access to all of the accumulated wisdom of the ages on the earth plane and throughout other parts of our solar system.

There is no jealousy, judgment, or selfishness. There is complete brotherhood. Most of man's inventions, scientific advances, poetry, inspired prose, art and music originate here and are passed down, through the process called intuition, to receptive minds on the earth plane. For this reason, the *intelligences of this level "cause" much of the good, beautiful and inspiring activities of the lower planes.*

This is the *final* opportunity to choose to return to the earth plane for more earth-life experience and growth; or, if all factors are favorable, then comes the *final* rebirth onto the **celestial planes.**

7. Celestial Planes

The nature of these planes of consciousness (as well as those still higher galactic, universal and cosmic levels 8, 9, 10 and 11) are largely beyond the comprehension of those now living on earth. The celestial planes are the location of the Christian God, of Buddha, and gods of other great religious persuasions on the earth plane. Biblically it is referred to as "the third heaven."

On these planes there is *preliminary* contact with the Universal Godhead, and understanding of the universal life and energy systems of which our solar system is composed. The tapping of such levels of consciousness enabled the Nazarene to perform "miracles." *This path is open to each of us.* This is what He meant when He said, "These things I do, you will do also; and *greater* things than these will you do."

After your initial study of Fig. 32, I suggest you lay it aside until you come to the end of Part IV. By then you will have increased your understanding through the study of 50 questions and their answers. These questions and answers will make it much easier to grasp the important concepts in Fig. 32.

Now you can comprehend how it is that we are functioning not only on the **earth** plane but also in the very lowest and densest portion of the **astral** plane. When the physical body dies and the etheric body disintegrates, we do not really have to go on a "far journey." We will be automatically on whatever vibrational level we deserve to be on, based on the quality of life we have lived while in the physical body.

As you ponder the answers to the questions and the implications of the blueprint, you will glimpse the sublime vistas and the grandeur of the overall scheme of life which God has created for ***all of humanity*** —

regardless of race, color, caste, sex or religion. You will note that while the blueprint forever strips away most of the controversial dogmas and creeds that *separate* the world's religions, it does not discredit the *central spiritual teachings* of the major religious systems.

Gradually, the overall concepts will become familiar and more *comfortable*. There will be less reason to cringe or become frightened by the implication that we are each a spark of the **Universal Godhead.** We have the opportunity to start living a life right *now* that will "lay up for ourselves treasures in heaven"—another of the Nazarene's gentle admonitions.

No longer can we fail to realize that our every act is a "cause"—and that *each* cause must have an "effect" on our lives in the countless centuries of life which lie ahead.

No longer can the scramble to meet the monthly payments on a never-ending list of material wants—or the effort to climb a little higher in the economic or social rat-race—be quite so irresistible.

No longer can we fail to recognize that no matter how dull, dreary and unrewarding this moment of life may be, the path which begins with the *next* moment can be the stepping stone into a glorious and ever-unfolding future of great promise.

No longer can a political system fail to recognize that its citizens are far more than one-lifetime, soulless cogs in a materially-oriented world, who face personal extinction at death.

Even if you disagree with many details of Fig. 32, your study of this book will have been of great value. You have come to realize that immortality **is** an alternative to your assumption of personal extinction at death.

And if the term "immortality" has any negative connotations for you, perhaps we should take a lesson from the men who edited the Bible. "Immortality" is not mentioned in the Bible. "Life Eternal" is mentioned 72 times. On that authority and on the basis of 20th-century research into the nature of man, let us close Part III with the assurance:

Life is Eternal

This is still just a glimpse, perhaps, but it is a clearer, more meaningful, exciting, stimulating, challenging and easily understandable glimpse than anyone can picture without full perception of the grandeur of "the many mansions" of infinite progression that lie ahead.

PART FOUR

Specific Questions and Specific Answers

Foreword

Sadly, too seldom do scientists, medical doctors, professors, philosophers, theologians, ministers, rabbis or priests, individually or collectively, even attempt to provide soul-satisfying replies to the age-old questions propounded by people about life after death.

Regardless of race, color, caste, or creed, each of us—totally alone—walks though the door called Death. It is then that certain basic questions cry out for answers. Nothing could be more important than to know them *beforehand*.

Using an entirely different approach from that of the foregoing chapters, I try here in Part IV to list the basic questions asked about death and give the answers which represent the best of all available conclusions.

CHAPTER 16

Unraveling the Mysteries

"Finding myself to exist in the world, I believe I shall in some shape or other always exist; and, with all the inconveniences human life is liable to, I shall not object to a new edition of mine, hoping, however, that the errata of the last may be corrected."   —Benjamin Franklin

The material that follows is possible only because of the inquisitive minds of dedicated researchers during the past century. First I honor the most dedicated of the serious (and honest) deep-trance mediums, primarily in England, Scotland, Brazil, the United States, Canada, Ireland, Italy, and South Africa. Second, I acknowledge the work of thousands of persons traditionally known as "sitters," whose presence seem to provide subtle energies that facilitate the best contacts with communicators from other levels of life.

These valuable contributions would have been lost, however, had it not been for dedicated psychic researchers and scientists who had the moral courage to investigate and report the work of these mediums and their sitters or circles. These researchers, even down to this year of 1987, have had to suffer ridicule from their peers and loss of their professional status. Men like Sir William Crookes in England, Schrenk-Notzing in Germany, Nobel prize winner Charles Richet in France, Ernest Bozzano in Italy, Dr. Holtacher in South Africa, T. Glen Hamilton, M.D. in Canada, Carl Wickland, M.D., Elizabeth Kübler-Ross, M.D. and William Tiller, Ph.D., in the United States, and Dr. Hernani Andrade in Brazil are the better known of scores of their kind.

Although the accumulated communications and data were fragmentary and often extremely contradictory, in time it became possible to piece together a reasonably consistent and experimentally valid picture of life after death.

Finally, in the past ten years, this type of research has intensified. Communications under *laboratory* conditions from recently "deceased" communicators with medical and scientific backgrounds have added still more validity to the emerging picture. These have greatly enhanced our understanding of the process of death and rebirth. It has pushed our knowledge far beyond that which grew out of the first hundred years of Spiritualism.

Hence, I acknowledge my indebtedness to all those referred to above, without whose effort the material that follows would not have been possible. Their conclusions appear to be *substantially* correct in their broadest aspects. In general, they confirm age-old teachings that form the core of the world's great religions. Of equal importance, however, they strip away a vast accumulation of dogma and creed with which these religions have been profaned over the past 3,000 years.

Regardless of race, color, religion, creed, caste, sex or educational level, we are beginning to see more clearly what happens when each of us, *totally alone,* passes through the door labeled "Death and Rebirth."

1. Let's take first things first. After all of this talk about life and death, what is the purpose of life?

I promised in the opening pages to cut out all of the philosophical, religious and scientific jargon. So here is the answer, just as simply as I can state it: *The purpose of each individual life (soul) is to grow mentally, emotionally and spiritually back toward the level of creative intelligence from which it originally issued.*

Please take a moment to refer again to Fig. 32 in Chapter 15 and note the vertical arrow at the left side of the page. The concepts presented in this diagram will go further toward answering this question than dozens of books.

2. Is it painful to die?

No. Even those whose terminal illness caused prolonged and excruciating pain find that *at the time of death* all pain is gone. This is one reason it is often observed that the face of a dying person relaxes and even has a smile.

The *actual* transition is so smooth and painless that often one cannot believe he is dead. Frequently when a patient goes to sleep during a painful illness he awakes to continuing pain. When he awakens after death, and finds no pain, the first thought is, "I must be dreaming"—or he may wonder if a sudden and miraculous cure has taken place. He has a feeling of lightness and buoyancy. The person sees his physical body lying still and dead and he observes the actions of the nurse or family members. Then it occurs to him, "I suppose I am dead! I did not expect it to be anything like this! I feel fine!"

3. Will I become a ghost? If so, how can I be released?

It is most unlikely that you will be a ghost. Ghosts, apparitions, shades or astral shells result only in the relatively rare cases when the etheric body (or "etheric double," as some call it) fails to separate from the physical and then disintegrate. Separation normally takes place in minutes, but may take up to 30 to 40 hours. Some persons, ignorant of this fact, may have a tendency to hold onto the etheric body and may appear as ghosts. Some people will be able to see this energy field as a bluish-white mist.

Until the etheric body has separated completely from the astral body, the person cannot proceed to his earned existence in the astral world. This failure to shed the etheric body often results from a very traumatic event—murder, fatal injury, or unpleasant emotional experience. Such a failure can also result if a person has never thought about an afterlife and has been wholly centered on his possessions and personal affairs.

A ghost can be released very easily from the area it is "haunting" by a good psychic. The psychic needs only to get in tune with the ghost and in a friendly, loving manner explain that death has taken place and that there is nothing to be gained by lingering in these old haunts. The psychic then encourages the soul to relax and look for any sign of light from persons who are willing to lead it into the realm where it should now be living.

4. There are many types of people alive today in what you have called the physical or earth plane. Let us assume that you are right when you say each person will shed his caterpillar-like physical body and start flitting around like a butterfly on some other level of existence. What I want to know is, "On what level am I likely to find myself?"

Not knowing you, I cannot answer your question. However, you can look at Fig. 33 and then look at yourself. Assuming the character groupings listed as A, B and C are reasonably accurate, you can answer the question yourself.

A. Individuals who have made more than average progress in this and/or past lives and whose souls have evolved to the point that they "just naturally" are living their present lives in harmony with the characteristics depicted in Fig. 34.

B. The average kind-hearted, considerate, well-meaning, hard-working adults, and all infants and children.

C. Greedy, cruel, selfish, materialistic, highly egotistic and unloving persons, including, for example, swindlers, rapists, drug addicts, alcoholics, sex perverts, suicides, murderers, hardened criminals, and political despots. This classification includes those persons who *failed* to benefit from the learning opportunities provided in their *just concluded* physical incarnation on planet earth.

The *width* of the individual arrow is roughly proportional to the *number* of people in each category.

5. Is there an actual place called hell? If so, where is it?

Yes, there is such a place. It is definitely not the fire and brimstone place of the New Testament, nor the place depicted in the famous Hieronymous Bosch painting. It is really more like the traditional purgatory that has for centuries been referred to by the Catholic church. It is a dark, dismal, uninviting place filled with countless numbers of souls who are lost and wandering about in great distress.

It is also occupied by some rather frightening life forms of non-

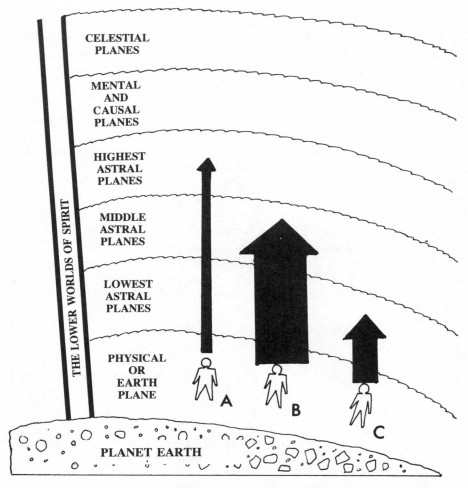

Fig. 33. The next stop for all people now living on planet earth

human lines of evolution. It is cluttered up with thought-forms accumulated over the centuries as a result of humanity's hatred, greed, lust, jealousy and other unvirtuous passions. These thought-forms can be as "real" as the shadowy "bodies" of the poor souls whose lives qualified them for *this* plane of existence.

Of all the levels in the lower worlds of spirit, hell is the lowest.

6. Is there a devil?

No, at least not a red-skinned character with a tail, a pair of horns and a pitchfork as has been pictured in centuries past. The lowest astral level—like all other levels in the worlds of spirit—*is largely a world created by thoughts*. This does not make it any less real. Far from it! Mental torments can be far worse than actual physical torments—as in the case of a person with delirium tremens.

In the darkness of the lower astral, imagination and conscience can create the most frightening devils of all shapes and sizes. To these are added the very real astral bodies of strange creatures of nonhuman lines of evolution.

Confirmation of what we are telling you about devils—and *light beings*—comes from a small research project reported in the May/June 1979 issue of *Parapsychology Review:* "A heart specialist from Chattanooga, Tennessee, has just finished a study of more than 100 patients brought back to life after being clinically dead. 'The good news,' he said, 'is that some of them had a blissful encounter with a being of light.' The bad news, however, is that over half of the patients 'had a perfectly appalling time,' walking through dimly-lit caverns....The doctor now firmly believes hell exists. 'Reluctantly,' he said, 'I have come to the conclusion it may not be safe to die.'"

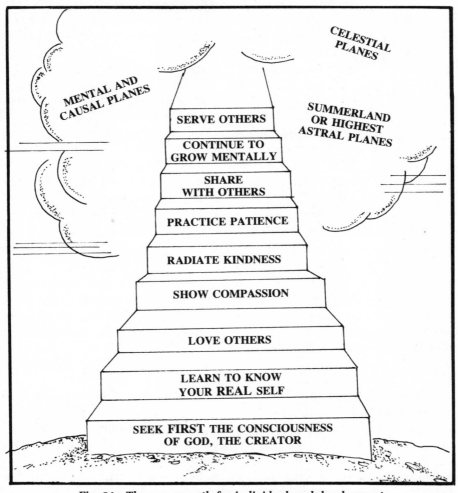

Fig. 34. *The proven path for individual soul development*

We can agree with the heart specialist's conclusion that "hell" does indeed exist on the very lowest of the astral planes. His second conclusion is certainly academic, since we all die. But the problem is neatly solved by living a life *now* that will entitle you to a "gate pass" to be used as indicated in the color version of Fig. 32, to be found inside the back cover.

In any event, if you do find yourself in the lowest astral planes, you can escape these torments if you persist in striving to find the light and in calling out for assistance. Sooner or later an encounter will occur with one of the compassionate beings who willingly give of their time to lead tormented souls to a place of rest and enlightenment.

7. What can or should I do to make certain that I am on a path which will bypass that dark and dismal level of existence you call the lower astral?

Quite frankly, you should not accept my answer to such an important question as this. In fact, you should not accept *any* person's answer! The only thing to do is to look at the question from every angle just as carefully as you can, considering all of the evidence that has been accumulated. Then, and only then, listen for guidance from that still small voice that is within you.

All I can do is to help you collect further information upon which to base *your* answer to this question.

Perhaps the most helpful single thing I can do is to share information that has come from wise old souls who have travelled much farther along life's high road than I have. One can place belief in far less than 10 percent of the information that comes from spirit entities through mediums. It is very rare indeed to obtain *direct communication* from those highly evolved persons currently living on the mental, causal and celestial planes. In our research in communication between the interpenetrating levels of life and consciousness, we have found and repeatedly tested a mere handful of communicators living on the higher levels. We have followed faithfully the admonition in the epistle of John to "try the spirits (to see) whether they be of God."

So in Fig. 34 I present not my answer, but theirs, to your very important question. Only time will prove for each of us whether these wise old souls know whereof they speak. All I can say is that our "still small voices" have told us we can safely consecrate our current lives to such a course of action.

Persons *now residing* on the higher astral and the mental-causal planes confirm the "central core" spiritual teachings of the world's great religions, once they have been stripped of the *dogma and creed* that each has acquired with the passing centuries.

From their vantage point, they state that the concept depicted in Fig. 34 is the only time-proven, safe, sure, quick and enjoyable route for each soul to travel—now and throughout the coming centuries.

8. I am miserable and unhappy. Will I be better off after I die?

Sorry, but the answer is *no.*

When you someday cast off your physical body, the real you — your mind, memory banks, personality and soul — will be precisely what they were before you left the physical body. If you are miserable and unhappy when you make the transition, you will still be miserable and unhappy in your new surroundings!

Today is the *first day of the rest of your life.* This is the day to start to follow Jesus' gentle admonition to "lay up for yourself treasures in heaven." Only by building into your life and actions many of the qualities listed in Fig. 34 will you enjoy *this* life and assure yourself of an exciting adventure in the centuries ahead.

9. Does a suicide succeed in escaping his troubles?

No, he only compounds them. There is no escape for any individual from the requirement that each one *must* evolve mentally, emotionally and spiritually. A person who fails to cope with everyday problems does not escape by suicide. He cannot "kill" himself. He is just as alive after destroying his physical body as he was before he pulled the trigger, jumped out the window, or took an overdose of sleeping pills.

He finds himself in the darkest, most dismal and frightening level of the astral plane. A long, hard and lonely struggle lies ahead before this soul achieves the level on which it would have arrived by natural death.

10. How long might a suicide or a murderer remain in the lowest astral plane?

We have been told that there is a big difference in the time spent on the lower astral by these two categories. The suicide has harmed only himself and his loved ones, if any. Usually he or she is immediately filled with remorse.* When an offer of help and guidance is given, the suicide is likely to respond readily. *How fast he absorbs the teachings* offered will determine how rapidly he moves to a more hospitable level.

The murderer is in much, much deeper trouble. His act in cutting short an earth life indicates that he has not only failed to learn much in his past lives, if any, but that he has not evolved spiritually in the present life. Usually, he has little readiness to accept teaching when offered, so his stay on the lower astral may be from many years to many centuries of our time.

11. I have heard that if one has chosen to have the body cremated, it should not be done immediately after death. Is this correct?

---

* There are exceptions, of course. Consider the person who commits suicide for wholly unselfish reasons — for example, the action of Titus Oakes of Scott's 1914 polar expedition.

Yes. However, some of our knowledgeable friends on the mental and causal levels have reminded us that in the Orient it has for countless centuries been the practice to burn the body before sundown on the day of death. This practice came about because in warm climates decay of the physical body starts promptly.

It is desirable that the etheric and astral bodies have ample time for a completely *natural* and *total* withdrawal from the physical body. Hence it is perhaps *advisable* whenever possible to wait for two or a maximum of three days before cremating the body. Where this is *not* possible and the soul or spirit is *forced* to make a sudden departure from its physical body, it will again become normal after a period of rest.

12. Where is the "next" world (or "astral world") located?

Only in the past few years have we become able to answer this question with a scientifically satisfying statement. Our five senses have given us a false, or at least totally inadequate, concept of reality, as if our material world were the whole of it. The material world—and our physical bodies—are not the "solid matter" we think we see and touch. All matter—the chair you sit on, the building in which you find yourself at this moment, the "solid" foundation upon which the building rests—consists almost entirely of empty space. That is why your vision can pass through "solid" glass several inches thick. This is why hundreds of radio and television signals carrying speech, music and pictures are at this moment traveling right through the solid walls of your room and your "solid body."

Only if you can comprehend the above concept can you begin to realize that it is possible to have two or more things occupying the same space at the same time. Your physical body dwells in our common, everyday, three-dimensional world of space and time. Your mind and soul live in another space-time system that interpenetrates your physical body and occupies substantially the same space as your physical body.

Hence the "next world" is the one in which your mind and soul *already* lives and in which your mind and soul *will continue to live*. When you have shed your worn-out physical body, you will be aware of the surroundings in which your mind and soul are living—the astral planes.

It is only for convenience in Figures 32, 33, 35 and 36 that I stack the various levels one above the other. This makes it much easier to grasp and to accept the idea of "many mansions."

13. Will I have to meet immediately that alcoholic spouse who mistreated me and the children, and whom I divorced? And what about my friend Carol, who had five husbands?

No, to the first of these questions. You will find yourself in a group where you are in harmony with all of the other members. As to the likely whereabouts of your former husband, take another look at C in Fig. 33.

As for friend Carol, I can only assume that she has a long way to grow, both spiritually and mentally. But again, she too will find herself with those persons for whom she has an affinity. If she does not want to be with any of her former mates, she will not be.

In due course, we do have to meet those with whom we have unfinished business. Each must sooner or later "balance accounts" if he is to grow emotionally and spiritually.

14. Do persons addicted to alcohol, tobacco and hard drugs lose their craving for such stimulation when they arrive on the next plane?

No, not right away. For example, an alcoholic, being on the lowest astral plane, is in close touch with the physical or earth plane. Often he is not truly aware that he is "dead." He may seek out his old haunts and get a vicarious thrill from visiting a bar. In fact, if he finds a patron who is depressed, muddled and psychically sensitive, he may obsess that person. By this merging of their respective energy fields, the dead person may become more directly locked into the physical aura of the bar patron and experience more directly the feelings to which he had become accustomed. If the possession of the patron continues, it may completely wreck his life, and in some cases may even cause the patron to commit suicide.

A person addicted to hard drugs is in the deepest possible trouble. He will be resistant to any offer of help and will persist in his craving. He will experience torments that equal anything pictured in the old ideas of hell. He may remain in this dreadful condition for what would be centuries of earth time.

15. Can a "dead" person look in on activities of a child or mate?

Yes, this happens all the time. For a period of days, months or years, the deceased person is very much attuned to the earth plane. If the transition is an unusually smooth one, the deceased may even *look in on his own funeral!* The records are full of examples of a mate or parent who lingers for months and enjoys daily contact with surviving family members.

It is not uncommon for a deceased mate to want to complete some item of unfinished family business. In those rare cases where a good trance medium is consulted, the deceased may reveal where a missing and badly-needed last will and testament or other document can be found. The settling of more than one estate has been accomplished by this means.

As the deceased becomes fully reconciled to his or her new life, the earth ties (primarily personal love and affection) become less binding. The deceased then becomes fully absorbed in the increasing challenges of the completely new world of living that has opened.

16. Is there any factual basis for the idea that the spirit of a dead person can intrude into the mind of a living person and adversely affect that person's behavior?

Absolutely, even though modern psychiatry has laughed at this concept. However, for those who were open-minded enough to do serious research on this matter, it quickly became clear that there is a solid basis of fact for the age-old idea of spirit or demon possession.

Perhaps the best single piece of research on this subject is Wickland's *Thirty Years Among the Dead*, which I discussed in Chapter 4. In it he tells of the technique he developed for getting into two-way conversation with the possessing entity and then proceeding by persuasion (and in some cases, shocks of static electricity) to induce the intruding spirit to depart on its way.

Wickland's work has been confirmed by research in which I have been personally involved.

The many ways in which entities in the spirit world influence or communicate with people in physical bodies is illustrated in Fig. 35. Item A deals with obsession; the other forms of communication are far more beneficial and healthy.

I have reason to hope that in less than a decade, "modern" medicine will have come to realize that there are at least some persons now locked up in mental institutions because of spirit possession. Today these poor unfortunate souls receive no help because many psychiatrists are unable to recognize and treat this problem.

17. All my life I have been taught that when I die, I will lie in my grave until some far-off judgment day, and then I will be raised from the dead. The material you have presented in this book disagrees with my religious teachings.

I said in the opening pages of this book that this is not a religious treatise. I have presented information from many sources to the effect that present and future lives are intertwined and even concurrent. The fact that you believe in some *far-off* day does not reduce the need for preparing *now* for your very own judgment day *whenever* it comes.

18. As a Christian, will I meet Jesus when I arrive in heaven?
As a Buddhist, will I meet Buddha?
As a Muslim, will I meet Mohammed?

It is possible, but not very likely, that you would have immediate contact with these or any other Being living on the celestial planes. Recall that I said in Part I that modern science has shown us that *everything* in the universe is vibratory in nature. As this is being written, the newspapers warn that it is dangerous to watch an eclipse of the sun without use of dark glasses to protect the eyesight. This is because the incandescent sun is sending out energy at such a high vibratory level

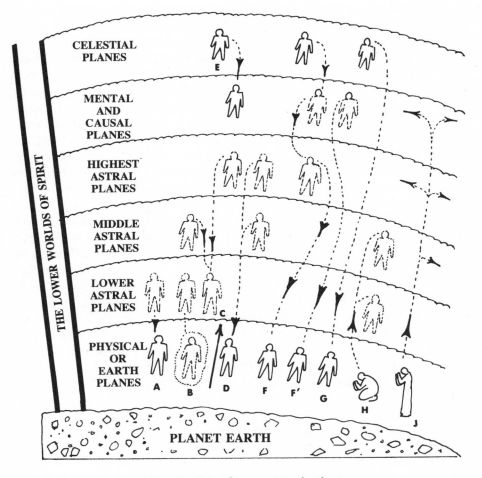

Fig. 35. *Interplane communications*

Key to the Diagram

A. The act of obsession
B. Ghosts, apparitions, "astral shells"
C. Rescue teams and invisible helpers
D. Teachers, masters, guides, protectors
E. Higher teachers, masters, angelic beings, light beings
F-F′. The sources of "intuition" and inspiration for the best creative activities of musicians, artists, poets, writers, sculptors, inventors, scientists, etc.
G. Guidance for Jesus, Buddha, Mohammed, and all divinely inspired souls
H. Prayers by the living for the newly "dead"
J. Skilled meditation and prayer

109

that it would permanently damage the light-sensing cells in the retina of our eyes.

The dwellers of the celestial planes, the location of all of Man's great religious figures and gods, are such bright and shining beings that their energy would damage a new arrival from the earth plane. Hence it is not likely that you would meet any of these beings *in person.*

All such enlightened and compassionate beings, however, do have the ability to lower their vibratory rate by coming down through a succession of other beings on the various levels. (This is what the scientists call transduction, or step-down transformers.) So yes, it *is* possible for you to "see" and meet a being who *fits your own image* of the being you desire to meet.

19. Are angels a figment of the imagination of the prophets and writers of the Bible, or do they really exist, as Billy Graham says they do?

Yes, angels do exist, as Billy Graham says. But they do not have wings as portrayed in some of the beautiful and imaginative drawings and paintings of the Middle Ages.

The subject of angels is a complex one. There are many types or classifications of angels. None of them developed from the human line of evolution. It would take several chapters to do justice to the subject, so we will have to be content with the following over-simplification of a very wonderful and helpful aspect of God's great universe.

The angels of the most numerous type are largely concerned with the health, well-being, and advancement of man, beast, fowl, plant and mineral life forms. They work at all levels on the astral plane as depicted in Fig. 35. They evolved from what in Sanskrit are called *devas,* meaning "radiant beings."

The highest form of angels are known as "archangels." They are concerned mainly with performing major tasks in the overall operation of our universe. For simplicity we might call them "God's Helpers." They are great beings of infinite wisdom, love and compassion who in every sense deserve the phrase, "the power behind the throne." Or we can say these are the top executives who help with the day-to-day management of our little part of the solar system.

An example of how an archangel tries to help modern man is given in my book, *Collapse and Comeback.* This booklet contains a transcript of a one-hour-and-twenty-minute discourse given by the archangel Hilarion in answer to my request for information as to what lies ahead in the way of economic, political and social changes in the remaining years of this century. It also contains comments by the archangel Michael, another of the seven archangels who make up what is called the Spiritual Hierarchy.

Both of the above categories are true angels and should not be confused with the term *guardian angel.* This is a broadly descriptive term that is applied to the friendly and helpful beings on the astral planes who are *assigned* to work with each of us as individuals in this present lifetime as well as those who are *attracted* to us at various stages of our own mental, emotional and spiritual growth. These beings are all of the human line of evolution. They are more properly called guides, masters, teachers, helpers, protectors, etc.

All of the above categories consist of loving and compassionate beings interested only in serving man and his Creator to the fullest of their individual capabilities. In ages past when a sage, seer, mystic or even a simple shepherd "saw" such a being, it was certainly natural to use poetic terms to describe it. Today it is possible for some highly clairvoyant persons and very advanced meditators to encounter angels and describe them as *light beings*.

20. Have beings in the worlds of spirit described what they see as "material things"?

Yes, this literature is full of such reports from dwellers on the different planes. A typical report from the middle astral planes about 60 years ago stated: "The surface of the zone is diversified. There is a great variety of landscape, some of it most picturesque. We, like you, have lofty mountain ranges, valleys, rivers, lakes, forests and the internal correspondence of all the vegetable life that exists upon your earth. Trees and shrubbery covered with the most beautiful foliage, and flowers of every colour and character known to you, and many that you know not, give forth their perfume. The physical economy of each zone differs from every other. New and striking scenes of grandeur are presented to us, increasing in beauty and sublimity as we progress."

In 1977, the first member of our research team made the transition from this plane to the higher astral plane. Melvin Sutley died at the age of 80 after a life full of love and service to his fellow man. When we talked to him a year later, through the telepathic channel Sarah Gran, he had this to say:

Sutley: This talk with you is something I have been awaiting for a long time. Yes, I think back to the days when we worked together and I had the privilege of sitting in on the information that was given us and the times you visited me when I was in bed in Philadelphia and unable to get up and go to meetings in the lab. This is marvelous. It is difficult to communicate in this manner, and I must get used to the medium.

This place where I have been living is so beautiful, George, so *beau-u-tiful.* I know that all that beautiful country that you brag about where you used to live in Florida cannot possibly measure up to this.

Meek: Good!

Sutley: The trees are so green, grass is so green and so velvety, air is just like breathing wine, if you could do such a thing. The sun is not too hot, the breezes are lovely. Oh, it is **marvelous.** I don't know why I hung around that place Philadelphia so long. I didn't *know* it would be like this.

Meek: That answers a question in my mind. I frankly wondered why you *did* stay quite so long in that nursing home when we could see what a terrible strain it was on you. When you were alone you couldn't have had the best of attention and help—it was a tremendous strain for you to stay there, those last few months particularly.

Sutley: Yes, if you and Paul and Hans and...[unclear]...had stayed there with me, I think I would have made it a few more years. But I'm so sorry I hung on so long because this is—Oh, they tell me I'll forget about it, you know, and I will.

Meek: I looked at the early transcripts from the Philadelphia lab where you and R.B. were present, and saw reference to the name "Margaret." I am ignorant in this situation. Was she your wife?

Sutley: Oh, yes! That's my wife [with great pride in his voice]. You know what, George? She waited for me [sounds almost like tears in this sentence]. I kept her waiting all that time. I didn't know. [He really feels sad about that.]

Nine months after the above contact with our friend Melvin, we were pleasantly surprised when he came through at the end of one of our scientific discussions. We had been talking, by means of a medium, about the nature of time in the worlds of spirit with Dr. William Francis Gray Swann, who had died in Philadelphia in 1962. Here is the relevant portion of the transcript:

Meek: All right, we will be glad to share this tape with Paul, Hans and Will. This is the extent of our questions. If there is anything else tonight, Dr. Swann, that you or one of your teammates wish to share with us...

Swann: Yes, we have two new arrivals in our midst: Melvin and Margaret.

Meek: Good evening, Melvin, and good evening to you, Margaret. Although I didn't have the pleasure of meeting you here on the earth plane, we have heard much about you and it is a great pleasure to greet both of you.

Sutley: You are very kind, George. Since I have grown stronger, we have given up the "old home" and decided to join our old friends and acquaintances and remind them that we were in communication with them before we came to this place.

We thank you very much for your kindness and your thoughtfulness over a period of time. We are glad that the experiment is again going forward. Frankly, it has gone so far afield from what we had in mind that I can foresee that when the breakthrough comes, it will be enormous.

Meek: Two thoughts come to my mind. First, you mentioned the help that we gave. It is deeply to be regretted that we were not able to give you more help, more assistance in the closing months. We felt very keenly that due to geographical separation and occupational problems, we were not able to share more with you. We deeply appreciate the great part that you played in the original activity in setting up this whole project. We recall frequently your initial contact with Paul and R.B. and the key role that you played. We also well remember the financial contribution which you made to our work.

Sutley: It was of great interest to me and still is. You are most kind, you and Paul and Hans.

Meek: What are you finding of interest these days, Melvin, to make use of that marvelous mind and soul you have?

Sutley: Margaret and I have not been here very long but we find there is quite a lot going on. We have been in on some very interesting discussions and we have fitted some of our knowledge gained in our last earth experience with some of the ideas being given out by some here who have not been involved in a life experience for a long, long time.

We have been circulating from group to group deciding where we belong. It is very wonderful to be here. For awhile I thought it had to be as it was before with the house* we had just like that one in Philadelphia and everything that I had before. But I found out that it just wasn't satisfying. It is going to be much, much more interesting here.

Meek: We are delighted with that news, Melvin. We hope that you find it possible to come in frequently in the months ahead as we get more regular communication with Dr. Swann and our friends.

Sutley: True. Tell Paul and Hans hello for me. I am most grateful to them.

Meek: We will share this tape with them so they can hear the inflections of joy and excitement in your voice. Speaking of old friends, we would like to share with Dr. Holmes a report on his project. Is he available this evening?

The significance of this second communication from Melvin is that it shows how rapidly this man and his wife have progressed from the "summerland" or highest astral to the mental and causal planes, where Dr. Swann and his teammates are. This rapid upward movement through the worlds of spirit can be attributed to three factors. First, Melvin and Margaret had led lives of great service to their fellow men. She was a renowned surgeon; he was a specialist in hospital administration and one of the founders of Spiritual Frontiers Fellowship. Sec-

---

* The thought-created house Melvin had constructed for himself when, after death, he arrived on the highest astral plane. Many mediumistic communications refer to thought-created structures and surroundings.

ond, through his lifelong friendship with Arthur Ford, the medium, he was well acquainted with the reality of life after death and some of the conditions in which he would find himself after death. (Readers of this book will have the same advantage!) Third, Melvin *himself* decided he wanted to move on upward to meet his friends. The Swanns and the Sutleys had been close friends and co-workers for many years in Philadelphia.

Thus, in this very personal experience with Melvin, the first of our research team to make the transition, we see confirmation of the answer to question 13—that like attracts like; that is, we will find ourselves with friends and former associates. We also confirm the answer to question 7—that living a life as portrayed on the stairway in Fig. 34 is the *fastest,* most *certain,* and most *pleasant* way to have a wonderful life **after** one dies.

21. *Will I retain all of my five senses when I leave my physical body? Will I acquire any new senses?*

You will no longer have any need for, and in fact will lose, the senses of smell, taste and touch. Your sense of hearing and seeing will be extended far beyond your present capabilities.

Beginning on the middle astral levels, you will know a person's thoughts by merely looking at him. You will know if what he is saying really agrees with his feelings. He cannot pretend to be anything but what he actually is. There is no place for "phonies" in the worlds of spirit. In general, your sensitivity to your surroundings will be greatly enhanced. You will *feel* far more alive than when you were in your earth body.

22. *To what extent, if any, does a person's formal education determine his new level of existence?*

Very little indeed, as you will understand by examining Fig. 33 carefully. Persons who are considered to be the most learned and with many university degrees may find themselves on the lowest portions of the lowest astral planes—if they have grossly misused their knowledge. Back at "square one," to use a current expression.

Persons who have had little or no formal education in this lifetime may find they have arrived on the highest astral in the Biblical land of milk and honey—*if* throughout earth life they have traveled the *proven path for individual soul development* diagrammed in Fig. 34.

23. *What about food in the afterlife? Do people have to prepare and eat food?*

No. Not having a physical body, you will have no need for food. The higher, finer, vibratory "bodies" in the worlds of spirit can draw all needed energies directly from cosmos.

24. Is there marriage in the next life?

No and yes.

Bear in mind that marriage is a device that evolved over the centuries as nature's efficient method of providing the necessary care for the well-being and growth of children until they could fend for themselves. Since there is no generation of new children on the planes of spirit, there is no compelling need for the institution of marriage as such.

On the other hand, if your present marriage is a completely happy one and you would find your greatest happiness in association with your mate when he or she arrives, then it is fitting that the relationship continue. If the present relationship is unhappy, then it will automatically cease. All will find themselves in surroundings and with people with whom they are attuned.

25. Is sexual intercourse possible between males and females when they no longer have physical bodies?

No. Intercourse between the male and female of most species of all life forms—humans, all animals, birds, plant life—was provided by the Creator for the purpose of *continuation of the species;* that is, for the production of offspring. In the worlds of spirit there are no offspring among the human dwellers therein. Hence there is no functional *need* for sexual intercourse.*

However, as was pointed out earlier, a new arrival on the astral plane is still filled with all the thoughts and bodily desires intact. A person who on the earth plane was filled with lust usually finds himself on the lowest portion of the lower astral. He is still steeped in his attachment to earth and may not realize that he is "dead." He is thus what we term "earthbound." He may, in this condition, get a vicarious thrill out of wandering into a bedroom as an undetected witness to sexual intercourse. Eventually, when he evolves and moves up to higher levels, such fascination gradually disappears.

I use the word "gradually" advisedly. I was somewhat amused to learn that "boys will be boys" even on the middle astral planes. It came as a surprise to hear an entity (a former university professor) tell us quite frankly that in his present plane of existence he missed having contact with the beautiful form of the female physical body.

However, there is another—and extremely important—aspect of sex

---

* A medical doctor friend, a good psychic diagnostician with much experience in the field of psychiatry, provides an additional insight. "In the lower astral there is a lot of so-called 'funny business' going on. This includes orgies. It is not uncommon for physically incarnate people to attend these during the hours when they are asleep. This accounts for a lot of dissipation of energy during sleeping and waking hours."

that we should mention. Any reasonably mature adult knows that there is far more to the matter of sex than the physical-pelvic aspect. The greater our comprehension of the cosmos and all we have encountered therein, the more obvious it becomes that a *duality of forces* appears to underlie everything. Some of the more obvious manifestations are day-night, love-hate, male-female, ying-yang, sweet-sour, cold-warm, positive-negative electrical charges, etc.

Each individual human being has within himself a *mixture* of male-female characteristics—physically, mentally and emotionally. A person with a female physical body may have the mental and emotional characteristics we usually associate with a male—and vice versa. The important point is to note that we are each—to a degree—*both* male and female.

We carry this *basic duality* with us when we die and proceed to move on to one of the worlds of spirit. Many of those persons on the mental and causal planes with whom we have come in contact in our research have referred to having lived some of their earth lives in male physical bodies and some in female physical bodies.

From our research it appears that the melding of the male-female polarity becomes complete only when we accept the final rebirth and move to the celestial planes.

26. Twenty years ago my daughter died at the age of six months. Did her soul or spirit remain that of a baby?

No. She was received on the middle or higher astral plane and given the most tender and loving care. She was given every opportunity for continued growth and development. She will reach adulthood. If you wish to meet this daughter after you have made the transition to your next level of life, you can do so—that is, provided you are not now living a life that will result in your arrival on the lower astral. In that case, there might be considerable delay before you could meet your daughter, because she almost certainly will not be found on that level.

If she has not been alerted to be on hand when you make the transition, all you have to do is to send out *mentally* a call for her with all the *love and longing you can muster.* She will come.

Children in the afterlife are cared for very much as they are here. There are those who find their greatest delight in mothering the motherless, and in teaching the young. So under such unselfish care the children reach mental and bodily maturity much as if they had remained in this world. In most cases, though, they will still return for additional learning experiences on the earth plane of existence.

The etheric process of development is interesting; children need mother love no less in spirit than in earth life.

Little do most people know how close the afterlife is, how close its inhabitants come to us, the influence they exert on us, or the result of our thought vibrations upon them. Then again, as the children grow, they keep in touch with us from day to day, and when we go out into the afterlife, they know and greet us as we enter the life that has no night.

There are in the next life institutions of learning just as we have here. What is more, the inhabitants do not cease to study and increase their store of knowledge when they have reached a certain age. I can assure you that your daughter will continue to grow in body, mind and spirit.

27. Both of my parents died in their eighties. Both had been in nursing homes for many years and had wasted away to skin and bones. Both were senile. When they "woke up" after death of their physical bodies, what was the condition of their minds and souls?

They were in excellent condition. The deterioration you had observed was limited to their physical bodies. For some months or even years before their minds and souls made the final transition, they were, in fact, spending time on short visits to their next plane of life. This, in part, accounted for their failing memory, the lengthening periods of forgetfulness, and "absent" look and behavior.

When the full transition of the mind and soul had been completed, they would be, in most respects, the same as they had been in the prime of life.

28. Can the passage of a loved one through purgatory (the lower astral) be speeded by payments of money to a priest?

No. This centuries-old practice does nothing except add to the coffers of the church, and perhaps give a small psychological consolation to the one who pays the money.

We are all bound by the absolutely impartial and inescapable law of cause and effect. In each of the first three gospels, Jesus is reported as saying, "For with whatever measure ye mete, it shall be measured unto you again." In Galatians 6:7, Paul says, "Be not deceived, God is not mocked: For whatever a man soweth, that shall he also reap."

If, during your life, you caused pain, hardship, and unhappiness to others; if you allowed yourself to become a drug addict or hopeless alcoholic; or if you were a murderer or a suicide, you will reap precisely as you have sown. You will find yourself in the lower astral levels. This most undesirable "place" has been described in religious lore by the words "purgatory," "hades" and "hell." A person who finds himself in this condition solely because of his own unwillingness to grow mentally and spiritually is totally on his own. No priest can post bail for such a person. Study Figs. 32, 33, and 35 for a deeper understanding.

Fortunately, the lower astral is completely *bypassed* by those whose lives included few if any of the above-mentioned activities.

29. In some religious groups it is customary to pray for the soul of the dead. Does this practice serve any useful purpose?

A very emphatic **Yes!** The newly deceased person is very much alive. As a pilgrim arriving in a new land, there are many strange and even bewildering experiences on every hand. (How can it be otherwise, when our religious lore has been so deficient in this area?)

It is a great comfort for this pilgrim to hear *your* spoken or unspoken prayer on his or her behalf. Tender thoughts of love, good wishes, encouragement, heartfelt thanks for shared experiences—these are all easily received by the deceased if he has arrived on the *middle* astral plane. Even if he is "asleep" or is wandering on the lower astral plane, such prayers are useful, although their effectiveness may be somewhat delayed until the departed has experienced the trials and tribulations which are the fruit of his life's actions.

30. How is time measured on the planes that make up the spirit worlds?

It isn't measured. There is no serial time as we know it. Locked as we are into our present space-time system, it is almost impossible for us to comprehend living in a "timeless world." Since our earliest childhood we have each been locked into a life that is rigidly bound into a system of seconds, minutes, hours, days, weeks, years, centuries, eons, and light years.

There are no trains to catch at an appointed time. There is no first of the month time-payment to be met. There is no growing old, wrinkled and senile with passing years.

(The more technically or scientifically inclined reader is referred to Appendix B for a more detailed answer to this question.)

31. What about political or governmental systems on the astral planes? Is there any equivalent of money?

There is nothing to resemble countries, states or nations. The principal divisions result from like souls being grouped with like souls. There are no presidents, dictators, kings or rulers.

Nor is there need for money or a unit of exchange. Supply is available for all wants to all individual souls.

The generating force is *thought*, difficult as this may be to comprehend. You can *think* and have beauty and happiness. You can *think* base desires and they will be fulfilled—which shows how a benevolent Creator can demonstrate to you the foolishness and triviality of those desires. It is very like the situation in which one finds himself today in life on the earth plane. You may have all the money you want, but you still are not happy. It is pretty clear that happiness on *any* plane does not depend on money. Sooner or later each will wake up to this fact and seek the only things that genuinely satisfy—continuing mental, emotional and spiritual *growth*.

118

32. Some mediumistic persons claim they get guidance from departed spirits—"counselors," "protectors," "guides," "angels," etc. Is there any truth in such statements?

Yes, there most certainly is. Such advancement as humanity has made in the past 4,000 years is in part due to such guidance, often explained as "intuition." Indeed, most "revelations" received by sages, mystics, prophets and spiritual leaders have come from such sources, as illustrated by paths D, F-F', and G in Fig. 35.

However, this is an area requiring much additional research in the decades ahead. The human mind is a fantastically complex thing with the ability to spin dreams that stagger the imagination. Hence, it is very difficult to make certain that a particular idea or thought is coming from a friendly and helpful intelligence in the worlds of spirit.

The daily practice of deep relaxation and a prayerful attitude over a long period of years seems to be the only proven way of hearing that "still small voice" within—a voice which may, in fact, be from your personal helper in the world of spirit. But, I repeat, this is a *most hazardous* business. The pages of history are filled with acts which stemmed from self-delusion with respect to "heavenly guidance."

33. Can I put much trust in what I am told by a Spiritualist medium?

Yes. No. And then again maybe, perhaps.

Today, the *very best* mediums almost never give sittings to any but their closest personal friends or to serious researchers. My sixteen years of searching over much of the world has disclosed only a few dozen such persons.

Communications from spirits closest to the earth plane—the easiest to obtain—are, for the most part, *useless* as well as *inaccurate*. This covers 95 percent of all survival information which comes through a medium on the platform of a Spiritualist church. The problem with such mediumistic communications is that the most readily contacted persons are those who are on the *nearest* astral planes. These are often recent arrivals and are no more knowledgeable than before they left their physical bodies. This, combined with the "noise"—or the sheer difficulty of communication—gives rise to misconceptions.

Communications from more *elevated* spirits also suffer greatly in transmission. A crude analogy is a game in which several people sit on chairs spaced closely together in a row or circle. A sentence is whispered into the ear of one person who quickly whispers it into the ear of the next person, and so on until the last person. When the message in final form is then repeated to the group, everyone has a good laugh at the gross distortion that has taken place in the transmission.

No specific rules of guidance can be given. In general, however, the communications that come through a medium who makes a "business" of his or her mediumship, charges for sittings, and handles one client after another, hour after hour and day after day, should not be taken too seriously.*

For this reason, a bereaved person should strictly avoid trying to contact the loved one through a medium. At best the medium will be tapping the sitter's mind for a description of the deceased. When the medium says, "I see standing beside you..." and then proceeds to describe fairly accurately the departed loved one, the medium is usually not in touch with the departed. Moreover, some of the more mischievous of the earthbound spirits—the only level which *most* such mediums can reach—delight in masquerading as the departed person and can be quite adept at putting on a performance that convinces the sitter that he or she is in touch with the loved one.

It is infinitely more useful for the bereaved to sit quietly every few days and send prayerful and loving thoughts to the loved one. Again, study Fig. 32 and Fig. 35. Visualize *where* the loved one is. Speak out loud as though the loved one is present. Often, in fact, he is! Wish him well in his new surroundings. Of course, tell him that you miss him but that you are no longer grieving because you **know** that he has *returned home,* that he is among loved ones who are looking after his every want. State that you are so very thankful for his love and companionship, and that you are content that you will again meet and continue your relationship—if that then suits your mutual purposes. All of this is a far more effective way to spend time than running from medium to medium—and it saves money!

34. Twice you have mentioned the many pitfalls that you and your fellow researchers were obliged to avoid in communicating through even the very best of mediums. What about the persons in spirit who try to communicate with you? Is it easy for them to communicate?

Yes and no. It is relatively easy for those on the lower astral or even the lowest part of the middle astral planes to communicate. But they

---

* There are exceptions, of course. In the past 50 years, few of the really great mediums had other means of financial support than the modest fees received from their sitters.

Robert R. Leichtman, M.D., in a private communication discussing this point, says: "There are those who assume *anyone* who dares to charge for a reading or sitting with a medium is instantly declaring himself to be a fraud. True, I see legions of half-baked, half-witted 'mediums' and 'psychics' running amok at meetings, hustling readings and making a lot of money. Nevertheless a *good* medium is worth something. Good advice is worth something. People have no problem paying their minister for his services. The pseudo-spiritual and sanctimonious often protest that 'what comes from spirit should be as freely given as it was freely accepted.' That sounds good but it is a bit impractical, as one does have to pay grocery bills and rent despite what may be great psychic talent. The time it takes to develop the talent takes time from other activities also, and this should be compensated."

are of little help in providing useful knowledge for mankind.

It is extremely difficult for those on the *mental and causal* planes to communicate, even through the best of mediums. The difficulties experienced by spirits in trying to communicate are outlined in great detail in the book *Gilda Communicates,* by Ruth White and Mary Swainson, in the chapter, "Technical Difficulties."

For a short explanation of these difficulties, consider the comments of Leslie Flint, the great English medium. Flint's mediumship is of a very rare kind. His helpers in the spirit world use ectoplasm from his body to create an etheric mass a few feet from his head. The spirit communicator "talks into" this substitute "voice box" and the spirit's voice becomes audible to all persons in the room. In the course of 50 years, many hundreds of spirit beings have communicated through this system. In his book, *Voices in the Dark,* Flint reports an important sitting as follows:

"A spirit with a marked French accent introduced himself as Richet and, in the course of conversation with him, we learned he was the late Professor Charles Richet, the eminent French physiologist who in 1905 was President of the Society for Psychical Research in London, and who was winner of a Nobel Prize in 1913.

"He told us that not only must the communicating entity lower his own frequency to the lower one of earth but simultaneously he must remember what his voice sounded like in his lifetime and recapture memories of happenings which will give proof of his identity to the person with whom he wishes to communicate. When the professor was asked by a sitter whether he could see and hear people at a seance, he answered that it depended on the amount of concentration he put into the effort to do so. If he focused his mind sufficiently, he could both hear and see people on earth; but he found it simpler to apprehend their thoughts before they were uttered as words.

"He grew quite testy when someone suggested that sometimes the voices of communicators from the spirit world did not sound exactly the same as their voices during their life, and he said it was hardly likely they would sound the same, seeing they were not using the same vocal chords they had in life. He added that we must take into account, also, that the communicating spirit was trying to concentrate on three different things at the same time while communicating. Most of what Richet said made sense to me. I had often heard communicators remark on the difficulty of 'speaking through this box thing which wobbles about all the time,' or say plaintively how confusing it was to remember some event which would prove beyond doubt who they were while concentrating so hard on other things. As the discarnate Professor Richet remarked rather grumpily: 'The miracle is that we can communicate at all.' "

Yes, indeed, it is a miracle that we *and* they can communicate at all.

But in spite of all of the troubles at *both* ends of the line, we are beginning to bridge the gap between our physical world and the worlds of spirit.

35. Mediums and other psychic persons speak about "raising the vibrations" when trying to contact those who have died. Is this just nonsense?

No. Recent advances in physics and related fields of science show that matter—indeed, apparently everything so far encountered in the cosmos—is composed of energy, which is vibratory by nature. Consider the following analogy. If we put a pan containing ice on the stove and apply heat, the atomic particles increase their vibratory action. Thus the vibratory rate of the newly-formed water is higher than that of the solid ice. Applying more heat to the water raises its vibratory rate still more. Then the application of still more heat can cause the water particles to fly into space. The resulting steam represents energy at an even greater level of atomic vibration.

Conditions relating to thought, both in this and in the astral world, represent energy levels and vibratory rates far beyond that of steam. We have every reason to believe that this admittedly crude analogy of changing vibratory levels of ice-water-steam apply to thoughts in the physical, astral, mental, and spiritual or celestial levels. Each succeedingly higher level of thought in the worlds of spirit represents even higher rates of vibration.

Look at this the other way around. People living on the mental and causal level cannot come directly through the mind of a medium. Their rate of vibration is so high that they might damage the medium's brain if they attempted direct contact. Communications from these higher levels have to be relayed down in steps. Look again at Fig. 35 and note particularly items D and F. Often the "relay stations" or "transformers" that serve to step down the vibratory level cause a loss in content, a loss in quality—and may even represent a gross distortion of what the higher-level being is trying to pass down.

36. Can a person ever visit the astral planes while still residing in the physical body?

A very definite "yes," and this offers one of the most exciting prospects for humanity's development in the century ahead.

Usually when we go into deep sleep during the early portion of each night's rest, the astral body leaves the physical body but remains connected with it via the so-called silver cord. As it is of course *already* existing in the astral world, it has no trouble traveling at that level. What it can or may do in such travel is too long and involved a topic for us to discuss here. I can say, however, that it is able to gain knowledge that will be of help to the conscious mind upon its return. (This is one reason why many people learn the habit of saying, "Well, let me sleep on that matter."

Senile persons and persons nearing death often find that their astral bodies are starting to spend time away from their physical bodies even in the daytime, when they are judged to be awake. This, of course, is the basis of so much of the research reported by Kübler-Ross, Moody, Osis, Crookall and others.

What is still more exciting is that through meditation techniques it is possible to sit down in a quiet and secure spot, relax, and then attune to the higher planes and let the astral body travel. Remember, the levels of mind and soul are contained in the astral body so that they, too, are out of the body. This allows direct mental contact with intelligences on the astral plane. Not only can such contact vastly increase the knowledge available to the meditator, but it can also bring to him the increased wisdom that can be gleaned from much older and wiser souls.

37. Often small children insist that they see and hear other children or playmates which are invisible to adults. When they get older they seem to grow out of this. Are their "playmates" a figment of their imagination?

Most certainly not! We have recently learned that up until the age of six or seven, the eyes of many children can see light at wavelengths considerably shorter than those detected by the eyes of adults. But they also have a high sensitivity to energies outside our known electromagnetic spectrum. Sensitivity to this latter type of energy in adults is possessed only by those relatively rare individuals who are known as clairaudients and clairvoyants. This ability of small children enables them to see and tune into what we call the astral or etheric world—perhaps into the middle astral planes.

A recent study has found that a large number of children today have imaginary playmates or companions such as an invisible older friend. What's more, the same study has found that having a make-believe friend is apparently good for a child.

A recent *Psychology Today* article says that up to 65 percent of the kids in a study group reported having imaginary friends. The article points out that only a generation ago, children with imagined playmates were thought to be hallucinating and "dangerously removed from reality."

Researchers have since found that children who have make-believe companions are different from those who do not—they are said to be less aggressive and more cooperative, they smile more, they show a greater ability to concentrate, they are seldom bored, and their language is richer and more advanced.

38. Why is the word "causal" combined with the word "mental" in

identifying the next to the highest plane shown in Figs. 32, 33, 35 and 36?

Many persons know little or nothing about the role that *thoughts* play in creating our material world. Hence, let me give some specific examples to show how thought actually *causes* things to happen in our everyday world—and in the worlds of spirit.

Consider this book; every facet of it is the result of many individual thoughts by hundreds of people. The words you read are the product of my thoughts. The paper was made on machinery perfected over decades by hundreds of individual thinkers. A typesetter had to utilize his thinking process to design the book and punch the correct keys on his machine. Then there were the contributions made by the printer, the bookbinder, the transportation company, the bookseller, etc.

Let's consider our own bodies. The knowledge acquired in the last 30 years regarding the subject of psychosomatic illness shows clearly that our thoughts can and do affect the several trillion cells in our own bodies and bring about either health or illness.

In Part I, I presented the concept that *your mind is the programmer* of your brain (the computer). Your brain is of no functional value unless your lower self—your very wise *unconscious* mind—programs the body on all details of its routine daily functioning. Unless your *conscious* mind thinks *thoughts,* you cannot turn from one page to the next, nor can you weigh and evaluate these *thoughts* that my fingers are pecking out and putting on paper.

In my book *Healers and the Healing Process,* I gave details of a scientific report of how Olga and Ambrose Worrall, seated in Baltimore, Maryland, focused their thoughts on a laboratory 600 miles away in Atlanta, Georgia. They undertook to use their *minds* to accelerate the growth rate of individual shoots of rye grass planted in a pot in the laboratory. They did increase the growth rate by more than 500 percent. Later Mrs. Worrall, still seated in Baltimore, focused her thoughts and healing energies on an atomic cloud chamber in the Atlanta laboratory. She displaced matter in the cloud chamber sufficiently so that it was possible to record the resulting disturbance on photographic film.

In subsequent research, Mrs. Worrall succeeded in changing the molecular bonding between hydrogen and oxygen in water—one of the most stable substances in our physical world. (Recall that your body and brain are largely composed of water.)

With these few examples of our growing understanding of how our thoughts can cause effects in the world around us, it will not be such a great step to explain why the term *causal* is coupled with the term *mental* in describing the levels nearest to the level of the Godhead. Most of what we have in this physical three-dimensional world, including most of our inventions, *first existed in the mental and causal worlds.*

Please refer again to Fig. 35. Note path A. This indicates how a soul or spirit in the lowest astral plane can obsess a person living on the earth plane—that is, *cause* that person to be possessed. Paths D and F indicate how friendly and helpful souls or spirits on the middle and highest astral planes can serve us as guides, protectors and teachers. If you can accommodate these ideas, then it should not be too great a step to contemplate that *extremely* wise intelligences on the plane nearest our Creator have thought up many *good ideas far in advance of anything we yet have on the earth plane.* This is the true source, the pathway of humanity's highest creative work—for artists, sculptors, writers, medical discoveries, inventions, etc. It is represented by path F'.

Thus we now have a rapidly growing basis for understanding the power that thought has in the whole scheme of creation. We can understand as never before the *causal* nature of thought.

39. How do you personally feel about reincarnation?

Perhaps I should put my personal experience on record. I grew up in a strictly orthodox, midwestern Christian Protestant denomination. As the decades of my study, searching and world travels passed, I continued to reject the subject of reincarnation. Not until I was well past the age of 60 had I assembled sufficient knowledge to change my views. Not until I had logged hundreds of hours of contact, via mediums, with beings in the worlds of spirit did I find the evidence overwhelming and convincing. Only then did my conscious mind accept the evidence so that I could become comfortable with the concept of reincarnation and convinced of its reality.

Hence, with this background, I understand the feelings of those who have closed minds on the subject. As stated at the start of this book, I have no desire to preach any dogma, gospel, religion, creed or "ism."

In the next nine questions and their answers, I deal with the subject of reincarnation. While some people in our western culture will consider these comments with an open mind, many readers will not. In fact, the latter may even label the whole subject "stuff and nonsense, unbelievable, obnoxious and distasteful."

If you are one of the latter, simply skip over the remaining questions and their answers and move on to Part V, so as to *concentrate on the overall theme of this book.*

40. Perhaps you should clarify what is meant by the term reincarnation.

Yes, that is very important. There are many misconceptions about the term. Webster's *New Third International Dictionary* defines:

Incarnate—invested with flesh or bodily form.

Discarnate—having no physical body.

Reincarnate—rebirth in new bodies or new forms of life, especially a rebirth of the soul in a new body.

I use the term strictly as "rebirth of the soul in a new body"—a new *human* body. The Eastern concept of metempsychosis, or the transmigration of souls, maintains that human souls can go into animal bodies. However, there is no evidence I am aware of to support this belief.

41. How can reincarnation be a fact when the majority of theologians, priests, rabbis and ministers do not accept the concept?

A good and obvious question. Let us assume that *back over the years* you had asked the following three questions of a prestigious panel of 1,000 of the world's leading medical doctors, psychiatrists and psychologists:

1. In 1930, you asked the question: *Is it possible that your theory that illness stems almost entirely from invasion of the body by bacteria, germs and viruses is seriously in error?* Probably 90 percent would have answered, "Preposterous! Our medical theories have evolved over many centuries of treating people. Modern medical science cannot be in error." Yet only a few decades later, it became recognized that most illness develops when stress and/or our thoughts and emotions trigger a chemical imbalance that only then allows the bacteria, germs or viruses in our body to take control. Thus, in only a few decades we learned that perhaps 75 percent of all illness is triggered psychosomatically—and that what we had *thought* we knew was only partially correct.*

2. In 1950: *Is there any truth in the ancient Chinese concept of acupuncture meridians at or near the surface of the body?* Probably 90 percent would have answered, "No, that is merely ancient superstition." Yet only thirty-five years later, perhaps the majority would answer with a qualified "yes." *Many of this group might be found using acupuncture on their patients.*

3. Today: *Is the brain the same thing as the mind?* It is likely that the majority would answer a resounding "yes." But a few who are actively engaged in brain-mind research are beginning to have doubts. Some frankly say it does not look as though we will ever be able to explain the human mind in terms of the brain.

Now, what is the significance of these questions and answers? Merely this: the human body has been under study for thousands of years, yet it is only in *this most recent instant in history* that some of our cherished concepts about the human body and its functioning have been found *to be false.* Is there any reason to think that our religious professionals (the theologians, ministers, priests and rabbis) have the final answer on life and death? Hardly! The next time you encounter one of these, ask, "Please tell me exactly what happens to me after I die."

---

* This changing trend is nicely detailed in *Beyond the Magic Bullet* by Bernard Dixon, published in 1978 by George Allen & Unwin, London, Boston and Sydney.

Do not judge them harshly if their answers to questions on *reincarnation* are not fully satisfying.

The current *explosion* of knowledge about our universe is cause for comment in a column by Vermont Royster, "Toward Understanding," in *The Wall Street Journal:*

"It seems hard to realize but in my lifetime man has learned more about the universe in which he lives than in all the lifespans of all the generations that went before.

"In little more than half a century we have made prodigious leaps in our knowledge about the infinitesimal particles that make up the physical world and about the powerful forces that govern the infinite space in which this world floats as a tiny speck.

"Yet here is a curious thing. In the contemplation of man himself, of his dilemmas, of his place in this universe, we are little further along than when time began. We are still left with questions of who we are and why we are and where we are going.

"So for all that growing knowledge we are left with the ancient cry from the Book of Job: 'Where is wisdom to be found? And where is the place of understanding?' "

Apropos of our *expanding knowledge*, there may be a parallel between the concepts of acupuncture and reincarnation. Both have been around for thousands of years. Until recently the medical profession in the western nations did not believe in acupuncture, and the clergy and people did not believe in reincarnation. After tens of millions of Americans heard about acupuncture as a result of former President Nixon's trip to China, they started questioning their physicians. The result has been that in just a very few years, American medical practitioners have investigated acupuncture, found it beneficial and are using it.

The recent books relating to past life readings and the use of hypnosis for regression to pre-natal lives have stimulated the thinking of millions of Americans to look carefully at the subject of reincarnation. A recent study showed that perhaps 20 percent of Americans now believe in reincarnation. Only time will tell to what extent the thinking of the clergy will move in the same direction.

So the fact that your religious counselor cannot answer your question should certainly indicate that neither he nor you has any basis for totally rejecting the concept of reincarnation. Generally speaking, religious spokesmen are as ignorant of known facts of life after death as modern medical scientists are of many of the factors determining the health and well-being of the body and mind.

42. I am mystified as to how reincarnation actually works. Can you give me some specific guidance on this bewildering matter?

I can certainly try. Let's cut out long, wordy discourses and take the simple picture story approach. But let me caution you that what follows is a highly simplified presentation of an *extremely* complicated subject, which we are only beginning to understand.

In recent years, as the world's raw materials have become scarce and higher in price, there has been a trend toward *recycling*. Whereas in the past we shipped vast quantities of materials to the dump or incinerator, today we have started to reclaim or recycle materials. Now we carefully gather up empty aluminum beer and soda cans and sell them back to the mill. At the recycling plant they are melted and molded into ingots. The ingots can then be used to extrude shapes for storm windows, automobile parts, or more beer and soda cans. Similar recycling plants are set up for reuse of automobiles, glass containers, newspapers, shipping cartons and many other useful and increasingly valuable materials.

Has it not occurred to you that if death is the end for each of us, our Creator's plan is a very wasteful one? What in all the world is more precious than a human soul? Stop for a moment and think about yourself. Do you have any material item that you consider more valuable than your very own self—your soul? Does it make any sense to think that an all-wise Creator is going to send your precious soul to the dump, the graveyard of your dreams, the incinerator? Has not science in this century shown us that energy cannot be destroyed—that it can only be changed from one state or vibration to another state or vibration?

What could be more logical than the *recycling of your soul*?

Therefore, if you will permit a bit of fanciful humor or a late 20th-century parable, let us consider Fig. 36, "The Original Recycling Plant."

Let's start our discussion at the bottom left of the diagram. Here I stand. At age 76, I have traversed much of this lifetime. I am headed for the elevator. Sometime in the years ahead I will cast off this worn old body. I will be ready for a free ride to some higher plane of being.

I see *three* elevator doors, all closed. Which one of these will open and offer a ride? Well, if I have learned anything in this life, I have learned that this is a world of *cause and effect*. I have learned that *nobody* can cheat or beat the rules of the game. Hence, the door that opens will be determined by the life I have led. I, like all others, will be judged as falling into one of the three categories shown in Fig. 33. on page 102. Please take a moment to reread the descriptions of levels A, B and C on page 101.

If I have failed to learn the rules that have been spelled out over the centuries by the enlightened souls who have done their best to illuminate the path to a happy, future life, I have no one to blame but myself. In the school of life I must then be judged a *failure*. I get an F on my report card for this life. The door marked C opens and I soon find myself in some very uninviting surroundings when I am kicked off at the second floor.

One who did somewhat better in learning his lessons and putting

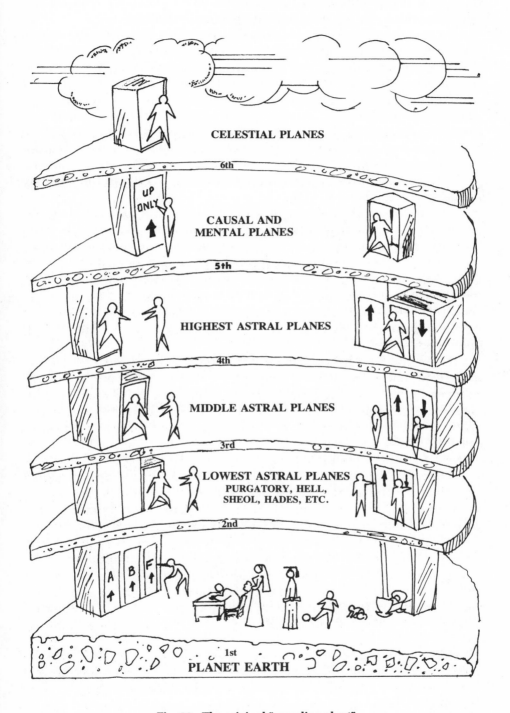

CELESTIAL PLANES

6th

CAUSAL AND MENTAL PLANES

5th

HIGHEST ASTRAL PLANES

4th

MIDDLE ASTRAL PLANES

3rd

LOWEST ASTRAL PLANES
PURGATORY, HELL,
SHEOL, HADES, ETC.

2nd

1st
PLANET EARTH

Fig. 36. The original "recycling plant"

129

them in practice will be welcomed for a ride on Elevator B to the third floor. On the other hand, for the person who has been very diligent in learning and putting into practice the admonitions illustrated in Fig. 34, bingo—door A opens and he or she takes the express to the fourth floor.

Let's assume that I get only as far as the second floor. I will have three options:

a. Stay where I now find myself—for a very long time, even centuries by earth time.

b. Start looking for some beings whose light shines through the gloom and who offer to lead me upward to the third floor where I can get some more schooling.

c. Because of my gross preoccupation with myself and burning desire to get back to my old haunts, I stumble into the *down* elevator.

If the latter happens, I find myself again squeezed into a small physical body for still another life on the surface of planet Earth. The recycling plant has done its job! Or to put it more crudely by using the terminology of the computer programmer—"garbage in, garbage out." I am merely back at square one and have to start all over again. In fact, if my life has been particularly hurtful to others, I may find I have some additional handicaps to carry in this new life. For centuries the oriental religions have used the term *bad karma* to cover this accumulation of unlearned lessons.

If a person finds himself on the third floor, the first order of business is to relax and enjoy life. In principle, it is possible to apply oneself sufficiently to earn a ride on up to the fourth floor. On the other hand, if the individual prefers to come again to the challenge of living and learning on the surface of this fascinating and often frustrating planet, he may eventually take the *down* elevator back to the first floor. There is no pushing for a decision. It is always up to the individual.

When a person finds himself on the fourth floor (having arrived by express from ground level, or the local from the third floor), he is really in for a delightful period of post mortem life. (One of my humor-loving friends says that in any description of the summerland we should abandon the old phrases of "pearly gates" and "streets paved with gold." We should talk in terms of wall-to-wall carpeting, air conditioning and celestial stereo! This is not as facetious as it sounds. We learned in answers to questions 6 and 32 the crucial role our *thoughts* play in forming our reality in this nitty-gritty everyday world. We will find that in "heaven" or "hell" our *thoughts* will play an even greater role in creating our "reality.")

Here, as always, the law of cause and effect is operating. If a person's mental and spiritual growth continues to the point of "graduating," he will undergo what has been referred to as the *second death*. This involves *shedding* the astral body that has served as a containment vehicle; then the mind and soul can progress to the higher level of vibrations of which the next planes are composed. The person is thus *born* on the mental and causal planes.

If, however, the soul is not qualified to move upward, it has the option of remaining on the higher astral plane until such time as it may decide to have another go at life on the earth plane.

Once the person arrives on the mental and causal planes, he loses most of the detailed interest in what is going on far below on the earth plane. However, if because of great altruism and compassion for his fellow beings the person wishes to return for still another earth walk, this is *the last level from which a return can be undertaken.*

Much of the material in this book has come from our friends now living on the mental and causal planes. Most of these left the earth plane within the last 35 years. There is much reluctance for any of these intelligences to come back to the chaotic world of today. Some say frankly that they will wait and take a look at things in the twenty-first century. Who are we to suggest they do otherwise? They need be in no hurry.

If they continue to work and study and grow mentally and spiritually, they eventually have the possibility of taking the *local* elevator which makes the short run to one higher level—the celestial planes. Again, due to the change in the vibratory levels of matter, this involves shedding what has loosely been called the "mental body" and accepting what is known as the *final rebirth.*

Since, as I've pointed out elsewhere, modern man can hardly conceive of the level of existence of the celestial planes, we can end our effort to explain reincarnation here. *There is no recycling from this level.*

43. Frankly, I just do not like the concept of reincarnation. I do not like the mechanical-like aspect. It is almost like being strapped to a big rotating water wheel where I come up into the invigorating air and sunlight, only to be submerged again in the murky waters of life on the earth. Isn't there any way I can get loose from the wheel and escape the cycle of birth, growth, death and rebirth? Be specific.

Yes, you and everyone can get off the wheel of death and rebirth. Here is a time-proven formula.

Let us assume you have lived your life in accordance with the precepts diagrammed in Fig. 34, the "Proven Path for Individual Soul Development." Hence, on departing your physical body, you will be entitled to "take the elevator" directly to the highest astral plane. Assume that your life here is joyful, beautiful and filled with happiness, and that you continue to develop mentally, emotionally and spiritually—what our enlightened forefathers termed *growing in grace.* Someday, in the great scheme of things, you may find yourself evolved to the very uppermost levels of the higher astral. Further growth is open to you by two different paths. You can gain more experience of growth by returning and taking on a new set of circumstances on the earth plane, or you can shed your astral body and become fitted to live in the more refined and invigorating mental and causal worlds.

Since your question indicates that you are bent on escaping the wheel of rebirth with its constant dunkings, trials and tribulations on the earth plane, you would probably decide to push on upward in your search for fulfillment. So you accept the second death and find yourself reborn on the mental and causal planes.

Arriving on these planes, you will find, in due course, that once more you have a choice of two paths: return again for further mental, emotional and spiritual growth on the earth plane, or shed your so-called mental body and take the one-way elevator going up to the celestial planes. You say, "Excelsior!" and take the final death and rebirth.

It's all there in Fig. 36. You may be amused at the seemingly child-ish representations in this diagrams, but you cannot go wrong in betting your life that this is *the way it is.*

Eureka! You have made it. Congratulations. No longer are you strapped to the wheel of rebirth.

Sorry. There is a catch. Recall my reference to *cause and effect.* Each of us can ride the desirable UP elevators *only* if we have *continued* to grow mentally, emotionally and spiritually. And what is the safest and most certain way to accomplish this growth? Simply by applying the precepts in Fig. 34, the nine-step staircase which has as its destina-tion everlasting life. (If this were the conventional "how to" book, we could observe: "Just take the nine easy steps and become a god yourself. No need to bother with reincarnation."

But, you ask, "Do you have any *proof* that this can be done? Be specific; give some example—some case histories."

While in trance, the psychic Edgar Cayce described the past lives of 1,200 people in readings that were in great detail and which involved many lives for each person. Violet M. Shelley, in her book *Reincarna-ion Unnecessary,* analyzed these 1,200 records. She found that in 18 cases the persons were told that *when this life was finished they might choose not to return.*

What was so special about these 18 persons? You will be happy to know that they were people like you. The list included housewives, a governess, a real estate salesman, a psychiatrist, an architect, an actress, a writer, a secretary, a life insurance representative, etc. What did these people have *in common?* From my study of the data carefully assembled by Ms. Shelley, it seems that *all had lived previously and were now living lives that had taken them far up the stairway in Fig. 34.*

Now for more specifics which confirm that you can get off the wheel of rebirth if and when you *make up your own mind that you want to.* With the aid of one of the deep-trance mediums mentioned in the first paragraph of the Acknowledgments, we discussed this subject with numerous friends we have acquired on the mental and causal planes. (The subject cannot be intelligently discussed with any dwellers below this level, as they know only what is *below* them. They lack the necessary perspective. And, since we the researchers are lacking in cosmic consciousness, our mentalities are not sufficiently developed to comprehend the perspective from the cosmic levels.)

One of our collaborators from the causal and mental level is the previously mentioned Dr. William F.G. Swann, cosmic ray scientist, former physics professor at the universities of Yale, Minnesota, and Chicago, and Swarthmore College. Swann died in Philadelphia in 1962.* In discussing reincarnation with our friend Swann, he said that he has made the decision that when the current research project on which his team is working is completed, he will accept final rebirth on the celestial planes.

A similar conversation was had with George W. Russell, the Irish writer, poet, artist and mystic known as A.E., who died in 1935. He is strongly tempted to return once more to his "beloved green isle," as he calls it. But for now he will delay the decision and see what develops during the next half century of earth time. His story, like those of Swann and many others contacted on this level, shows that it is possible to escape the wheel of rebirth. So also do the lives of the 18 persons mentioned in the Cayce readings.

Thus the answer to your question is a *qualified* "yes." But we must be completely honest and say that so far our research has not turned up any formula for accomplishing this objective other than that which is diagrammed so explicitly in Figs. 32 and 36.

To all of this, one more comment should be added. Several months after writing the first part of this answer, the scientist, mystic and author Itzhak Bentov, one of my closest friends, was one of 271 people who died in the Chicago DC-10 air crash.† Some months before this accident, Bentov, in an interview published in the March 1978 issue of *New Age,* expressed his thoughts as follows:

"*New Age:* In your cosmology, what about the concept of death?

"*Bentov:* The universe is an information storage system. It is a teaching and learning machine, and it's ridiculous to think that the universe is going to throw out that information that has been collected

---

* A preliminary copy of the manuscript of this book was submitted for criticism to H.T.E. Hertzberg, anthropologist and parapsychologist. When studying his marked-up copy of the manuscript, I was interested to find the following penciled note, with an asterisk placed as above: "My brother-in-law, an astrophysicist, studied with Dr. Swann in Swarthmore in the 1930's. My wife, also a Swarthmore graduate, remembers Swann also. I even met him there myself."

† Author of *Stalking the Wild Pendulum: On the Mechanics of Consciousness,* Dutton 1977.

over, say, eighty years. I look at the body the way you might look at a car. You may use a car for, say, 80,000 miles and then junk it—but you wouldn't junk the driver along with the car! The driver goes on. So naturally consciousness goes on and keeps collecting information over many, many lifetimes.

"*New Age:* So you feel we just keep getting reincarnated on this planet.

"*Bentov:* Until we learn how the system works. The purpose of the lesson is to find out how it works, and once you know, then you're out of the system. Then you stand aside and look at the other people finding out for themselves."

Here Bentov, with his great ability to put important ideas into easily understood form, is telling us, "Yes, you *can* get off the wheel of rebirth—just as soon as *you* find out *how the system works!*"*

And after all, this is the purpose of this book. When we fully comprehend the concepts in Figs. 32, 34, 35 and 36, our consciousness will arrive at the point where we have most of what we need to know about *how the system works.*

44. We hear much about people getting "readings" of their past lives. Some of these come through mediums. Some are obtained through hypnosis. How valid are these readings?

They have *very little* validity, as I see it. My associates and I have researched this question rather carefully.

In my case, I sought out seven persons in the United States and England who are said to be among the best such past-life readers. Among six personal readings there was absolutely no correlation, even for identical time slots! None of these contained anything that could be considered in the least evidential or meaningful. Only one reading, said to have come from an elevated being, fell into a totally different category, and three years of painstaking study of the material indicates that it has considerable validity.

The batting average for hypnotic regression to past lives seems to be slightly higher than the readings through mediumistic persons—but not by a wide margin. For example, some of my research colleagues regressed a number of persons and carefully recorded all of the detailed information on the purported past lives. One year later the entire activity was repeated. *Not one item was the same!* The fantasy creating capability of the human mind is staggering.

---

* A few of the many persons who submitted criticisms and suggestions on the early draft manuscript of this book—*before* the inclusion of this quotation of Bentov's views—expressed the opinion that I made it sound too easy to break the recycling system. One critic wrote several paragraphs on this subject. I feel that his views should be made available to the serious seeker and have therefore included them in Appendix C.

Let me make my position clear. *Past life records are a reality.* Everything that ever happened, every thought ever held, every word ever spoken is permanently embedded in the fabric of the cosmos—on the master recording tape, if you want to call it that. But very few souls on earth today can easily and accurately tap this material and operate the retrieval system so as to get an accurate and precise readout of the data.

In 1973, twenty-seven years after his death, Edgar Cayce expressed his present thoughts on this subject of past life readings. As reported in the book *Edgar Cayce Returns,* by Robert R. Leichtman, M.D. and David Kendrick Johnson, Cayce had this to say of his latest thoughts on the subject:

"Past life reading is a relatively rare gift. There are maybe twenty people in the United States who can really do it, although there are many more who say they can. I believe there are only four on the West Coast at the moment, in spite of the fact that it looks like thousands. Most of these other people are making something up. I am talking in particular about people who have perhaps four standard plots which they give out to their clients, with only little shadings of difference.

"It would be interesting for someone to go through your records or David's—or even mine. It would be seen that no two life readings are the same, and that each reading is helpful to the client. There's always a helpful reason why the client is being made aware of this information—it's not just another pretty story.

"But when you begin to find a pattern of similar plots in a psychic's file of past life readings, then you begin to realize that perhaps this psychic is behaving in a way that's not quite proper.

"I would like to add, too, that there are several games on the market which purport to help people remember their past lives. They are almost entirely worthless. The people who developed them are really not what they pretend to be. As a matter of fact, the two people I am thinking of at the moment are knowingly fraudulent. They are after the aggrandizement of their bank accounts."

Thus, in view of the scarcity of mediums who in fact *do* have the ability to use helpers in the realms of spirit to tap the Akashic records, and in view of the vast amount of deception—self and otherwise—surrounding the use of hypnosis for past-life regression, my personal advice for anyone who cares to take it is, "Forget about trying to pull away the veil. Start in *right now* to concentrate ever more sincerely in building into *this* life the tenets set forth in Fig. 34."

45. I have had intelligent pets with wonderful personalities. What happened to them when they died?

A long cherished pet is just as certain to survive death of its physical body as you are. Cats and dogs have provided a substantial amount of evidence on this point over the years. There are even well-documented cases of the survival of pet monkeys and favorite horses. If the survival of well-loved pets were not a fact, "heaven" or the afterlife would be a less happy place for animal lovers all over the world.

Unlike man, the lower animals do not normally possess individual souls. Each species has what is known as a group soul. All wild animals and animals raised by man for food return to their respective group soul upon death of their physical body. However, it seems that a domesticated dog or cat that becomes a pet takes on a certain individuality from its very personal association with its master. According to Barbanell and others, it seems to develop a *humanness* that it did not formerly possess, as a part of the friendship.* It may be a part of man's contribution to the evolutionary scheme to confer this attribute on those animals who come within his care.

It could be this quality that determines the survival of a beloved pet. Beyond the grave, the domesticated animal will not continue the process of perfecting its individuality but will return ultimately to the group soul of its species. But for all animal lovers, yes, when you come to your next life, you will find your favorite pet waiting.

46. Those who believe in reincarnation talk a lot about "karma." What is karma? Is karma good or bad?

Many lengthy books have been written on this subject. I'll try to keep it simple.

This universe seems to run on two tracks, labeled *cause* and *effect*. In my daily life, I carry out activities that help or hinder my mental and spiritual growth, and that of others. These actions by me are labeled *causes*. The results of these actions are called *effects*. If my actions are beneficial and help me and my associates or family to grow mentally and spiritually, the effects will be good. This is called good karma. If the actions hurt my mental and spiritual growth or that of others, they are called bad karma.†

A day of reckoning comes for each of us. It is as sure as the proverbial "death and taxes." My good and bad actions will be considered in determining which of the three astral planes will be my new home.

Being human, we each generate good and bad karma. As in the game of baseball, it is the *batting average* that counts. Hence it is prudent to try to store up far more good karma than bad.

---

* Maurice Barbanell, *This is Spiritualism*, Spiritualist Press, London, 1959.
† A reader well versed in the eastern religions and/or Theosophy may think that this is an excessively simplified discussion of good and bad karma. It is intended as such. There is reason to believe that much of the traditional concept of karma is as distorted and nonproductive as are many portions of the dogmas and creeds of the various religions. Discussions with present occupants of the mental and causal planes indicate that until man evolves sufficiently to understand the true nature of karma and the whole reincarnation process, he will do well to stick to basics.

To be honest, I must acknowledge that the concept of karma is not universally accepted. There are those who think that no matter how greedy, lazy, dissolute, jealous and hateful a person may be in this life, all such actions are forgiven, and a life of eternal bliss awaits the saint and the sinner alike. As the evidence shows, however, such thinking is unfounded.

47. I might want to look more deeply into what people around the world have thought about reincarnation. Where can I find the best source of information?

Just as I finished writing on reincarnation and constructing the diagram in Fig. 36, a friend lent me *Reincarnation: The Phoenix Fire Mystery*, by Joseph Head and S.L. Cranston. If I had had this book thirty years ago, it would have greatly speeded up my own research. It is by far the finest summary I have found of the centuries of East-West dialogue on death and rebirth from the worlds of religion, science, psychology, parapsychology, philosophy, art and literature, and from great thinkers of the past and present.

It is gratifying to learn that what I have presented in this book on the subject of reincarnation is in no way contradicted by this monumental study by Head and Cranston.

48. Now a final but very important question on reincarnation. Let us say that I accept the concept of reincarnation. Will such a belief assure that the quality of my life will be any better here—and hereafter?

An emphatic—in fact, a most resounding—no!

Did the *beliefs* of the Crusaders who swept down through Europe to Asia Minor cause them to refrain from ruthless slaughter of 80,000 of their fellow human beings in just one of their many battles?

Did the *beliefs* of members and leaders of the Church in Europe prevent the infliction of the most horrible torture and death on many unfortunate people during the Inquisition?

Have the religious *beliefs* of the millions of people who make up our Western civilization prevented us from trying to exterminate each other in two devastating wars just in my lifetime?

Of course not, even though all such actions were totally at odds with the basic teachings of love and compassion which form the very core of such *beliefs*. Why should we expect that *any* belief—even a belief in reincarnation—will automatically be translated into a better life for those who hold such a belief?

In the very nature of things even good beliefs are of value only when through *constructive action* they are translated into deeds that enhance and glorify life. As an example, consider southern Asia, where reincarnation has been actively embraced for more than 2,000 years but has often been misused. Religious and secular leaders have repeatedly used it to keep the masses under control. Hundreds of millions of believers in reincarnation in both the past and present have used it as a crutch or an excuse to refrain from putting forth the effort to grow mentally, emotionally and spiritually and thus better their animal-like lives. It is all too easy to rely on the explanation that *present* life problems are a result of bad karma carried over from previous lives—and that one must be content with life, no matter how miserable.

What folly. What loss of God-given potential. Practicing a belief in reincarnation—in the recycling of the human soul—should result in an effort to surmount life's present problems victoriously and thereby accumulate a supply of good karma.

Failure to use the belief in reincarnation *constructively* is not confined to the people of southern Asia. As I travel throughout the Western world, I am appalled to see how a small amount of misinformation about reincarnation cannot only spoil the quality of a current life-time—but also create problems that will have to be solved sooner or later in future lifetimes. Olga Worrall, world famous healer and participant in healing research as reported in question 38, traveled almost constantly, meeting with individuals and large groups. She once expressed her opinions on this subject in a personal report to me, a portion of which follows:

"As I travel here and abroad I am shocked and dismayed at some of the things that are happening to people because of false teachings about reincarnation. I have met dozens of St. Pauls—and I can't even begin to recall how many St. Johns I have met—as well as the mother of Christ. These phony past life readings are causing the breakup of many families—with immoral behavior stemming from the concept of 'soul mates.' Let me give one example.

"I have just been asked to help in the case where a man, aged 45, at the peak of his career, met a divorcee at a party who told him that she was an expert on 'life readings.' She proceeded to disclose that she and he are 'soul mates' and that they must immediately take up life where they left off in the last incarnation. Result—the man moves into her home; she has a six-year-old son; he has a lovely and loving wife and three children; he cannot understand why his wife objects—after all, his 'soul mate' must come first!

"When the man's mother appealed to the woman to think of the lives of the four children, the woman's answer was, 'We have absolutely no responsibility for these four children. They chose to be reincarnated into such a family situation, and they will just have to live with the problem. This is their karma.'"

Mrs. Worrall concluded: "At the New Life Clinic in Baltimore, we have many such people whose lives have been broken up by 'soul mates' and 'life readings'—and by many who think that their specific illness or poor health is a required carry-over from a past life. With this latter category we in most cases find that their illness stems directly from emotional stresses and strains *in this current life."*

Because of many similar experiences encountered in my own travels, I have pondered as to why a person's life can get so messed up— and what can be done to avoid such happenings. I have concluded that at least two main factors are involved. First, there is no fully authenticated bible or handbook that sets forth the true facts on reincarnation. Second, even if such a bible or handbook existed, many people would fail to put its principles to work in their daily lives. The examples of the crusaders, the inquisitors and the instigators of the wars mentioned earlier are examples of this factor.

As to the lack of a "Reincarnation Bible," we find that none of the Theosophical books, none of the Rudolf Steiner or Alice Bailey books and none of the many books on occult lore presently treat the subject in the clear and easily understood way that the spiritual teachings of Buddha are set forth in the Eightfold Path of Enlightenment and the central teachings of Jesus are presented in Matthew, Mark, Luke and John.

This leaves a person in the situation where, "A little knowledge is a dangerous thing." As Professor William A. Tiller of Stanford University has remarked, "We have many indications that nature does a recycling job on the individual human soul and that reincarnation is a fact. But it seems that our present level of ignorance regarding the workings of the cosmos is such that we really cannot comprehend more than the merest outline of a theory of reincarnation. Hence we should refrain from any attempt at day-to-day interpretation until we know vastly more about this subject than we know today."*

It is in an effort toward taking the first step at eventually creating the much needed "Reincarnation Bible" that friends in the worlds of spirit and I present herein Fig. 32, "The Interpenetrating Levels of Life and Consciousness," and Fig. 34, "The Proven Path for Individual Soul Development." But until others, working on both sides of the veil, carry the work much further, it is well to put aside all such concepts as "soul mates" and look upon "life readings" as intriguing mysteries that have absolutely no significance for guiding one's daily life. For now, the material embodied in Figs. 32 and 34 will, *if put into practice,* assure a better life now, and hereafter.

49. Immortality and eternal life certainly appeal to me. How can I comprehend such a mind-stretching concept?

---

* Of course, my personal research has influenced me to include this statement. It is hard to overlook or explain away the fact, as mentioned in the answer to question 44, that readings of my purported past lives by six highly recommended persons in the United States and England did not agree with respect *to even one lifetime.*

Locked into our little individual lives as we are, it seems almost presumptuous to think we are made of the same stuff as God our Creator. But this is the truth of the matter. We have no trouble thinking that God will be alive for ages to come. Therefore, if we think of ourselves as some small part of Him, we can visualize more clearly that we already have eternal life. Stop thinking of *eternity* as something in the far-distant future. You live in eternity *now*. Eternity is this instant, the next instant and so on. You *already* live in eternity. After all, *you cannot die!*

50. One final question: Of all the messages received from all the persons you have contacted in the worlds of spirit, can you single out one which is the most helpful to those of us trying to understand these issues?

Yes. Wilfred Brandon dictated four books through the mind and hand of Edith Ellis of New York City during the period of 1935 to 1956. In 1935, Brandon gave his credentials in *Open the Door* as follows:

"I was killed in 1132 in France, again in 1373 in England, and once more I fell by the sword in 1647. I was too weary to incarnate again until 1762, when, like many other adventurous spirits, I wished to try life in America, a life of free democracy. The New World was for me only a soldier's grave. No use of my heart or mind was made on Earth for six centuries. Whatever I have made of myself as a thinker was accomplished here. I hope to incarnate once more, but only when an Age of Reason arrives. How far distant that time seems now!"

Here is the Brandon statement which I single out as a fitting and helpful conclusion for Part IV:

"There is no death. That is the key to what you have to learn in the years to come on Earth. You are all preparing to end your lives with bodily death. You have made no preparation for going on with existence. Most people, if they do have a belief in immortality, have such a fantastic idea of what it will be like that they are not making plans for anything but an eternity of idleness and some singing, for which they perhaps haven't the least talent.

"What a picture!

"Here we are far more interested in getting on with life than you are. We see our wasted incarnations and wish we might have been sure of life after death. We could have fitted ourselves to meet it had we known what we know now."

Having just finished reading these question and answer pages, you may feel like the person who came out of a mind-stretching meeting and humorously remarked, "Well, I am *still* confused, but now I am confused on a *higher level!*" I hope you are not confused, but in the remaining portion of this book you will find exciting information that should go far to clear away any fears and doubts you may still have as to whether or not you *really will live forever.*

PART FIVE

The Certainty of Living Forever

Foreword

Down through the ages, mankind in all portions of the globe has speculated that life must continue after disintegration of the physical body. In the foregoing pages, we have assembled and examined the experiences and data that confirm this speculation.

Now, in these closing years of the 20th century, *the long-sought proof of survival is being generated.*

Dwellers in "heaven" or "paradise" are in fact now collaborating with more than one thousand earth dwellers in many countries in an effort to create man's ultimate communication system. This present decade has witnessed the first two-way electronic communication between the living and the so-called dead—in one case *more than twenty hours of meaningful two-way conversation* on a variety of topics.

A start has been made at *rending the veil* between heaven and earth.

CHAPTER 17

Perspectives, Predictions and Parallels

In order to comprehend the step that mankind is starting to take in his efforts to tap higher levels of consciousness by pulling aside the veil between heaven and earth, it will be helpful to develop some perspective. Throughout mankind's history, there have been men and women who have dared look beyond the present moment and dream of ways by which the quality of life might be improved. These "dreamers" often developed an idea that left its impact on the forward movement of society. This movement in every field of human endeavor has resulted from what has been called "constructive discontent" with things as they were.

Late 20th century man looks out from his present perspective and is horrified by what he sees—a materialistic world seemingly running amok. He watches helplessly as some fellow passengers daily do their utmost to destroy each other—and even the space ship on which all are moving through the cosmos. It is in such situations that prophecies are born.

For most of this century, there have been predictions that mankind would develop an instrumental system to permit the enlightened souls of "heaven" to converse with, and bring enlightenment to, persons in fleshly bodies. Of the several dozen predictions that have been made, these five illustrate the point:

1931. Sir Arthur Conan Doyle, medical doctor, creator of Sherlock Holmes, and an untiring exponent of Spiritualism, returned *after* his death by way of a series of messages channeled through the mediumship of Grace Cooke. Portions of this material are the subject of two books edited by Ivan Cooke: *Thy Kingdom Come* and *The Return of Arthur Conan Doyle.* Some of the *unpublished* material referred to design details for electrically-activated devices to serve as an instrumental communication system from the spirit world. I made a visit to the Cooke home in 1974 to investigate. I found that indeed serious effort had been made to build the equipment, but there had been no success.

1935. *Open the Door,* a book telepathically channeled by Wilfred Brandon through Edith Ellis of New York City was published. On page 23 he states: "Yet science is on the verge of discovering the secret of life after 'death'; it is all but able to connect with our plane. Marconi and those who study the marvels of the ether will in time find *the connecting wave length* and we shall then be united in a common understanding of the Law of Life." On page 31 he continues: "We speak and the sound is forever there. We are continuously pictured there also, as on a cosmic photographic plate." On page 86 he says: "Your radios have already made that plain to you. Every sound is there in space. It needs only a mechanized device to connect the etheric world with the mortal world. How? By discovery of the laws of vibrations which are universal and hold on all three planes of matter—and possibly beyond them." And on page 179 he adds: "All of these [automatic writing and trance mediums] are *makeshifts* which we must use until we can, through them, work with your radio engineers, *until we can perfect a mechanism* that we can use automatically. This is possible and will doubtless be the next step after television."

1944. *Psychic Press* published an article containing prophecies and predictions about a heaven-to-earth communication system. The technologies already available at that time, including electronic systems, induced the spirit world to envisage research in this field and to provide for technical means to talk to human beings, making the hitherto-used mediums redundant. In trance sessions, *recorded in 1944,* spirits of departed scientists talked about fluidal electronic rods, covered with layers of ectoplasm to produce human voices. In a lengthy talk through a medium, further details were discussed. The main obstacle was how to overcome the problems of high frequencies in the spirit world.

1944. The book *Esoteric Healing,* channeled through Alice A. Bailey, carries a "Letter to a Scientist" dictated by the Tibetan master Djwhal Khul. On pages 376 and 377 he prophesizes: "Towards the close of this century, electric devices will be used to contact departed souls, together with photographing of thought forms, thus opening a new area of spirit photography." On page 378 he adds: "The astral body will be susceptible of photographing, but never the mental vehicle," and then goes on: "Yet the first demonstration of existing after death, in such a way that it can be registered upon the physical plane, will be *via the radio* because sound waves always precede vision. No radio now exists which is sufficiently sensitive to carry sound waves from the astral plane."

1972. From the Stainton Moses recordings: "...ere long there will be *an instrument* that will make contact between the two worlds a fact, so that the most highly skeptical will be convinced of life after death. When that time comes, all the barriers that now stand will be broken down."

This small sampling of dozens of available predictions gives valuable perspective for judging the developments we will be reporting in the next chapter. But our capacity for understanding these new breakthroughs can be enhanced even further by taking a moment to briefly review the key events which led to the development of mankind's already existing communication systems.

In 1558 Giovanni Battista della Porta proposed a message sending device that would utilize magnetism. Man had known about magnetism since ancient times, but it was almost 300 years before the development of electromagnets made della Porta's dream a reality.

Fig. 37. Giovanni Battista/Magnetism

In 1838, Samuel F.B. Morse, a portrait painter with an inventive bent, built a crude contraption which demonstrated that clicks from an electromagnet could carry a message along a wire. After much experimentation and assistance from Joseph Henry, a message was sent over 45 miles of wire stretched from Washington to Baltimore: "What hath God wrought?"

Fig. 38. Samuel F.B. Morse/Telegraph

In 1867, Alexander Graham Bell, a teacher of speech, demonstrated with a very crude device that wires could carry not only Morse's dots and dashes, but the tones of the human voice itself. The first words were transferred over a wire only 17 feet long.

In 1877, Thomas Edison, with no formal education, used a sewing needle to capture the vibration of the telephone mouthpiece, first on paraffin paper, then on tinfoil, and then on wax. Crude as his device was, he had invented the forerunner of today's magnetic audio and videotape recording systems.

Fig. 39. Alexander Graham Bell/Telephone

By 1896, Guglielmo Marconi was demonstrating that dots and dashes of telegraphy could be transmitted *without* a wire over long distances—even over the Atlantic Ocean! It did not take long for Lee DeForrest to show that Marconi's signal could be detected by a device that used the flame of a Bunsen burner and platinum electrodes with a coating of hydroxide. He followed this device with the invention of the first "audion" vacuum tube detector, and by 1907

Fig. 40. Thomas Edison/Voice Recording

the voices of singers could be heard on the airwaves. Following in the steps of these pioneers came dozens of inventors bringing regenerative circuits in 1912; superhetrodyne radio in 1918; the first complete television system in 1926; and the first broadcast from a commercial station of color television in 1940. In 1969, when mankind made its first landing on the moon, millions of persons participated in that historic action via both radio and television. Today we regularly see photographs sent back to earth from cameras traveling more than a thousand million miles out in space.

With this veritable flood of inventions and technical achievements over the past 80 years, it is easy to see that the stage has been set for a whole series of breakthroughs that will fulfill the *predictions* and *prophecies* quoted in this chapter. The next chapter deals with *breakthrough number one.*

CHAPTER 18

History in the Making

No library in the world contains the information we will be presenting in this and the following chapter. Some of the material, in fact, has never before been reduced to printed pages.

The idea itself—building a wireless, a telephone or a radio which will make it possible to converse with the dead—has been around in *both* heaven and earth for at least 100 years. Marconi and Edison spent the closing years of their earth lives trying to develop such a system. Neither succeeded. The reasons, as we see from our present vantage point in time, are obvious. Scientific knowledge had not matured to the point where enough was known about the nature and types of energy that make up our physical and nonphysical universe. Moreover, the whole subject of solid-state physics had yet to be born. We will summarize the pertinent early history by reporting on two major breakthroughs which set the stage for yet a third.

Breakthrough Number One:
The Electronic Voice Phenomenon

Following in the footsteps of Marconi and Edison are some pioneers whose names will not be as familiar to you. In 1956, two men in California, a photographer named Atilla von Szalay and a writer named Raymond Bayless began an era of what has come to be known as EVP (Electronic Voice Phenomenon). They recorded on magnetic tape some paranormal voices—voices that should not, logically, have been there. Bayless reported their experiments in the *Journal of the American Society for Psychical Research* in the winter of 1959. The announcement made hardly a ripple. Not a single person contacted the society or the researchers to inquire about their work.

But across the Atlantic, things were about to heat up in the field of EVP research. In the summer of 1959, a Swedish film producer named Friedrich Jurgenson came up with some extra voices on his recordings as he was trying to capture bird songs on tape in the countryside. Amid the bird songs he heard a faint human voice, a male voice speaking Norwegian, saying something about "bird voices of the night." Like anybody would in that situation, Jurgenson wondered if the voices weren't just stray radio signals. But the more he listened carefully to his tapes, the more voices he detected that could not be explained as radio transmissions. The voices included some personal messages, such as "Friedrich, you are being watched." A few weeks later, he recorded what he recognized to be the voice of his mother, who had died four years earlier, saying in German, "Friedel, my little Friedel, can you hear me?"

Jurgenson continued his experiments and published a book about them in 1964. In addition to using the tape recorder with a microphone, he experimented with making recordings from the radio, then studying them to see if he could detect extra voices.

His book was read by Dr. Konstantine Raudive, a psychologist and author of books on philosophy, who lived in Germany. After visiting Jurgenson and listening to his tapes, Raudive decided to experiment himself in order to answer the question of whether or not the voices were somehow connected with Jurgenson's particular personality. For three months Raudive could detect nothing paranormal on his tapes. Then he heard a whispered, "That is correct," in the Latvian language. This was in response to his remark that spirit world inhabitants, like those on the earth, might face certain limitations.

Raudive was encouraged, and he went on to collect a huge number of voice recordings. By the time he published the first book on his work in 1968, he had recorded some 70,000 phrases. Also, he had added some new techniques. He learned that if he tuned his radio to the so-called white noise between stations, the tapes recorded at those wavelengths would contain voices. Word of Dr. Raudive's work spread, and scientists and engineers in Europe tried to duplicate his experiments. One of those was Alex Schneider, a Swiss physicist, who helped Raudive develop a new method of recording. The two discovered that voices not heard by the human ear at the time of the recording could be detected on the tape when it was played back.

Other pioneers who cooperated with Raudive included Theodore Rudolph, a high-frequency engineer who worked for Telefunken. Rudolph developed his own recording device, called a goniometer. Another colleague of Raudive was Dr. Franz Seidl, an electronics engineer in Vienna who developed a device he called a psychophon.

Engineers and scientists were not the only people to become interested in experimenting with the electronic voice phenomenon. Many lay people did also, after reading Raudive's book. So many began experimenting, in fact, that a German woman, Hanna Bushbeck, started a newsletter in 1969 to help the experimenters keep in touch and exchange ideas. Today, there are more than a thousand people in Germany alone recording, analyzing and cataloging paranormal voices. One Catholic priest in Switzerland, Father Leo Schmid, has recorded thousands of phrases.

And that is only in Europe. Not until 1971 was Raudive's book brought out in English, under the title of *Breakthrough: An Amazing Experiment in Electronic Communication with the Dead*. It was published by the British firm of Colin Smythe, which is a fascinating story in itself. Mr. Smythe was handed a copy of Raudive's book at a book fair in Germany with the suggestion that he might want to consider publishing it. He turned it over to an associate, Peter Bander, who was skeptical about the whole matter—until, that is, Smythe himself tried some experimenting with the voices and came up with the voice of Bander's mother, who was dead. The two publishers decided to have Raudive brought to England so that his tapes and his methods could be checked out by scientists and engineers under controlled conditions. Convinced that Raudive had, in fact, come up with unexplained voices on tape, they published the book, along with a recording of some of the voices. As a result, many more scientists and laymen throughout the world are now experimenting with EVP.

As with so many aspects of the serious research into the almost un-explored realms of the lower worlds of spirit, it is necessary to be constantly on guard and try to separate the wheat from the chaff. So far, I have said little about the content of the messages these researchers are receiving. Frankly, there have been serious problems with these record-ings. Up to this time, the voice heard in the majority of such words or sentences purported to be coming from other planes is so weak that only a person who has spent many months trying to attune his hearing can distinguish the words from the background noise or sound that is a necessary part of the energies involved. This fact naturally results in much of the material being subject to misinterpretation.

There is also another problem. It has been found bits and pieces of the experimenter's own thoughts can be impressed on the recording tape. To date, only a very few researchers have obtained sentences or groups of sentences which are distinct enough that ten people listening to them can agree on what it is they are hearing. Moreover, it is very rare to get a complete sentence. Alexander MacRae, a Scottish researcher, made a statistical study of many hundred EVP voices and found the average length to be only 1.8 seconds.

In spite of such discouragements, the membership of the two German electronic voice associations and the American Electronic Voice Association are diligently pursuing this line of research to perfect a communication system for conversing with persons who are very much alive but no longer have physical bodies. More than 2,000 persons in many countries are today following this line of research.

Breakthrough Number Two:
The Metascience Research

My reading over many years in the fields of psychiatry, psychology and psychic research opened up exciting vistas for research into the basic nature of the human being. In 1970, I terminated my professional career as an engineering and management consultant who had special-ized in the direction of industrial research laboratories in the United States and Europe, in which role I had made 44 trans-Atlantic trips. With the prospect of royalty income from certain inventions I had made for Swedish clients, I then embarked, at age 60, on what I hoped would be a 15-year, self-directed and self-financed research program.

The Ghost of 29 Megacycles, by John G. Fuller, gives an indepth report on my work and that of others during this period. It was published in England in 1985 and in the United States in 1986.

Since the answers I sought did not exist in any laboratory any place in the world, I drafted my personal research program, using the same techniques and principles that had made millions of dollars in profit for my professional clients. Knowing that no one, or a combination of, the major sciences could supply the answers I sought, I conceived a *meta*-science approach. In the sense that *meta* means "over, above, transcending," I drafted a research program that was "over, above, transcending **all fields of science** and including the best of the world's accumulation of religious, psychic and metaphysical lore."

Over the next decade, five trips around the world and many shorter foreign trips brought me into personal contact with a few dozen creative thinkers in the fields of medicine, psychology, parapsychology, psychic research, metaphysics, science, religion, psychiatry, etc. My close collaboration with these persons, often leaders in their specialties, resulted in the eventual formation of an International Advisory Panel of more than two dozen members in twenty countries.

In 1971, I and two electronic specialists opened a small private research laboratory in Philadelphia to work exclusively on the project that had foiled Marconi and Edison—a communication system capable of two-way conversation with the higher levels of consciousness. Through good fortune this laboratory activity had the benefit of two outstanding telepathic channels, an advertising executive in his sixties and a minister in her late fifties. Through the superb clairaudient abilities of these two persons, contact was established with Dr. William Francis Gray Swann, mentioned earlier. Dr. Swann, prior to his passing eight years earlier, had been a physics professor at several distinguished universities and had written the then-definitive book on cosmic rays.

Dr. Swann desired to help us in our research and assembled a large team of colleagues from the highest astral and the mental-causal planes. Many weekend sessions with Dr. Swann and his colleagues gave invaluable insights as to the nature of our design problems—numerous, and of great complexity!

During this period, my twice-yearly trips for research in Europe delved deeply into the electronic voice phenomenon research just reported. By 1975, my engineering analysis indicated, at least to me, that the EVP approach held very little prospect of achieving meaningful and extended two-way conversation at higher levels of consciousness.

Several decades of organizing and directing research had taught me at times it is prudent to carry on simultaneously two or more somewhat parallel lines of research. Hence, in 1975 I established a second research activity in the home of William J. O'Neil, a colleague who was a radio and television technician. I have already told you part of Bill's story—how he came to develop remarkable clairvoyant and clairaudient abilities and how he was encouraged to develop his healing skills by "Doc Nick"—in chapters 7 and 8.

Wonder of wonders, it developed that Doc Nick had been a ham radio operator. He suggested that instead of the "white noise" traditionally used by the EVP researchers, we should use certain audio frequencies. These would serve as an energy source against which the sounds produced by Doc Nick's vocal cords (in his rather dense astral body) could be projected. He said that the result would be that our ears and the tape recorder would then be able to pick up his voice. This suggestion sounded plausible to us because we had observed that *all* of the EVP voices had to "steal energy" from radio frequencies, spoken or sung words, music or artificially created "white or pink" noises or sounds.

After some experimentation, we had the great thrill on October 27, 1977 of hearing Doc Nick's first words just barely coming through the quite loud mixture of tones Bill had provided as a starting point.

Bill: Try it again.

Doc Nick: All right. Do you hear me now, Bill? Can you hear me, Bill?

Bill: Yeah, but you make it sound just like—oh boy—a robot on television [chuckling].

Doc Nick: Yes, we always will, when we...we will. The one thing... you hear, Bill. You hear, Bill?

Bill: Yeah, okay [sounding as though he is shaken up by the happenings]. You have to forgive me but—I know this is—you have to admit this is kind of scary.

Doc Nick: [Unintelligible.]

Bill: It's all garbled. I can't understand you.

Doc Nick: I said, why are you...leave it alone, leave it alone. Did you hear me, Bill? Do you hear what I say?

Bill: Yeah, I got it now, Doc. You asked what I was doing on the Vidicom, right?

Doc Nick: Yes.

Bill: Dr. Mueller wants me to get busy on this, you know.

Doc Nick: Oh yes, *that* man.

Bill: Yeah, that man [chuckling]. You have to forgive me, but it is not that easy, it is not easy. [Tones shift slightly in pitch.] That frequency changed again.

Doc Nick: Yes, I know, Bill. It is much better now. I feel [echo effect], I feel, I feel more comfortable with this frequency. Don't change it anymore. As I told you before, you must be careful of these frequencies. Mark the frequency change.

Bill: Oh, yeah—yeah, sure. I am supposed to guess what these frequencies are. I don't have any way of monitoring these frequencies.

We really can't blame William for being a bit scared when he had his first communication with someone who had been among the so-called dead for seven years. But he showed his own good sense when he remarked to Doc Nick, "Who do you think will believe anything like this?"

Our position in releasing a tape recording of this communication was precisely that of Doc Nick when he replied, "Don't worry about that. It is not important, believe me!" Those who scoff at this information, even after carefully evaluating the tape and the related printed materials,* may later find themselves in the embarrassing position of one member of the French Academy of Sciences years ago. He told his learned colleagues, "I personally have examined Mr. Edison's phonograph and I find it is nothing but the clever use of ventriloquism."

Noise-filled, broken and disjointed, and disappointingly brief as it was, *this was history making at its best.* It was the first meaningful two-way conversation of this quality of which we have any record. None of the tens of thousands of EVP phrases achieved as of this date were of such significance. And it certainly ranks in importance with what is said to have been the first communication over Alexander Graham Bell's first crude telephone, "Come here, Watson!" or Mr. Edison's squeaky tinfoil recording of "Mary Had a Little Lamb" on his first phonograph.

In some respects, this historic voice exchange between Doc Nick and William O'Neil may be even more momentous. It could be called the start of a communication system between the living and the dead— between heaven and earth, between mankind on planet Earth and higher levels of consciousness. But science demands replication, and in this case further instrumental voice contact with Doc Nick was not accomplished. And thereby starts the trail to the **third major breakthrough.**

---

* Available by writing Metascience Foundation, P.O. Box 737, Franklin, NC 28734.

CHAPTER 19

History Repeats Itself

Of course it was disturbing, even disheartening, when shortly after that historic conversation, Doc Nick seemed to go off in a disgruntled manner. What happened was, however, most interesting. You will recall that Bill mentioned he was also doing some work with a Dr. Mueller. At that point, Doc Nick remarked, in seeming disapproval, "Oh, yes, *that* man!" and Bill answered, chuckling, "Yeah, that man."

At this period in our research, in 1978, Bill was clairaudiently and clairvoyantly collaborating in his research with *both* Doc Nick and Dr. George Jeffries Mueller. These two dwellers in the interpenetrating worlds of spirit had totally different personalities and professional backgrounds. Doc Nick had been the first to collaborate with Bill, and he definitely regarded Dr. Mueller as a "Johnny-come-lately." However, sad as we were to see our friend Doc Nick break off contact, he had made an historic appearance, helped Bill to further develop his already great psychic abilities of clairaudience and clairvoyance, had introduced the idea of using certain audio frequencies and generally set the stage for what was, within three years, destined to become the third major breakthrough.

Earlier we mentioned the Apostle Paul's admonition 2,000 years ago to "test the spirits" to make sure they were who they professed to be and were not mischievous imposters or pranksters. Bill had learned this lesson well and between us we proceeded to put Dr. Mueller "on trial." The research over the next two years resulted in notebooks filled with data and reports. It must be one of the best documented cases of survival in more than 100 years of psychic research. Here are the highlights in abbreviated form:

Education: Dr. Mueller told us of his undergraduate work at the University of Wisconsin in Madison, social and glee club activities, his earning a master's degree in physics, his doctoral work at Cornell University in Ithaca, New York, and his subsequent instructorship in physics at Cornell. Parapsychologist Dr. Walter Uphoff visited the registrar's office at the University of Wisconsin and was able to verify Dr. Mueller's statements. Dr. Norman Uphoff, Walter's son, was at this time on the staff at Cornell, and was able to verify Dr. Mueller's statements regarding his work at Cornell.

Death: Dr. Mueller *voluntarily* gave the name of the small town in California where he had been living when he suffered a fatal coronary attack. We were able to obtain a copy of the death certificate, confirm the cause of his death and get additional vital statistics.

Social Security number: Dr. Mueller obliged us by providing his social security number! We were able to verify this and learned the names of two persons to whom payments were being made, 14 years after Dr. Mueller's death.

Survivors: We verified the existence and names of four suviving members of his immediate family. They were as he gave them to us.

Personal appearance: Bill described Dr. Mueller the way he saw him clairvoyantly. We then wrote to a surviving wife and asked her to describe her former husband. Then a comparison was made of the two descriptions. They agreed as to body build, height, weight and mannerisms. They disagreed in one particular. Bill described him as having wavy brown hair, whereas in fact he was bald at the time of his demise. This discrepancy is easily explained. Even if you, the reader, make the transition at the age of 90 and are old and decrepit, you will have the privilege of "manifesting" a spirit body that suits your fancy. Most persons choose their appearance at what they consider the prime of life. Dr. Mueller had wavy brown hair as a younger man.

Intimate conversations: In the period from 1978 to 1981 (prior to the two-way instrumental conversation with Dr. Mueller), Bill recorded on tape dozens of extended conversations on a great variety of subjects. Our investigations confirmed some of the intimate items Dr. Mueller shared.

Personality: Again in deference to Dr. Mueller's privacy, we will refrain from anything presenting a personality profile, but from his dozens of hours of one-to-one contact with Bill, we got a very clear picture of his personality and mannerisms. We found our observations were confirmed by a few contacts we made with persons who knew him. Basically we can say he was a warm-hearted man with a wonderful sense of humor. Due to his great intellect and scientific expertise, he naturally had a communication gap with Bill, a high school dropout. Dr. Mueller could never "bend" to the point of addressing William as "Bill."

Professional Resume: Dr. Mueller dictated to Bill two pages of details, which he said were contained in the last printed copy of his professional resume. Apparently the details were quite accurate, because one family member was of the opinion that we "must have done some research and uncovered this material in the files of one of Dr. Mueller's consulting clients." While we certainly had *not* had any access to files of Dr. Mueller or his clients, it was evidential to have such a statement from a family member.

His book: Dr. Mueller referred to a "small booklet" he wrote in 1949 for the U.S. Army. Several times he requested that Bill "locate a copy and read pages 66 and 67." After searching for two years involving contacts with several departments in the Pentagon, the Library of Congress and the Army library at West Point, a copy was located in the

Army section of the archives of the State Historical Society of Wisconsin, Dr. Mueller's home state. Comments regarding these two pages and their amazing relevancy are presented in Appendix A.

Scientific knowledge: On several occasions, Dr. Mueller dictated a scientific discourse—at least as scientific as possible with Bill's limited knowledge of scientific terms. One of these, dealing with the origin of music in the earliest civilizations, is a most enlightening document.

A useful invention: Dr. Mueller, prior to the death of his physical body, had a deep interest in arthritis. He gave Bill the wiring diagram for a device to treat arthritis. He called it the Integrated Frequency Response Therapy Unit. We built samples and had them tested in several locations. We have received dozens of affidavits signed, voluntarily, by patients who benefited. My wife Jeannette and I, as well as some of our friends, are among the many persons who have benefited from the use of this device.

Our main interest in contacting Dr. Mueller, of course, was not just to gather evidence, as impressive as it may be. We wanted his help in our research work. And one of the most dramatic examples of Mueller's help was the way he applied the knowledge he had acquired from a life-long hobby—the study of the theory of music. From this background, he provided a suggestion that helped make his voice audible in Bill's laboratory. He instructed Bill to create a recording on a cassette tape of 13 specific tones that spanned the adult male voice—from 121 to 701 cycles per second—for use as a source of audio energy in the instrumentation Bill was devising. Wonder of wonders—the third breakthrough! It occurred on September 23, 1980. Here it is:

Mueller: William, I think that's much better, right there, William. Now, William, did you understand? Williiaamm?

Bill: Yes sir, I understand, Doctor.

Mueller: Very well. I will give you a count from one to ten. One. Two. Three, four, five, six, seven, eight, nine, ten. One moment, William.

Bill: Okay.

Mueller: Very well, then. [Reciting] Mary had a little lamb, its fleece was white as snow. And everywhere that Mary went, the lamb would go-ooo-goooo [deliberately holding last syllable]. Play that back for me, William. William?

Bill: Yes sir.

Mueller: Play that back for me.

Bill: All right, Doctor. I am sorry, I was lighting a cigarette.

Mueller: Oh, those cigarettes again! [Bill played the tape back, then they resumed their conversation.] Did you change it, William?

Bill: Yes I did, Doctor.

Mueller: Very well. I am back about three feet now, I am back

155

about three feet. I will give you another test. One, two, three, four, five, six, seven, eight, nine, ten. I'd change that frequency again, William.

Bill: Very well, Doctor.

Mueller: One, one, one, one, two, three, four, five. This is somewhat better, William. Play that back, if you will.

Well, Mary's "Little Lamb" certainly is adding to its claim to immortality! But since one of the first rules of science is that of replication, nothing could be more gratifying than to have Dr. Mueller's conversation confirm that we had at last established meaningful instrumental communication with a person who had shed his physical body.

Now, thanks to Dr. Mueller's contributions to the new communications system, we want to share a remarkable conversation with another communicator. What makes it remarkable is that he says he died 151 years ago! Fred Ingstrom, which is how he identifies himself, says he lived in a rural area of Virginia and died in 1830. Our check of the scanty birth records of that time and place have not yet confirmed his existence then.

Fred's voice, while still robot-like, was vastly better than the quality of Doc Nick's voice at the time of our first breakthrough.

Bill: Could you give me a count of ten?

Fred: One, two, three, four, five, six, seven, eight, nine, ten.

Bill: Yes?

Fred: Did you, did you understand me, Bill?

Bill: Yeah, I understood you. Let me make a little change here, okay?

Fred: Okay. [Next part is inaudible.] Oh boy!

Bill: What's the matter?

Fred: Oh boy. Do you mind if I laugh?

Bill: No, go ahead and laugh.

Fred: Ha, ha, ha.

Bill: Okay—ha, ha [chuckling]. Let's see. I'll make a change here. Now say something. Give me a count of five.

Fred: One, two, three, four, five.

Bill: You sound more like a robot.

Fred: I do? Well, maybe I am a robot.*

Bill: I doubt that very much. I am going to change it back again. Now give me a count of five.

---

* The perceptive reader may wonder how a person who died 150 years ago could understand expressions such as "robot" and "oh boy." While Bill could not see Fred *clairvoyantly or hear him clairaudiently,* Fred had been visiting Bill's laboratory for many weeks and had been listening to all of the conversations with Dr. Mueller. From these and similar experiences, Fred was quite at home with modern slang and terminology.

Fred: One, two, three, four, five.

Bill: Again! Wait a minute!

Fred: One, two, three, four, five. Did you get this? Did you hear me? Did you hear me, Bill?

Bill: Yeah, I heard you. Wait a minute. [Changes pitch of tones.] Now, give me another count of five.

Fred: One, two, three, four, five. Do you mind if I laugh? I am having fun. Ha, ha. Let's get this thing...

Bill: [Chuckling] Oh boy. Okay. [Changes pitch again.] Wait a minute now. [To his wife] Yeah, hon? Okay, sweetheart.

Fred: What did you say, Bill?

Bill: I was talking to my wife.

Fred: Oh, that's right. You are married. Oh boy. Ha, ha, ha.

Bill: Okay. Oh boy, I am glad you have a sense of humor. If you can hear me, you will be able to hear that, because I'll make a tape of it, okay?

Fred: Okay. Oh boy, that will be fine, oh boy. That's right, you mentioned that, you said you were married. How long have you been married, Bill?

Bill: About eight years.

Fred: Oh well, if I ever get out....How old are you, Bill?

Bill: I am 63.

Fred: Oh boy, I had you, thought maybe you are in your 20's, something like that, in your 20's.

Bill: Well, mentally I feel like I am in my 20's, but when I, when I shave, my mirror says: "Who are you fooling, old man?"

Fred: Yes, I know what you mean. Well, I better get going. Oh boy, I have to go right now. Sorry about that. See you later, okay?

Bill: Yeah, that's okay, Fred. Good night.

Fred: Good night.

The great value of the technical assistance given by Dr. Mueller is dramatically shown by this next excerpt, taken from a conversation in April 1981. Near the start, he gives his reactions to one of the audio frequencies and then proceeds to pinpoint an electronic circuit problem on the video apparatus on which he and William were working.

Spiricom is the name we gave to the electronic device we used to talk to these spirits. Vidicom is the name we coined for the video device which will do the same thing, but with pictures as well as sound.

Bill: Just a minute, Doctor. Yes, I know you are here, but I got to—I am gonna cut down the volume of these other frequencies.

Mueller: Very well, William.

Bill: I want to cut them down to a level that won't, ah...

Mueller: I am not sure, William, but—I don't feel too comfortable with that one frequency.

Bill: Well, we will see. Maybe we can change it later on, Doctor.

Mueller: Very well. Oh yes, William?

Bill: Yes?

Mueller: Ah, I think we have a problem with the Spiricom we are working on.

Bill: Spiricom? Oh, you mean Vidicom.

Mueller: Oh yes, William. I am sorry, Vidicom. I think the problem is...I know that your wife's relatives...television receiver. However, William, I think the big problem is an impedance mismatch into that third transistor.

Bill: Third transistor?

Mueller: Yes, the transistor that follows the input.

Bill: I don't understand.

Mueller: The pre-amp, the pre-amp!

Bill: Oh, the pre-amp?

Mueller: Yes, I think that I can easily correct that by introducing a, by introducing a 150 or 100—I am not sure, William—a 150 ohm one-half watt resistor in parallel with a .0047 microfarad ceramic capacitor. I think we can overcome that impedance mismatch.

Bill: Oh boy, I'll have to get the schematic back.

Mueller: You'd rather have the schematic?

Bill: I'd rather mark it on the schematic, Doctor.

Mueller: Very well.

Bill: The schematic is over there in the file.

Mueller: Very well.

I hope you noticed how very specific Dr. Mueller was in pinpointing the problem on the experimental video device on which he and William were working. He said the problem lay near the third transistor in the pre-amp unit. The problem was an impedance mismatch, and could be corrected by using a 150 ohm half-watt resistor in parallel with a .0047 microfarad ceramic capacitor. What better *proof* could science want that Dr. Mueller's mind, memory banks and personality are still alive and functioning in a useful and most dramatic way!

And now we share an excerpt in which they further discuss our Vidicom research project. Incidentally, the problems of developing a workable Vidicom system seem even more monumental than those of perfecting Spiricom.

Bill: What's that again?

Mueller: The television set with the metal screen—I didn't put that in the magnetic input from the signal generator in conjunction with the input...from the camera to the television system. You understand, William?

Bill: Yes, I think that's it.

Mueller: Oh, by the way, William. Did you get that multi-faceted crystal?

Bill: No, I didn't, Doctor. I got that five-faceted from Edmund's.

Mueller: Edmunds? Edmunds? Who is Edmunds?

Bill: Edmund's is a company—Edmund's Scientific.

Mueller: Oh, I understand. What were the results?

Bill: Well, I inserted it into the lens of the camera, but all I got was a lot of crazy colors of light. But I didn't get any imagery.

Mueller: Oh, I see. Well, very good. Well, I think if we follow this other procedure, William, and I am not absolutely sure but I have a feeling, that this will help clarify the image, so we can discern features on the subject. We have the form, we have the face, we have the...we know...the human form. However, we must be able to discern the facial features, so we can identify the subject. I don't know yet [talking to another entity. Just a minute, William. [To the other entity] What's that?

Bill: What's that, Doctor?

Mueller: No, no, William, I am not....Someone is talking to you. William, do you know Nathaniel? There is a fellow here, William. He says his name is Nathaniel. He says he knows you and you know him.

Bill: Nathaniel? I don't know anybody by the name of Nathaniel.

Mueller: He says he knows you.

Bill: I don't recall knowing anybody [named Nathaniel].

You perhaps noted that Dr. Mueller turned aside from the microphone to talk with another spirit person standing in the lab. William was unable to *see* him visually or clairvoyantly, or to *hear* him clairaudiently. The spirit, who told Dr. Mueller his name was Nathaniel, *seemingly could not talk through* Spiricom. In the following days, with Dr. Mueller serving as intermediary, William and Nathaniel discussed boyhood activities, including pranks in which they had participated more than half a century ago.

The contacts with Dr. Mueller were sporadic. Days and even weeks would pass with no contact—even when William left the electronic equipment on. Then Dr. Mueller would pay an unexpected visit like this one:

Mueller: Wiillliiaam...William...William...Wiiilliiiaaammm, William...Wiilliiaammm. Are you there, William?

Bill: I'm coming, Doctor, I'm coming. [Out of breath] Oh boy. I am sorry, Doctor, I am sorry. I just went downstairs for a cup of coffee. I am sorry, Doctor.

Mueller: That's all right, William.

Then, equally frustrating, there would be a totally unexplained *termination* of contact in the midst of a very useful conversation. Here is an example:

> **Mueller:** What's that, William? Did you understand what I mean?
> **Bill:** Oh, I understand, but a lot of things I don't understand. Do you have any suggestions, Doctor? [Pause.] Do you have any suggestions? Dr. Mueller? Dr. Mueller? Oh boy. Dr. Mueller? Are you there, sir? Oh my God. Dr. Mueller? Oh boy.

In the early months of our conversations with Dr. Mueller, electromagnetic factors, the phase of the moon, sunspots or other unknown factors resulted in poor quality of Dr. Mueller's voice. Still, we recorded a lot of material. In this segment, Dr. Mueller responds to William's mention of possible surgery. These comments and his observations of his own death 14 years previously, are worth careful consideration.

> **Mueller:** I am very happy, William, that surgery was not necessary. There are times when surgery becomes necessary. Don't worry about it, William. Don't worry. Worry does not help the situation. Should surgery become necessary in the future, since it's not a malignancy—it's benign—there's nothing to worry about, William. Did you understand? Hopefully you will not have to have that surgery, William, but should you have to have that surgery, please, William, please—worry will not help. Do you understand, William?
> **Bill:** Yeah, I understand. But do you understand, Doctor? I know I am not getting any younger.
> **Mueller:** I know. I understand, William. Well. In my case, well, I was fortunate. It was sudden. However, you know in advance. The important thing, the one benefit that you will find as the result of our contacts, *you are aware!* I was not aware of this side. I didn't know the potential over here before. So when I got over here it was like waking up in the morning and not knowing where you are at. Like having a bad dream...

There are many discussions on more joyful subjects than surgery and death experiences! Often Dr. Mueller displayed his delightful humor. In this excerpt, he speaks of his fondness for carrots and cabbage.

> **Bill:** Yeah, I just turned on the tape recorder, Doc.
> **Mueller:** Very well, William.
> **Bill:** You said to hurry back, and I did. That has been exactly one week ago.
> **Mueller:** Ho-ho.

160

Bill: Yes. Ho-ho yourself. Cold weather has left us, temporarily anyway. It's raining, it's nice and warm. Of course, you never know what to expect. I am going to try to put in a little garden this year.

Mueller: Oh, wonderful. Send me a couple of carrots.

Bill: What's that again?

Mueller: I said you can send me a couple of carrots.

Bill: A couple of what?

Mueller: A couple of carrots.

Bill: Oh, carrots!

Mueller: Yes, William. And a nice head of lettuce.

Bill: A nice head of lettuce! I'm not going to plant acres, Doctor. What's that? I think you were talking at the same time I was.

Mueller: Well, perhaps I said if somebody had some cabbage, I like fried cabbage. Oh, I love fried cabbage!

Bill: Fried cabbage! Well, I love sauerkraut.

Mueller: Well, you know what sauerkraut can do?

Bill: Yes, I do. You know, Doctor, I never thought I'd see the day when I could talk to someone like you in the way we are doing. If ten years ago someone had told me this was possible, I would have recommended that they be sent to the "funny farm."

Mueller: Well, perhaps you are right.

Like Bill—and his fellow researchers—you readers may have difficulty believing these really are conversations with a scientist whose funeral took place 14 years ago. After all, it does take a bit of getting used to!

Fig. 41. William J. O'Neil

161

I should explain that these transcripts were prepared from recordings made simultaneously on two cassette recorders, and often on the audio portion of one video camera tape. Fig. 41 was made by taking a still photograph of the television screen during the replay of a video tape in which Bill was conversing with Dr. Mueller in August 1981. (Bill's lab was only dimly lit.) Bill is standing in front of the Spiricom equipment where he must remain alert to "fine tune" the signal and tone generator to maintain the best quality of Dr. Mueller's voice.

Fig. 42. Dr. George Jeffries Mueller

The following exchange is one of several in which Dr. Mueller states that serial time as we know it does not exist in his world.

Mueller: What did you say, William?

Bill: I said I am sorry, Doctor, but—oh boy—it's almost 4 o'clock in the morning. The last time we talked it was what? About a quarter after two, I forget what time it was.

Mueller: Oh, there we go with that—time again. William, you know better than that.

Bill: What's that, sir?

Mueller: You know better than that. I am not aware of time over here.

Bill: Well, I know. That's what you said, sir.

Mueller: I am not joking, William. I am not joking. Now listen, William, please listen very carefully.

Bill: Yes?

Mueller: Adjust that frequency, William!

Bill: All right, sir. Oh boy!

We were constantly amazed that Dr. Mueller could "see" everything in the lab. Often Bill would lay out letters or magazine articles, which Dr. Mueller would proceed to "read" and then discuss. Here he asks about a new instrument that had just been placed in the lab.

Mueller: Very well, William. What is that in there? What is that instrument there?

Bill: Which one is that, sir?

Mueller: The little one there.

Bill: Oh, the blue one, yes? The blue one, sir?

Mueller: Yes William.

Bill: That's a bio-feedback, sir. A bio-feedback unit.

Mueller: Oh really! Do you have any nerve problems, William?

Bill: [chuckling] No sir. You know what that's for, sir.

Mueller: Well, I am just joshing, William. I am just joshing. Let's get on with it.

During our years of working with persons in the worlds of spirit, we have learned that most great inventions are conceived in the mental and causal levels of consciousness and are then implanted in the mind of a person called an inventor. We refer to this process as intuition. Some time in the decades ahead, ideas will be transmitted directly by instrument from a scientist in the higher planes. Dr. Mueller gave us a taste of what that will be like in this excerpt from August 1981.

Mueller: Not very well but...now, William.

Bill: I think I've got it, Doctor.

Mueller: Very well. Try it just to make—just a little bit, William. You understand me, William? William?

Bill: Yes sir.

Mueller: Try adjusting that frequency. I'll give a count of five, William. One, two, three, four, five, fivvve. I think that's the best frequency, William. Now, the next project, William. William?

Bill: Yes sir, I am listening.

Mueller: Very well. The next project, William, is the elimination, as you call it, the zombie like sound of my voice. You know we have more...at this moment. Is that about right, William? [Raising his voice, as Bill was dozing off.]

Bill: Yes, that's right, Doctor. [Chuckling] I am sorry, sir. Please forgive me.

Mueller: That's all right, William, that's all right.

Bill: All right, sir.

Mueller: You know, in order to figure that, we are going to have to have a more stable frequency. By more stable, I mean we have to do away with the AC frequencies in the background. We are going to have to find a way to eliminate it—to eliminate the fractional frequencies. You understand me, William?

Bill: I understand you, Doctor.

Now for an evidential item that will gladden the hearts of even the most strict parapsychologists. On one occasion, Dr. Mueller suggested we refer to a small book he wrote in 1947 entitled, *Introduction to Electronics.*

Mueller: Did you obtain that book of mine yet?

Bill: Oh, that book of yours. No sir. By the way, our friend Mr. Meek is really going all out to find that, because I want to read those two pages you mentioned.

Mueller: Very well. And I want you to read that, William. There must be copies available somewhere.

Bill: Well, I think George—that's Mr. Meek, our friend...

Mueller: Your friend!

Bill: Yes, even if he has to go to the Library of Congress. He'll probably do that.

Mueller: Oh, I see. Oh, all right.

Even the Library of Congress did not have a copy. However, we located the book in the archives of the State Historical Society of Wisconsin, Dr. Mueller's native state. The two pages he specifically asked me to locate, and ponder the implications of the statements thereon, are reproduced in Appendix A.

We conclude this series of excerpts from the Spiricom recordings with a most prophetic exchange:

Mueller: William?
Bill: Yes sir.
Mueller: Did you make that telephone call yet?*
Bill: No sir.
Mueller: May I suggest you do, William. Now, you must understand one thing, William.
Bill: Yes sir?
Mueller: I cannot be here forever. I cannot guarantee how long I'll be visiting here. However, I will do my best. Do you understand, William?
Bill: Yes sir.
Mueller: There is a time and a place for everything. So as I have mentioned before, this is something I think you should be aware of.

Dr. Mueller's statement that he would not "be here forever" was most prophetic. As the months passed, I was able to observe that he was beginning to shed his dense earthly vibrations and was starting his progression upward, as depicted in Fig. 32, "Interpenetrating Levels of Life and Consciousness." Within one month of his having made the statement about not being able to stay forever, he had increased his consciousness to the point where our electronic system called Mark IV could no longer be used for contact. In anticipation of that event, we had already started to design equipment that may someday enable us to resume contact with him.

Any reader who wishes to know more about the eleven years of research which preceded these conversations between the "living and the dead" will find the detailed story in *The Ghost of 29 Megacycles*, by John G. Fuller. Fuller was given access to more than 300 documents—correspondence, research reports, agreements, library references, death certificates, social security dates, news releases, audio and video tapes, etc. He supplemented study of these with travel in the United States, England and Germany to interview my associates and other researchers who were independently engaged in electronic voice research. In his resulting book, he used his investigating and reporting skills to create a balanced analysis.

---

* Occasionally Dr. Mueller would give Bill the unlisted telephone number of a professional colleague. I checked two of these and found them to be valid.

Let Us Pause for a Moment

Ponder the significance of the preceding pages.

Their message is loud and clear. As a result of these breakthroughs, the prophecies and predictions of the past 80 years, sampled in Chapter 17, *have been fulfilled.*

The veil between heaven and earth has been rent

And from the standpoint of 20th century materialistic mankind, nothing in the past 2,000 years has done this so effectively. Man in the flesh on planet Earth has devised electronic instruments that enable him actually to talk with persons who were at one time *buried in the ground or cremated.* Man has discovered that these people are still very much alive. Their minds, memory banks, personalities and souls are still intact and in good working order. They think and speak just as they did *before* cremation or burial.

What are the implications of this rending of the veil? Changes so momentous that within only one, two or three generations, the developments that will naturally follow this humble start could *beneficially modify the course of civilization and human evolution.* The profound questions generated will undoubtedly be the subject of many books that will be written worldwide in the next decade.

We can anticipate some of the more obvious questions.

CHAPTER 20

Questions—Questions—Questions

At this point, it is certain that various questions have flooded the mind of the reader. And the more perceptive the reader, the longer and more profound will be the list of questions! Let us consider the most obvious ones.

1. Are the Mueller-O'Neil tape recordings a hoax?

An emphatic *no!*

The obvious and completely factual answer is that neither O'Neil nor I had either the funds or the talent to dream up the script and then stage more than twenty hours of recorded exchanges on a vast variety of subjects.

But this is an important question and it deserves a satisfying answer. It took mankind twenty years and tens of billions of dollars to launch himself into outer space. Having achieved solid "two-way" communication with the "dead" after long, hard, frustrating, discouraging, costly and lonely years, we realized we had merely taken the first small step toward launching man into "innerspace."

Our miniscule effort is comparable to the role played by Robert H. Goddard who, 70 years ago, spent his time trying to develop rockets beyond the size and usefulness of the "sky rocket" created centuries ago by the Chinese for firework display purposes. Goddard dreamed of using the rocket as a means of launching men and women into outer space, so they could some day visit other parts of the solar system.

The American press promptly labeled him "Moony Goddard." But when at last he sent one of his rockets to the stupendous height of one mile above the prairie, he began to get financial backing. He began to write learned texts that laid the foundation on which to launch man to the moon, park satellites in orbit and create our space shuttle system. More than any other person, he propelled mankind into outer space.

In 1981, eleven years into our research, it became obvious that skills and financial resources far beyond those at our command would be needed to achieve our dream of launching mankind into *innerspace*— that is, of permitting earthbound persons in physical bodies to have dependable, daily, static-free two-way instrumental communication with enlightened souls on higher planes of consciousness. Thus, it was obvious that the time had come to acquaint the world with the fact that a modest beginning had been made—time to publicize our modest beginning and stimulate inquisitive and pioneering minds all over the globe to *take upon their shoulders* the challenging goal of creating a

167

heaven-to-earth communications system. Like Moony Goddard, we were prepared for the ridicule that would come from the public press.

The first step was to reserve the ballroom of the National Press Club in Washington, D.C. for a press conference to be held on Good Friday, April 6, 1982. The next step was to take a two-week trip around the world to personally give information regarding the Mueller-O'Neil communications to my colleagues in Tokyo, Manila, Bombay, Rome, Frankfurt, Zurich, London, Paris and other cities and put into their hands material which they could distribute to the radio, television and press in their own countries during the week following the American press conference. I later made two more trips through seven countries in Europe and three trips across the United States to meet and talk with individuals whose interests in our research had been stimulated.

At the close of the Washington press conference, there was a question and answer period. One reporter asked, "Meek, do you really expect us to believe this story?" My answer was: "Of course not! You do not possess enough knowledge in this special area either to believe or to disbelieve. But I predict that in the months ahead, one or more of the world's great electronic laboratories will take a copy of the voice recordings on the cassette, a copy which I freely distribute to all of you today, and do some exhaustive research. Only if they publish their findings will you have any sound basis for deciding whether or not this is a hoax."

A few months later, a letter and a check came from one of the world's great complexes of communication laboratories ordering a copy of the cassette and the 100-page manual, *Spiricom—An Electromagnetic-Etheric Systems Approach to Communications with Other Levels of Human Consciousness.* Five more months passed. Finally, an employee of said company telephoned. Obviously their laboratory had done its homework, using some of the world's most sophisticated voice analyzing and synthesizing research facilities. The twenty-minute conversation concluded with this question: *"What can we do to help you? We have thousands of engineers and scientists, some of whom have spent 30 or more years in their specialties. The expertise of these men is as available to you as is the telephone at your elbow, at no charge."* *

So here at last, five years later, is the answer in print to the press reporter's question—*and*, no doubt, yours. By this offer to help, the scientists and engineers in the laboratories of the Bell Telephone system clearly indicated that they had detected *no evidence of hoax.*

---

* For reasons of their own, they did not publicize their results and conclusions. I tested the sincerity of their offer to help by asking for some literature and references on a specific type of ultraviolet light sensor. They willingly complied, supplying the desired information. I did not follow the connection further. Twelve years earlier, at the start of our research, I had resolved to stay free of all entanglements with commercial operations. I want to be free to share results, if any, with all peoples on planet Earth.

2. Is the instrumental communication readily repeatable by other persons?

Not yet.

This work involves one or more energies *outside* the four basic forces known to present-day science—electromagnetic, gravity, strong nuclear and weak nuclear. At least one unknown energy was generated by the highly psychic Bill O'Neil. We have no way, as of now, to measure or otherwise identify it. This is why, in our technical manual, we referred to Spiricom as "an electromagnetic-etheric" system.* In the most outstanding case where there was a partial replication of our work, it was quickly apparent that the operator and designer of the equipment, Hans Otto Konig of West Germany, contributed his psychic energy. Konig is a psychic who is clairvoyant and clairaudient, and works with a spirit guide. In some way, Konig's body contributed psychic energy to the system. It is important to add, however, that neither O'Neil or Konig acts as a medium. The communication does not in any way come via their minds. They are objectively wide awake and in complete control of all activities with their conscious minds. The voice of the communicator is *formed* in the room where they are working.

But if a person does possess this special energy, then the answer is yes, the activity is repeatable. In 1985 and 1986, Konig visited many cities in West Germany and demonstrated his equipment. In a radio and television station in Luxembourg, he assembled his equipment in front of its engineers and the studio audience and then proceeded to establish contact with recently deceased relatives of one or more persons in the audience. In one program that went out all over northern Europe, his contact was so solid and so dramatic that he and the station received more than 2,000 letters of inquiry and encouragement in the next 72 hours.

3. Is there any such equipment currently available for purchase or can do-it-yourself components be obtained?

No. Neither now nor in the foreseeable future.

A simple assembly of tape recorders and other components can be used, as is being done by more than 1,000 men and women in the United States and in Europe who are working with EVP, Electronic Voice Phenomenon, as previously mentioned. But this approach is primitive, resulting only in simple phrases and an occasional complete sentence. The words are so faint in most cases that it takes months of attuning one's hearing. No sustained two-way conversation is possible now.

Inherent limitations, now obvious after 20 years of research, will prevent the development of a practical system along these lines.

---

* See Appendix D for more information regarding the nature of these energies.

4. Well, then, what about duplicating your Spiricom equipment with which you talked to Dr. Mueller, Nathaniel, Doc Nick and others?

We are faced with the realization of three factors. First, the "Mickey Mouse" type equipment we assembled for Spiricom was, relatively speaking, even more crude than the crystal radio set I built more than 60 years ago with a coil of wire wound on a Mother Oats box I had obtained from our kitchen. A tremendous leap in technology, contributed by many inventors in the next ten years, was needed to make radio practical.

Second, the Spiricom system had no possibility of reaching beyond the tuning range of the lower astral planes, some portions of which include what, over the centuries, have been called Hell, Hades and Purgatory. (See Fig. 33.) Contact with the astral levels holds *real dangers for the experimenter*, from the standpoint of possession by some low-level spirit in the great cloud of such dwellers who, vibrationally, are stuck in close proximity to the earth plane. (One experimenter in Vienna was so taken over by such a spirit that he committed suicide.) Bill O'Neil himself has had occasional contact with such low-level occupants, with and without Spiricom. One tape-recorded communication included more foul language than we have encountered on the earth plane!

Third, it became apparent that to extend the "tuning range" for "long distance" (in radio parlance, DX), more inventions would be required. As of 1986, we know that these will involve certain wavelengths of light instead of radio waves, the use of laser and holographic imaging techniques, persons of a high level of spiritual evolvement and other considerations, *and the willing cooperation of persons dwelling on the mental-causal planes of consciousness.*

Our Spiricom-type instrumentation has served its purpose. Like the experiment of portrait painter Samuel F.B. Morse, showing he could send an electromagnetic signal over a piece of wire seventeen feet long; like the speech teacher Alexander Graham Bell, whose first telephone message came over a wire from a nearby office; and like the first radio transmission of Guglielmo Marconi from one part of his laboratory to another; *Spiricom has shown that instrumental voice contact with the "dead" has been achieved.* Just as the work of Morse, Bell and Marconi, within only a few years, was picked up and extended by hundreds of other inventors, history is certain to repeat itself in the case of instrumental communication with the higher planes of consciousness. And since the inventive search stimulated worldwide by Metascience has now been undertaken in at least ten countries, there is now no way that such work can be "bottled up," even if an individual or a vested interest were so short-sighted and foolish enough to make the attempt.

5. How soon can we anticipate the perfection of a really practical communication system with the higher levels of consciousness?

When the first edition of this book was published six years ago, Chapter 19, "Electronic Communication with the World of Spirit," concluded with these words: "Our lifetimes have witnessed the development of such communication devices as the radio, telephone and television. We have also seen the transmission of information to and from objects millions of miles in space and on other planets—all of this during that instant of history in which we have been privileged to live.

"The first such interplane instruments are bound to be crude—to be filled with static—and frustrating to operate. Such is the nature of research and development. But when the reality of such communication is proven, the world and its inhabitants will never again be the same. When that day comes, it will no longer be necessary to write chapters like these which *suggest* that survival is true. On that day, it will forever become a *reality*."

And now we can report that the very special day in history came *just 24 months later*—when we held the press conference on April 6, 1982. We announced the recording of more than twenty hours of conversation between the "living" and the "dead."

This new edition is being written in 1987. It is written from the perspective of 16 years of continuing research to create a practical and dependable system. It is made from the perspective of more than half a century of experience in creating products and processes which are daily of considerable use to this civilization. It is made from the perspective of many qualified collaborators on the higher levels of consciousness who are desirous of reaching this objective through us and other researchers.

From this threefold perspective, we answer with this unequivocal statement: a workable, dependable, repeatable two-way communication with the mental-causal levels of consciousness *should be demonstrated in Europe, the United States or South America well before the end of the century.*

There are obviously many additional questions that will occur to the perceptive reader. We will choose just one and strive to answer it in our final chapter: "What immediate implications do these three historic breakthroughs have for me and my loved ones **now**?"

CHAPTER 21

Unlimited Horizons

The implications of the material presented in the preceding 20 chapters are enormous, profound and sweeping. Consider first the implications for mankind as a whole:

1. For the first time in mankind's history, it has been proven incontestably that death is merely a new birth into a continuing life.

2. It is now certain that *individual* consciousness—often referred to as personality—continues to exist and to function in a disease-free and pain-free environment.

3. The needless and destructive fear of death can be removed, as well as the deep concern over the passing of a loved one.

4. The taboo our culture has imposed on the whole subject of death can be removed.

5. The knowledge that the mind and soul transcend death of the physical body will help man begin to understand that it is his own thoughts and emotions that largely determine whether *he will experience sickness or enjoy vibrant physical and mental health* in this life.

6. Each individual can begin to realize that he or she is a *permanent inhabitant* of an apparently limitless cosmos, and not just a soulless maze-running rat or corn-pecking pigeon, as proclaimed by present-day behaviorist psychologists.

7. In the decades or centuries ahead, when instrumental systems evolve to the point where they can be used to communicate with the mental and causal planes, mortal man will have access to the *accumulated wisdom of the ages on any subject.*

8. This book has developed solid confirmation to date in support of the *key spiritual teachings* assembled in what Christians call "the Sermon on the Mount" and in the *basic moral teachings* of Judaism, Hinduism and Buddhism.

9. We can begin to jettison some of the accumulated *nonproductive* religious dogma that has ruined countless lives over the centuries to the extent that it imposed burdens of fear and guilt.

10. Finally, the material in these twenty chapters suggests the possibility of constructing a bridge by which science and spirituality can meet on common ground, with the resulting changes in science and organized religion benefiting both you and me personally.

Yes, the implications are indeed staggering. They necessitate, for example, tremendous changes in our present theories and practices for treating both physical and mental illnesses. They do the same for our existing political and social structures, and for *all* religious creeds, not to mention the whole economic industry built around funerals and life insurance.

There will never be a better world until there are better people in it. Since society is composed solely of individuals, major changes in individuals will be reflected in *civilization as a whole*. Therefore, the important thing at this point is to consider a better *means* for achieving major changes *individually*.

Since I have already shown that scientific research into life after death has confirmed the core truths of the great spiritual traditions, it behooves us to pay attention to what those traditions have to say about "better." In my judgment, two points stand out.

First, all of them have some form of the Golden Rule. What Christians learn as "Do unto others as you would have them do unto you," members of other faiths also learn, although the language differs slightly. Whether it be Judaism, Buddhism, Taoism, Confucianism, Jainism, Zoroastrianism, Islam, Hinduism or Sikhism, the same idea about *how to relate to others* is at the heart of each ethical system or program for self-improvement. In all cases, it is the basis for a happy life.

If the first point offers a simple rule to govern our relations with other people, the second point does the same for our relations with our Creator—our God. Since God is *all*—omnipresent, never apart from us—we do not have to die in order to know the reality of His many mansions in which we live *simultaneously* during life on the earth plane.

I've shown throughout this book that your astral body—your butterfly body, if you please—can and does travel while your physical body is asleep. Some persons, in a meditative state, learn to visit the various planes or levels of the diagram I have called "The Interpenetrating Levels of Life and Consciousness" (Fig. 32). You don't have to wait until death of your physical body. Ordinary psychics regularly go to the *lower* levels. Extraordinary psychics such as those I have been working with go into the *higher* levels. The truly enlightened, however, have become familiar with *all* levels, from the lowest to the highest, and have realized that those levels are present within us *here and now*.

This enlightened condition is rare, of course, and has been limited to a mere handful of sages, seers, mystics, prophets and holy men— people who reached levels of cosmic consciousness while still in the flesh. What they tell us is that their condition is possible for us, too— you and me—if we were genuinely set in our hearts and minds on having God, not ego, as our center of self.

Moreover, they have often condensed their experience into systems designed to help people in their quest for God. These spiritual systems provide efficiency and security for the unwary beginner. Their essence is not a moralizing lecture on good behavior, but rather a *method* by which one can experience personally a deepening of wisdom, a growth in character and a realization of higher values in life. *All* of these systems have some form of prayer and meditation as a major part of the discipline involved.

Why meditation and prayer rather than psychic development? Why the emphasis on spiritual growth rather than, say, becoming a deep trance medium?

With all due respect and love to my good friends, the mediums and psychics in many countries who have assisted in my research over the years, I must say there are inherent limitations and shortcomings in psychic development. It is no substitute for spiritual growth. Those who follow and teach the spiritual traditions have recognized this for the past three thousand years.* They are quite familiar with the pitfalls. Therefore, they have placed injunctions on students not to pursue psychic abilities because they are obstacles to a full flowering of a consciousness rooted in God. Psychic talents are often spectacular and alluring, but they are by no means always satisfying. One of my dearest friends, for instance, has been a superb psychic for more than fifty years, but now in old age greatly regrets having failed to seek what the Apostle Paul two thousand years ago referred to as "fruits of the spirit." Without concentration on an ethical foundation, and without wisdom to apply such talents properly, great harm can come to the psychic and to others. When one fails to open himself *first* to God, the seeking of psychic abilities all too frequently leads into self-aggrandizing power trips.

Prayer and meditation, however, have the effect of dissolving the ego—the petty little personal self that wants to remain in control and "get the glory." And as ego goes, the light and love of God shine forth more and more clearly, so that the personal becomes transpersonal. There is an outreaching, a selflessness, an all-embracing attunement with the human race and all creation. The "other side" becomes more and more integrated into your awareness in *everyday waking life*, not occasional transcendental states. The various "levels" then become perfectly obvious aspects of the single reality which is none other than *here and now*. You can learn to tap daily the wisdom of the astral and higher planes without waiting until you shed your present physical body.

It is no accident that society's models of the fully-developed human being, the worthy examples, have included many saints and holy people. They have been revered for many reasons: their compassion, devotion, inspiring words of wisdom, service to the world, *lack of fear about death*, tranquility and peace of mind and heart in the face of circumstances that for most others would be extremely stressful, if not overwhelming.

---

* Buddhism is 2,500 years old; yoga is more than 3,000 years old.

What has been their secret? Each of them, in his own way, arising from his particular tradition, has discovered the truth of the sayings, "Let go and let God" and "Thy will be done." *A sense of the infinite* replaces the usual narrow self-centeredness. The personal becomes transpersonal.

Their secret—and the message of this book—was captured in only four lines by R.W. Raymond:

"Life is eternal;
and love is immortal;
and death is only a horizon;
and a horizon is nothing save the limit of our sight."

Yes, of course there is a funeral at the end of the road—be you a mighty ruler, an office or factory worker, banker, scientist, international financier, homemaker, billionaire industrial tycoon, minister, priest, rabbi, janitor or pope. Everyone of the more than five billion souls occupying a physical body travels a similar road. But now you understand the seeming magic by which soul and mind, memory banks and personality will still be very much alive. You can now understand that you cannot "cop out" by the suicide route. You cannot be destroyed even by an atomic holocaust. There is just no way you can terminate the wonderful total being that is *you*. This is the magic of living forever: **you cannot die!** And though you will be living forever, the *quality* of life—here and hereafter—depends on *you*.

You can now be *certain* that after *your* funeral your own precious mind, memory banks, personality and soul will be vibrantly alive and ready to continue a journey that has *unlimited horizons*.

Man in the closing years of the twentieth century has at last rent the veil between *heaven* and *earth*. You have peered through to the "other side" and have acquired the priceless knowledge that:

YOU WILL LIVE FOREVER

Afterword

As momentous as are the communication breakthroughs presented in Part IV, with the faint spoken words heard by the EVP researchers, the static-filled exchange with the "deceased" Doc Nick and the more than twenty hours of solid two-way conversation with Dr. Mueller, these are merely analogous to the faint dots and dashes over Mr. Morse's first telegraph, the squeaky voice over Mr. Bell's first telephone, the faint, static-filled voices I received more than sixty years ago on my crystal-set radio, and the wiggly images on the first broadcast television of Mr. Baird.

Research now under way leads us to predict with confidence that when the third edition of this book is published, a few years hence, the advances then reported will parallel the developmental history of mankind's other communication equipment breakthroughs.

The reactions of critics and of many thousands of readers of the first English edition, as well as the Japanese and other foreign language editions, testify to the substance and lasting value of the concepts presented in this book.

Appendixes

A 1949 Prophecy by Dr. George J. Mueller
which he helped to fulfill 14 years after his death

While helping O'Neil and Meek develop Spiricom in 1981, Dr. Mueller referred them to pages 66 and 67 of a small booklet he wrote for the U.S. Army in 1949 under the title, *Introduction to Electronics.* After months of searching, we located the book in the Army section of the archives of the State Historical Society of Wisconsin, his native state. Little did Dr. Mueller realize when he wrote the following prophetic material in 1949 that, in a most dramatic way, *he* would provide the "sparks of genius to reconcile the irrational, and so accomplish the impossible." Here is what he wrote:

"By 1895, the people of the world felt that their men of science were due for a long-deserved rest. It was the popular belief of the time that everything of importance had already been discovered and that the great inventions had already been contrived. With justifiable pride the scientific achievements of the eighteenth and nineteenth centuries were considered the ultimate in all that could possibly be accomplished in the universe. The predictions of the era were that future generations would have to be content with making minor refinements and rearrangements to the established order of science.

"Within the past fifty years, the events which have transpired prove how erroneous were these predictions. Even before the celebration which marked the arrival of the twentieth century, Pierre and Marie Curie had announced a discovery which was to have far-reaching effects and was to change the theories on the structure of matter. The Curies, working in France, had discovered radioactivity and had manufactured a radio-active element, radium, from pitchblende. The subsequent developments of the twentieth century continued to prove how mistaken were the predictions prior to 1900.

"Today, men are eagerly searching for the undiscovered in electronic research. Men are at work exploring the known and unknown portions of the frequency spectrum—from sound waves to supersonics, from the lower radio frequencies through the infra-red, the visible, and the ultraviolet regions, up into the area of the x-rays and gamma rays, those minute wavelength radiations associated with radioactive elements. Men are reaching even into the spectrum heights of those fabulous cosmic rays. Out of this work, new techniques and instruments of electronic wizardry will emerge, but only after seemingly impossible problems have been solved. These solutions will require the careful thought and patient work of many people, whose findings will be correlated with other efforts, verified by experiments and aided now and then by sparks of genius to reconcile the irrational and so accomplish the impossible.

"As a conclusion, a salute is given to all men of electronics and a greeting is extended to newcomers in the field. Through their zeal, new magic will be created from electrons in motion and electromagnetic waves in space. Through their initiative and industry, future accomplishments will be achieved to challenge those of Oersted, Faraday, Franklin, Bell, DeForest, and the other masters of earlier years."

Certainly in the years ahead, the name of Dr. George Jeffries Mueller will be ranked with those of "Oersted, Faraday, Franklin, DeForest and the other masters of earlier years."

APPENDIX B

Additional Information on the Nature
Of Time in the Worlds of Spirit

The answer given to question 30—*How is time measured on the planes which make up the worlds of spirit?*—was very elementary. The true situation is so far beyond the comprehension of lay readers that we sidestepped some of the complexities. For the technical or scientific reader, the following may be of interest.

Several times a year for more than a dozen years the electronic specialists connected with Metascience Foundation have utilized the services of two of the most capable mediums who have been discovered by searches in this country and abroad. These sessions have been for the purpose of discussing our research efforts with a team of former scientists and inventors now residing on the mental and causal planes. The team in the worlds of spirit was organized and is directed by Dr. W.F.G. Swann, who in the 1950's was reported in *Who's Who in Science* as follows:

SWANN, William Francis Gray, physicist; b. Ironbridge, Shropshire, Eng., Aug. 29, 1884; s. William Francis and Anne (Evans) S.; student Brighton (Eng.) Tech. Coll., 1900-03, Royal Coll. of Science (London), Univ. Coll., King Coll., City and Guilds of London Inst., 1903-07; B.Sc., London, 1905, D.Sc., 1910; asso. Royal Coll. of Science, 1906; hon. M.A., Yale, 1924; hon. D.Sc., Swarthmore Coll., 1929; hon. F.T.C.L., London 1936; Litt.D. (hon.), Temple U., 1954; m. Sarah Frances Mabel Thompson, Aug. 14, 1909 (dec. 1954); children—William Francis, Charles Paul Sylvia; m. 2d, Helen Laura Diedrichs, Dec. 23, 1955. Came to U.S. 1913. Chief Phys. div. Dept. Terrestrial Magnetism, Carnegie Instn., Washington, 1913-18; mem. faculties U. Min., U. Chgo., Yale, 1918-27, dir. Sloane Lab., 1924-27, also chmn. advisory research com. Bartol Research Foundation of Franklin Inst., 1924-27; dir. same, 1927-59, dir. emeritus, 1959-62, sr. staff advisor Franklin Inst. Labs. for Research and Development, 1945-62. Fellow Imperial College of Science and Technology (London, Eng.), Phys. Soc., London, Am. Physical Soc. (v.p. 1929, 30; pres. 1931-33); mem., sometime officer, numerous profl. assns. Mem bd. dir. Phila. Musical Academy, chmn. 1951-58. Recipient Elliott Cresson Gold Medal, Franklin Inst., 1960. Author: The Architecture of the Universe, 1934; (with other) The Story of Human Error, 1936; Physics, 1941. Contr. to study cosmic rays, atomic structure, relativity, and atmospheric electricity. Died 1962.

Of course, in keeping with the Biblical admonition to test the spirits to see that they are who they say they are, we established in 1972 that our communicator was in fact the man referred to in the above biographical sketch. This was made easier in the case of Dr. Swann because, as reported in our answer to question 20, one of our team members, Melvin Sutley, had been a very close personal friend of Dr. Swann. The Swanns and the Sutleys both lived in Philadelphia and had the closest of friendships. Melvin, who died in 1977, was the first of our research team members to make the transition.

After reading the above biographical sketch, the reader might say, "This certainly shows the intellectual level Dr. Swann reached during his recent stay on the earth plane. I wonder on what level of Fig. 32 he is now functioning?"

We have contacted Dr. Swann many times during the past seven years and have had many hours of discussion. He has told us that since his death in 1962, he spent only a short time in the level of existence we have colored yellow (in the foldout version of Fig. 32) and is now at the upper boundary of the levels we have colored green. He tells us that he is almost formless and is largely pure mind. He is the organizer and leader of a large team of scientists, philosophers, mathematicians and inventors, most of whom passed over within the last fifty years. Dr. Swann has already made the decision that upon the completion of the project on which his team is now working, he will accept the "final rebirth," shed his mental body and move into the levels above.

In preparation for a session in July, 1979, my associates and I had carefully composed six questions for submission to Dr. Swann and his associates—questions which had an important bearing on decisions we were facing on the design and operation of some very sophisticated electronic equipment. Here is a portion of the transcript of our session through the medium.

Meek: All right, question number five: Can your energy be made to interact with a stream of electrons in a vacuum tube such as a cathode ray tube or in a traveling-wave antenna?

Swann: If so, it would have a scattering effect. A wave guide as we understand it would possibly be the better equipment to work with than the cathode ray idea. We do *not know* if it would interact with that, but we believe it would.

Meek: And the sixth and last question, of a somewhat different nature. First, by way of explanation, we speak of the vibratory nature of all creation. To identify vibratory rate, you and we speak of higher and lower frequencies. Yet you and other communicators have told us that there is no time in your dimension. Therefore this question: How can we discuss "frequency" and "frequency stability" without a time base? The word frequency denotes cycles per unit of time. Yet you say you have no time in your dimension. How is it possible to discuss vibratory rates and frequencies independently of time?

Swann: [chuckling] We feel that there is a great deal of misunderstanding in this area. Our lack of time relates to days, hours, minutes and seconds such as we knew on the physical plane. Our area of dimension is a *type of frequency* in itself. The vibrating energies here are those which comprise that which we are, vibrating energies which we are. They even now comprise a portion of your own being but you will experience them more fully after you lay aside the physical body and lose the connection with your present etheric body and astral form and frequency. So that is the nature of "dimension of being"—that which is at a higher frequency.

On the physical plane, atoms are in motion and are vibrating at such a high rate that although there are great spaces between them, the surface actually appears to be solid. Here the spiritual atoms far outnumber your physical atoms and are vibrating and interacting with each other at a far greater rate than on the physical plane or on the astral plane. They are also somewhat different in composition. It is what many others have called "finer matter," because all energy is matter in some form or another.

This energy which comes into our area from other sources functions according to the numerical atomic numbers governing such energies. They are different from those on the physical plane inasmuch as they *are not measured by time.* They are not measured by so many vibrations per second. They are composed of extremely fine substance which does not follow the laws of the physical plane. In making the transition from the physical plane, a person must go through an intermediary area which is known to many on the physical plane as the astral world or the "summerland" and comprises a number of areas where vibration changes, or the nature of energy changes.

At last on the upper planes, the being dies or lays aside the astral body, much as he laid aside the physical body and proceeded in a body of finer matter into the area where we now live. The energies which come into this area are from a great—a much greater being, and one who has evolved far beyond the imagination of most beings upon the physical plane where you now reside. This energy is a pure light and as it comes into our area, it becomes differentiated. *This* is the energy that we use. It is not possible to find words to describe it.

We have said "frequency" several times because it seems to fit that which we work with, but it is not frequency measured in days, hours, minutes or seconds. There is very little with which to describe this energy. Let us say that it is very fast. It comes in *spurts.* So far as our measurements are concerned, it could be slowed down if we could get it to be constant. We could possibly hope to compress it into a more solid beam that would provide exactly what we are looking for: a carrier of voices.

We would desire to use this because of our plans to place these instruments in many dimensions, in each of many dimensions in the world of spirit. We thought that since this energy comes into many of the higher dimensions, it would be more native than anything else that we could plan to use.

Perhaps I have not made it clear that to us frequency is that which we can *see,* which we can *feel* or which *affects* us in any way. It has no magnetic qualities. It is a pure energy although tinged with the rate of atomic energy existing on our plane. One cannot now measure it in any way. You express a vibration in giga hertz and we say, "Yes, it is akin to that."

We have no true measurement here. We have a name for it, but we have no true measurement that you would understand. (And I can already hear your associate Paul saying, "Try us!") It is only a term, just as your term "giga" hertz was coined to name something which previously had no name. So that is what we have done here—coin a term for what we are working with.

Meek: All right, we will be glad to share this tape with Paul, Hans and Will. This is the extent of our questions. If there is anything else tonight, Dr. Swann, that you or one of your teammates wish to share with us—

Swann: Yes, we have two new arrivals in our midst, Melvin and Margaret. [The continuation of this transcript involving the Sutleys was presented in the answer to Question 20 in the text.]

From these comments by a scientist with the qualifications of Dr. Swann, it is obvious that we earthbound mortals, locked as we are into our little three-dimension sequential-time system, cannot explain the workings of the cosmos within the framework of what we now know of the electromagnetic system.

APPENDIX C

Notes on Reincarnation by Robert R. Leichtman, M.D.

The footnote at the close of the answer to question 43 promised additional views on the complex subject of reincarnation. Here they are, drawn from the comments of Robert R. Leichtman, M.D. on the early draft manuscript of this book. Dr. Leichtman is a psychic of outstanding ability and the author of *From Heaven to Earth*, a 24-book series of mediumistic interviews.

You make several statements about reincarnation that sound a bit too permissive to me. I have never found that the personality (which is what survives physical death initially) can make simple choices such as "to go on the causal planes or reincarnate." If that were the case, I doubt that more than a very tiny percentage would ever return to the earth plane. While free will and the development of wisdom to choose are objects of incarnation, this free will choice rarely would extend to deciding whether or not to reincarnate. The soul, in the average person, is impelled to reincarnate again and again because there are magnetic ties which keep pulling it back to earth again until it is complete. There are various laws of karma (or call it universal law, if you like) which demand this. It is unfortunate that the surviving astral personality and even the surviving mental essence of the personality would like to believe differently, but this is usually not the case. The soul is concerned with the evolution of consciousness and the work of service. Many can stay a long time on the inner levels working toward that, but there is often unfinished business in the life of that soul—business that can only be worked out here in the earth plane. There is a certain "magnetic" appeal that this unfinished business applies to call people back into incarnation.

I have seen the tomes that are written by people who get overheated with the notion that God is a Loving Father who would not permit his children to suffer, so "of course He would not make us come back here!" Unfortunately, some lessons are a bit painful, but are necessary anyway. Every good parent feels some anguish at times when his own children fight to stay home from school or fight to stay away from the dentist or rebel against getting cleaned up and doing their chores, but the long term progress of their children toward maturity demands that parents discipline their children to ensure their progress and to avoid creating a monstrous and childish mess which demands indulgences and has temper tantrums during the adult years. When the life of the personality gets too strong, it often tries to speak for the spirit within and begins to make up a self-serving concept of God that is something resembling a Santa Claus who showers a lot of gifts on "nice" people but not quite so many on "bad" people.

While it is true that a lot of difficulty and immaturity does get worked out after passing over, and many new talents and insights are gained, this is similar to the lawyer who learns a lot of theory in law school but still hasn't had any real life, personal practice in the field. Insights, compassion, talent and harmony—whether gained in heaven or in an earthly school—must be grounded, eventually, in the physical plane. That is the way new light enters the physical plane and collective humanity is enriched. Escape to heaven, however desirable, is not always possible, except for short bursts between lives. Not liking that idea has nothing to do with its reality.

—Robert R. Leichtman, M.D.

APPENDIX D

The Role of Subtle Energies

Only the merest fraction of one percent of the readers of this volume will have the interest or technical and scientific knowledge to cause them to seek information on the energies which are involved in creating a communication system capable of "talking with the dead." Hence, while we are not justified in adding the many pages to this book which would be required to present such specialized information, we wish to assist such readers in their search for enlightenment.

In 1982, at the time we made the public announcement of the third breakthrough, we published a 100-page technical manual, *Spiricom: An Electromagnetic-Etheric Systems Approach to Communications with Other Levels of Human Consciousness.* This manual reported in detail our research from 1971 to 1982 and shared the very limited knowledge we had then acquired about the nature of the subtle energies involved in instrumental contact with the higher worlds of consciousness. In retrospect, perhaps the most important parts of this manual were Chapter 9, "Spirit Energies—Their Nature and Problems for Spiricom Researchers" and Appendix A, which also touched on the subject of etheric energies.

While this manual does not present any plans for a "build-it-yourself" communication set, or provide an outline of the eventual solution, it does contain useful information not to be found in any other publication. A copy of the manual and a packet containing a 90-minute cassette tape with sixteen excerpts of two-way conversation with "deceased" persons and other informative printed matter may be obtained by sending $25 in U.S. funds to Metascience Foundation, P.O. Box 737, Franklin, NC 28734. Please make checks or money orders payable to Metascience Foundation.

A color poster of Fig. 32 is included at no extra charge with this book. If you would like extra copies of this poster, they are available from Metascience for $1 apiece, postpaid.

How To Die

All of us spend all of our earth years in temporary occupancy of this current physical body. Quite naturally, all of us are concentrating our thoughts and actions on the business of *living*. But what about the important business of *dying*?

As we move through our sixties, seventies and eighties, what guidance is available to ease us through the gates of death? Suddenly, we find we are really going through the *birth process*—rebirth into an exciting new world. What steps are involved? Who is there to help us?

For those who want a good but short overview of the subject, we reprint herewith the substance of an address presented in various cities in the United States by Mabel Rowand more than forty years ago. It was issued as a small booklet in 1942 and sold widely in the following decades. It is now out of print. Since our own sixteen years of fulltime, worldwide research in this area fully *confirms all details* of the Rowland material, we use this occasion to help all readers in this and the coming decades.

How To Die
by Mabel Rowland

Regardless of who we are and how we feel about it, each one of us must one day leave the body. But there is absolutely no reason to fear this change, for *life* is continuous and, what is still more comforting, *consciousness* and individuality are continuous.

What happens is that the soul leaves the body we now dwell in and starts anew in its next phase of existence, vibrating at a different rate. The change is as natural as breathing and we should be as trusting and fearless concerning it as we are about breathing. There is nothing to fear any more than when we lie down to sleep for the night.

As God's creatures, we are *privileged* to live life, and this privilege includes stewardship of a body—a body housing this dynamic, precious and most wonderful thing in the world—*life*. We must take care of the body, but we are not to presume that we own it. We dwell in it. We do not own it. The Creator put us into these bodies "for the duration" of our earth lives, and we are to follow the first law of Nature and strictly observe "self-preservation." We are to fight for our lives to the very last ditch and to protect our bodies to the very best of our ability. Even an insect does as much, instinctively.

Painless as we know "dying" to be, *it* is nature's own process and is arrived at upon the Creator's exact moment scheduled for us in the great plan. When will it be for *me?* Forget it! It is none of our business, but preparing for *life* afterward *is.*

It is only fair to yourself to take in these few facts which I shall give you and remember them—you may not believe them, nor do you need to—but it is necessary for you to read and remember them. That is the intelligent thing to do. Then when you need the information, it will suddenly pop up out of your subconscious mind and be useful.

Now when we have completed this cycle of our earth life and *it* is over—finished—we awaken in the next state of existence, discovering that our thought and feeling reactions are exactly the same as they always were! Remember that. You are *you.* There is no death. There is only a change of apparel, so to speak. You have shed the body, but your thoughts and feelings do not undergo any change in the passing out.

However, you become quickly conscious of the fact that things *other* than yourself are slightly, but definitely, different, and it is for *that very reason* I am making this talk. So please heed this, that you may not be at all *panicky,* but know exactly what to do.

You probably at some time have dreamed you were falling. If so, you know that the dreamer never hits and hurts himself. He wakes up. In the experience of "dying," sometimes the individual realizes he is going—or he may merely suspect it—but the truth is, that while people rarely admit it, even to themselves, most of them *fear* it.

There is no need to. There is no death: it is a misnomer. The *truth* is that the actual passing out is not only painless, as I told you a few moments ago, but often beautiful—a *natural* transition, never to be dreaded.

We do not get whisked to a city with "golden streets" and see angels flying around—no. If there is any such place, which was held out to us as "bait" to be "good" in the theologies we were raised on, then we are certainly not ready, in our present state of being, to take up residence there, anyway.

The *real* of the person leaves the body—very much as a butterfly leaves its old chrysalis. Many, many persons everywhere have seen this passing out. I have seen it myself. Ask any experienced nurse. She will probably tell you of seeing a vaporous cloud of ectoplasm—that's what it looks like to our human vision. It is the silver cord that holds us to our bodies. Everyone has it and here in our earth life it is never severed, but it stretches when we are asleep to let our souls or entities, the real of us, go from the body and experience dreams. Then it shortens again and comes back to the body. It holds "body and soul" together. There might be four or five people present at a bedside when a soul passes out and maybe only one or two of them will have their human vision stepped up to the frequency even to see this much.

Some of us have seen a great deal more. There *is* no death.

Now you understand that you are the same individual after you leave the body as before. No wings, no thrones, no crowns. You may be pleased with conditions, or you may at first be a little disappointed. It just depends on what you expected.

For the first few days, everyone's fate is the same, whether saint or sinner, and after that there are spheres of life where you will belong— and nothing can keep you out of your sphere. You are drawn into it by the *law of attraction*; that law which proves that like attracts like. We will be with people of the same tastes and degree of spiritual interests as ourselves, just as we naturally gravitate to and choose suitable associates here.

Individual reactions are just that—individual reactions. And there are some people who have lived a sheltered earth life to a ripe old age, steeped in theological tradition and with fixed ideas about streets of gold, gates of pearl, harps and so forth. These good souls are oftentimes their own worst enemies, being stubbornly unwilling to adjust to anything even similar to their earth life conditions, although the next plane is similar—surprisingly so. Some people, through theological training, actually expect, when they realize they have "died," to find the streets made of gold. Certain it is that if they believed that literally while here, they will be of the same opinion still.

Some theologies teach that when we die, the body, soul and entire entity lie in the grave and sleep until the "judgment day." Well, these dear souls actually believe that literally. And when helpers on the other side of life try to tell them they are the same John or Annie Smith they've always been, but that now their life is going to have a few changes in its working out, they are skeptical and react as they might to a Bunko man at the county fair. Some folks of this persuasion insist on sleeping until "Gabriel" shall blow his horn. They often sleep for years.

Let us consider now, a soul just out of the physical body, through a natural, leisurely process. It is *yourself* perhaps. You are greeting your parents. How wonderful they look and they have been gone for years! They were quite old and a little bent when you last saw them in earth life. It used to grieve and tug at you a little to see them aging and failing. But here they are as lovely looking and as smiling and happy as you remember them when they were young and you were very young, just starting to school back in the little home town.

Perhaps you are dreaming—something like this has happened to you before in dreams. No, they were very brief and fleeting flashes, those dreams. This is real and enduring. Still, your parents aren't saying very much—that is like a dream, too. But their gaze is fond and steady and they smile so reassuringly. It is real. And what a nice cool light feeling you have! They embrace you. It is real!

Lovingly, they lead you off into their own circle or vibration, where you will rest and talk. Soon you will experience a lovely drowsy, but

very safe feeling, and letting yourself go, will fall into a sleep of anywhere from three days or so to several weeks. Even the most spiritual
personalities we have any record of remained and rested the first sixty
hours or a few days, in the astral, then sometimes reappeared here on
earth, briefly, before ascending into higher realms.

The "dead" person doesn't feel nor act any differently for having
"died," but adjustments have to be made, just as they have to be made
here on earth. For instance, when summer is waning, we move in off
the sleeping porch, wrap up a bit and get out our furs and make a hearth
fire. That is all there is to it: it is that simple.

When you have slept for your few days or so after "dying" and
wakened to start living in your new environment, you never sleep
again. You rest as all do in the spiritual realms, but they do not sleep.
The exception is those people I just mentioned, waiting for Gabriel.

Please bear in mind that when the soul leaves the body it doesn't go
anywhere. The change geographically is no greater than you would
experience in life if you walked from one room to another, from a darkened room into a lighted one or from a warm room onto a cool balcony.
Please realize also that while your body is to be protected and cherished, leaving it, in God's own time, is no more to be feared than is sliding out of your overcoat, letting it fall on a chair and walking away from
it. And at first there is no consciousness of this "shedding" as it were, of
the body of flesh. Our rate of vibration has changed, that is all. And the
life we have entered is so very much like the earth life the new arrival is
often quite confused, particularly if he has been taught all his life to
expect something different.

Should you ever experience the baffling sensation of walking up to
your loved ones, embracing them, while they, completely unaware of
your presence, walk through you, just do not get panicky. Do the same
as you should do in an earth emergency, or any situation which you do
not understand. We are told by the Psalmist to "Be still" (Psalms 46:10).
It matters not what your religious belief is, or whether you have
any—that is perfect advice. Just be perfectly still, within your own
mind and lift your thought to your highest concept—whatever you think
of a God. Call to It or Him or breathe His name silently or aloud, just so
it is from the heart, which it will be then—it will be you "as a little child"
and immediately—even more quickly than I can tell you this, help
comes. Pleasant, friendly aid and you are never in that "spot" again.

The helper finds your relatives and loved ones for you. This is
necessary when deaths occur accidentally and suddenly. Remember
what you are reading please. Simply raise your consciousness. It is
your same old consciousness you know, to your own heavenly father.
Just say as much as "Father" and help will come. The astral realm is
organized. I repeat: you need not believe this that you are reading, but
please remember it. In accidental death and in wartime it all happens

so suddenly that the soul may be hurtled out of the body and stand amidst a hellish scene of disaster and destruction and see his own body lying there. It isn't a pleasant experience, but it is *life*. Life is progressive. It blooms and fades and grows again and lifts us from sphere to sphere *individually* according to each one's consciousness. Stand still and pray. Death is a natural part of life.

If your life here has been devoted to the accumulation of material things or to the making of money, to the extent that you have come to be steeped in it—to enjoy it, say, more than anything else, you are building up a hazard for yourself in the "next world." Be wise enough not to have your chief interest a material one like collecting or selling to make money, because when we leave the body, we go where there is *no economic standard*—money is not used. You will be a fish out of water unless you have a hobby which is something less material, more intangible and important than buying and selling.

Things "of the earth earthy" are just that. Be careful not to grow so fond of them to be obsessed by them, for once we actually *love* things or money, then we are in danger of being drawn and held by this earth vibration. Briefly, that would mean that we should, as a disembodied soul, yours or mine, after we have died, hang around others still in earth life, whose tastes and activities are the same as ours used to be. Our satisfaction would be merely vicarious. There are hoards of these pitiful earthbound souls haunting clearing houses, counting houses and money markets and trade centers of all sorts. Also we see the souls of the morally weak and depraved in drinking joints and low places.

While you are still living your physical existence, realize that money is important to you merely for body-comfort needs. This is temporary, so don't feed your soul to it. In the next plane you see no "business as usual" sign. It is then that your artistic attainments may be enjoyed and you will receive instruction for far more noble service than money grubbing.

So, my advice is to be prepared—to prepare while still living here. Cultivate your *soul side*. Learn to love and serve your fellow man. If it is not easy for you to love people, it can be an impersonal kind of love until you become a more loving creature. Cut down on the criticisms of others and magnify their desirable qualities. I mean just to yourself, as they start to "irritate" you when you think of them. The way they walk or talk or some little fault—forget that and refuse to see it. The Hindu, when he passes another human soul, mutters "pronom," meaning, "The God in me salutes the God (part) of you."

I am not being sentimental. I am giving you the key to the situation of living, more fully, both here and now and *afterward!* Let us live with our thought upon God and with this attitude of mind we shall be living the right way—and then surely we will "die" the right way.

About the Author

As a teenager, George Meek began a study of the world's great religions. Being of a scientific bent, he began early to follow the Biblical admonition "to seek, to knock and to ask." He sought to get answers to questions about God, man's relationship to God, heaven and hell, the purpose of life and the possibility of life after death.

His professional career was largely devoted to industrial research and development in the United States and Europe, to which he made more than forty trips for this purpose. This work was paralleled with extra-curricular reading in the fields of medicine, psychiatry and psychology.

At age 55, he decided to get into a position to terminate his professional career at age 60 and spend the remainder of his life on self-financed research into the basic nature of man. To make this possible, he utilized his knowledge of the mind to turn on his own creativity. In the next five years he made a series of inventions which his clients patented in 13 countries.

At age 60, he embarked on an intensive full-time library and literature research program and worldwide travel to locate like-minded researchers. He developed working contacts with several dozen medical doctors, psychiatrists, psychologists and scientists in many disciplines in twenty countries. He organized and led teams of these colleagues to travel to various countries for research purposes.

The first fruit of this collaboration was the book *Healers and the Healing Process*, co-authored with fourteen of his colleagues living in six countries. This book is recommended by the World Health Organization as *must* reading for health professionals in all emerging countries.

Now, almost sixty years after embarking on his search for answers to life's greatest mystery and after sixteen years of full-time worldwide research, he is happy to share the findings in this expanded edition of *After We Die, What Then?*

In order that he and the younger researchers who follow him can push further into *human dimensions research*, Meek has organized and manages Metascience Foundation. This activity is permitting still deeper exploration of man's energy fields and interpenetrating space-time systems.

Bibliography

The libraries of the world contain thousands of books that relate to life after death. The following listing is representative only.

For the convenience of the reader who may want to pursue seriously a particular aspect of the subject, this sampling of books has been listed under these headings:

1. Apparitions, Hallucinations and Ghosts
2. Communications through Mediums
3. Deathbed Experiences
4. Direct Voice
5. Electronic Communication with the Dead
6. General
7. Materializations (solid ghosts)
8. Out-of-body Experiences
9. Obsession and Possession
10. Philosophic Speculations Regarding Life after Death
11. Reincarnation
12. Spirit Photography
13. Light
14. Spirit Descriptions of After-Life Experiences

1. Apparitions, Hallucinations and Ghosts

Assorted Authors. *Ghosts and Things.* Berkley, 1962.

Bayless, Raymond. *Apparitions and Survival of Death.* University Books, 1973.

Fodor, Nandor. *Encyclopedia of Psychic Science.* University Books, 1966.

Fuller, Elizabeth. *My Search for the Ghost of Flight 401.* Berkley, 1978.

_____. *Poor Elizabeth's Almanac.* Berkley, 1980.

Fuller, John G. *The Airmen Who Would Not Die.* Transworld, 1979.

Green, C. and McCreery, C. *Apparitions.* Hamish Hamilton, 1975.

Holzer, Hans. *Yankee Ghosts.* Ace, 1966.

MacKenzie, A. *Apparitions and Ghosts: A Modern Study.* Barker, 1971.

Roberts, Nancy. *An Illustrated Guide to Ghosts.* McNally and Loftin, 1982.

Tyrell, G.N.M. *Apparitions.* MacMillan, 1962.

_____. "Six Theories About Apparitions," *Proceedings of the Society for Psychical Research,* Vol. 50, 1953-1956, pp. 153-239.

West, D.J. "A Mass Observation Questionnaire on Hallucinations," *Journal of the Society for Psychical Research,* Vol. 34, 1948, pp. 187-196.

West, L.J., ed. *Hallucinations.* Grune and Stratton, 1962.

2. Communications through Mediums

Borgia, Anthony. *Life in the World Unseen.* Corgi Books, 1975.

Brandon, Wilfred. *Incarnation, A Plea from the Masters.* C. & R. Anthony, 1958.

_____. *Open the Door!* C. & R. Anthony, 1935.

_____. *We Knew These Men.* Alfred A. Knopf, 1942.

_____. *Love in the Afterlife.* C. & R. Anthony, 1956.

Burke, Jane Revere. *The One Way.* E.P. Dutton, 1922.

_____. *The Bundle of Life.* E.P. Dutton, 1934.

_____. *The Immutable Law.* E.P. Dutton, 1936.

Cooke, Ivan, ed. *The Return of Arthur Conan Doyle.* White Eagle, 1968.

_____. *Thy Kingdom Come.* Wright & Brown.

Cummins, G. *Swan on a Black Sea.* Routledge and Kegan Paul, 1965.

Darby & Joan. *Our Unseen Guest.* Borden, 1947.

Duguid, David. *Hafed, Prince of Persia.* W. Foulsham, 1935.

Ebon, Martin, ed. *True Experiences in Communicating with the Dead.* New American Library, 1968.

Edwards, Harry. *The Mediumship of Arnold Clare.* The Psychic Book Club, 1942.

_____. *The Mediumship of Jack Webber.* Healer Publishing, 1962.

Findlay, Arthur. *Looking Back.* Psychic Press, 1961.

_____. *On the Edge of the Etheric.* Psychic Press, 1945.

_____. *The Way of Life.* Psychic Press, 1962.

_____. *Where Two Worlds Meet.* Psychic Press, 1951.

Ford, Arthur. *The Life Beyond Death.* G.P. Putnam's Sons, 1971.

Greber, Johannes. *Communication with the Spirit World of God.* Johannes Greber Memorial Foundation, 1970.

Hapgood, Charles H. *Voices of Spirit through the Psychic Experience of Elwood Babbitt.* Delacorte, 1975.

Hayes, Patricia and Smith, Marshall. *Extension of Life: Arthur Ford Speaks.* Dimensional Brotherhood, 1986.

Hilarion. *Nations.* Marcus Books, 1980.

_____. *The Nature of Reality.* Marcus Books, 1979.

_____. *Seasons of the Spirit.* Marcus Books, 1980.

_____. *Symbols.* Marcus Books, 1979.

Homewood, Harry. *Travis is Here.* Fawcett, 1978.

Kardec, Allan. *The Medium's Book.* Psychic Press, 1971.

_____. *The Spirits' Book.* Allan Kardec Editora Ltda. (Saõ Paulo, Brazil).

Lees, Robert James. *Through the Mists*. Philip Wellby, 1906.

Leichtman, Dr. Robert R. *From Heaven to Earth*. Ariel Press, 1978-1982. A collection of 24 books of mediumistic interviews: *Edgar Cayce Returns, Shakespeare Returns, Cheiro Returns, Jung & Freud Return, Leadbeater Returns, Sir Oliver Lodge Returns, Thomas Jefferson Returns, Arthur Ford Returns, H.P. Blavatsky Returns, Nikola Tesla Returns, Eileen Garrett Returns, Stewart White Returns, Schweitzer Returns, Rembrandt Returns, Churchill Returns, Yogananda Returns, Mark Twain Returns, Einstein Returns, Franklin Returns, Carnegie Returns, Wagner Returns, Burbank Returns, Lincoln Returns* and *The Destiny of America*.

Litvag, Irving. *Singer in the Shadows*. Macmillan, 1972.

Lombroso, Cesare. *After Death—What?* Small, Maynard, 1909.

Magus. *The Magian Gospel of Brother Yehshua*. Magian Press, 1979.

Mandel, Henry A. *Banners of Light*. Vantage Press, 1973.

Meek, George W. *As We See It From Here*. Metascience, 1980.

Montgomery, Ruth. *Threshold to Tomorrow*. G.P. Putnam's Sons, 1982.

Moore, Usborne. *The Voices*. Watts & Co., 1913.

Peebles, J.M. *Seers of the Ages*. Progressive Thinker, 1903.

Ramala Centre. *The Revelation of Ramala*. Neville Spearman, 1978.

Roberts, Jane. *The Unknown Reality*. Prentice Hall, 1977.

Roberts, Ursula. *Mary Baker Eddy, Her Communications from Beyond the Grave*. Max Parrish, 1964.

Smith, Suzy. *Life is Forever*. Dell, 1974.

_____. *The Mediumship of Mrs. Leonard*. University Books, 1964.

_____. *The Book of James*. G.P. Putnam's Sons, 1974.

Wetzl, Joseph. *The Bridge Over the River*. Anthroposophic Press, 1974.

White, Ruth and Swainson, Mary. *Gildas Communicates*. Neville Spearman, 1971.

White, Stewart Edward. *Across the Unknown*. Ariel Press, 1987.

_____. *The Betty Book*. Ariel Press, 1987.

_____. *The Gaelic Manuscripts*. Pantheon Press, 1977.

_____. *The Unobstructed Universe*. Ariel Press, 1988.

Wickland, Carl A. *Thirty Years Among the Dead*. Newcastle, 1974.

3. Deathbed Experiences

Barrett, W.F. *Deathbed Visions*. Methuen, 1926.

DeVita, Diana. *Be Not Afraid of Death*. DeVita Institute, 1982.

Hunter, R.C. "On the Experience of Nearly Dying," *American Journal of Psychiatry*. July 1967, p. 124.

Kübler-Ross, Elisabeth. *Death: The Final Stage of Growth*. Prentice Hall, 1975.

_____. *On Death and Dying*. Macmillan, 1969.

_____. *Questions and Answers on Death and Dying*. Macmillan, 1974.

Matson, Archie. *Afterlife*. Harper & Row, 1975.

Moody, Raymond A., Jr. *Life After Life*. Bantam Books, 1976.

Osis, Karlis and Haraldsson, Erlendur. *At the Hour of Death*. Avon, 1977.

Osis, Karlis. *Deathbed Observations by Physicians and Nurses*. Parapsychology Foundation, 1961.

_____. "Deathbed Observations by Physicians and Nurses: A Cross Cultural Survey," *Journal of American Society for Psychical Research*. Vol. 71, 1977, pp. 237-259.

Pattison, E. Mansell. *The Experience of Dying*. Prentice Hall, 1977.

Ring, Kenneth. *Life at Death: A Scientific Investigation of the Near-Death Experience*. Coward, McCann & Geoghegan, 1980.

Rogo, D. Scott. *Nad, A Study of Some Unusual 'Other World' Experiences*. University Books, 1970.

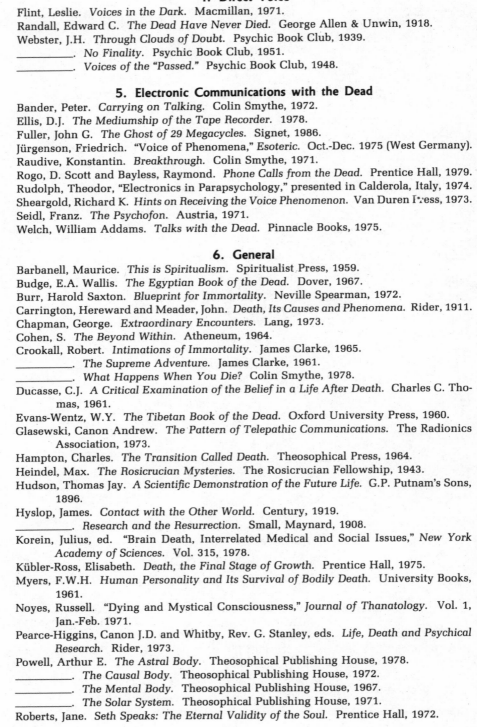

4. Direct Voice

Flint, Leslie. *Voices in the Dark.* Macmillan, 1971.

Randall, Edward C. *The Dead Have Never Died.* George Allen & Unwin, 1918.

Webster, J.H. *Through Clouds of Doubt.* Psychic Book Club, 1939.

_____. *No Finality.* Psychic Book Club, 1951.

_____. *Voices of the "Passed."* Psychic Book Club, 1948.

5. Electronic Communications with the Dead

Bander, Peter. *Carrying on Talking.* Colin Smythe, 1972.

Ellis, D.J. *The Mediumship of the Tape Recorder.* 1978.

Fuller, John G. *The Ghost of 29 Megacycles.* Signet, 1986.

Jürgenson, Friedrich. "Voice of Phenomena," *Esoteric.* Oct.-Dec. 1975 (West Germany).

Raudive, Konstantin. *Breakthrough.* Colin Smythe, 1971.

Rogo, D. Scott and Bayless, Raymond. *Phone Calls from the Dead.* Prentice Hall, 1979.

Rudolph, Theodor, "Electronics in Parapsychology," presented in Calderola, Italy, 1974.

Sheargold, Richard K. *Hints on Receiving the Voice Phenomenon.* Van Duren Press, 1973.

Seidl, Franz. *The Psychofon.* Austria, 1971.

Welch, William Addams. *Talks with the Dead.* Pinnacle Books, 1975.

6. General

Barbanell, Maurice. *This is Spiritualism.* Spiritualist Press, 1959.

Budge, E.A. Wallis. *The Egyptian Book of the Dead.* Dover, 1967.

Burr, Harold Saxton. *Blueprint for Immortality.* Neville Spearman, 1972.

Carrington, Hereward and Meader, John. *Death, Its Causes and Phenomena.* Rider, 1911.

Chapman, George. *Extraordinary Encounters.* Lang, 1973.

Cohen, S. *The Beyond Within.* Atheneum, 1964.

Crookall, Robert. *Intimations of Immortality.* James Clarke, 1965.

_____. *The Supreme Adventure.* James Clarke, 1961.

_____. *What Happens When You Die?* Colin Smythe, 1978.

Ducasse, C.J. *A Critical Examination of the Belief in a Life After Death.* Charles C. Thomas, 1961.

Evans-Wentz, W.Y. *The Tibetan Book of the Dead.* Oxford University Press, 1960.

Glasewski, Canon Andrew. *The Pattern of Telepathic Communications.* The Radionics Association, 1973.

Hampton, Charles. *The Transition Called Death.* Theosophical Press, 1964.

Heindel, Max. *The Rosicrucian Mysteries.* The Rosicrucian Fellowship, 1943.

Hudson, Thomas Jay. *A Scientific Demonstration of the Future Life.* G.P. Putnam's Sons, 1896.

Hyslop, James. *Contact with the Other World.* Century, 1919.

_____. *Research and the Resurrection.* Small, Maynard, 1908.

Korein, Julius, ed. "Brain Death, Interrelated Medical and Social Issues," *New York Academy of Sciences.* Vol. 315, 1978.

Kübler-Ross, Elisabeth. *Death, the Final Stage of Growth.* Prentice Hall, 1975.

Myers, F.W.H. *Human Personality and Its Survival of Bodily Death.* University Books, 1961.

Noyes, Russell. "Dying and Mystical Consciousness," *Journal of Thanatology.* Vol. 1, Jan.-Feb. 1971.

Pearce-Higgins, Canon J.D. and Whitby, Rev. G. Stanley, eds. *Life, Death and Psychical Research.* Rider, 1973.

Powell, Arthur E. *The Astral Body.* Theosophical Publishing House, 1978.

_____. *The Causal Body.* Theosophical Publishing House, 1972.

_____. *The Mental Body.* Theosophical Publishing House, 1967.

_____. *The Solar System.* Theosophical Publishing House, 1971.

Roberts, Jane. *Seth Speaks: The Eternal Validity of the Soul.* Prentice Hall, 1972.

Roberts, Jane. *The Nature of Personal Reality.* Prentice Hall, 1974.

_____. *The Seth Material.* Prentice Hall, 1970.

Roll, W.G. "A New Look at the Survival Problem," in *New Directions in Parapsychology* (J. Beloff, ed.), Elek Science, 1974.

_____. "Survival Research: Problems and Possibilities," in *Psychic Exploration: A Challenge for Science* (E.D. Mitchell and J. White, eds). G.P. Putnam's Sons, 1974.

Samuels, Mike M.D. and Bennett, Hal. *Spirit Guides.* Random House, 1974.

Sandys, Cynthia and Lehmann, Rosamund. *The Awakening Letters.* Neville Spearman, 1978.

Tiemeyer, T.N. *Jesus Christ Super Psychic.* ESPress, 1976.

Tuella. *The Dynamics of Cosmic Telepathy.* Guardian Action Pub., 1983.

Vasilev, L.L. *Experiments in Mental Suggestion.* I.S.M.I. Pub., 1962.

White, John and Krippner, Stanley. *Future Science.* Doubleday, 1977.

Whiteman, J.H.M. *The Mystical Life.* Faber and Faber, 1961.

Yes, Inc. *Wellness.* Yes, Inc., 1977.

7. Materializations (Solid Ghosts)

Bolton, Gambier. *Ghosts in Solid Form.* Psychic Book Club, 1957.

Crawford, W.J. *Reality of Psychic Phenomena.* Watkins, 1916.

_____. *Experiments in Psychical Science.* Watkins, 1919.

_____. *Psychic Structures at the Goligher Circle.* Watkins, 1921.

Crookes, William. *Researches in the Phenomena of Spiritualism.* James Burns, 1874.

_____. *Crookes and the Spirit World* (M.R. Barrington, ed.) Souvenir Press, 1972.

D'Esperance, E.O. *Shadowland.* Redway, 1897.

Dingwall, E.J. *Some Human Oddities.* Hoore and Van Tha, 1847.

Edwards, Harry. *The Mediumship of Arnold Clare.* Rider, 1940.

_____. *The Mediumship of Jack Webber.* Healer Publishing, 1962.

Fielding, Everard. *Sittings with Eusapia Palladino and Other Studies.* University Books, 1963.

Geley, Gustave. *Clairvoyance and Materialization.* Bern, 1927.

Gray, Isa. *From Materializations to Healing.* Regency Press, 1972.

Hack, Gwendolyn Kelly. *Modern Psychic Mysteries.* Rider, 1929.

_____. *Venetian Voices.* Rider, 1937.

Hamilton, T. Glen. *Intention and Survival.* Regency Press, 1977.

Holms, A. Campbell. *The Facts of Psychic Science and Philosophy.* Kegan Paul, 1925.

Neilsenn, Einer. *Solid Proofs of Survival.* Spiritualist Press, 1950.

Price, Harry. *Rudi Schneider: A Scientific Examination of His Mediumship.* Methuen, 1930.

_____. *Stella C: An Account of Some Original Experiments in Psychical Research.* Hurst & Blackett, 1925.

Rizzini, Jorge. *Otila e a Materlizacion de Uberaba.* Editora Cultural Esperita (Brazil).

Sudre, Rene. *Treatise on Parapsychology.* 1961.

8. Out-of-Body Experiences

Battersby, H.F. Prevost. *Man Outside Himself: The Methods of Astral Projection.* University Books, 1969.

Box, Oliver. *Astral Projection: A Record of Out-of-the-Body Experiences.* University Books, 1962.

Crookall, Robert. *The Mechanisms of Astral Projection.* Darshana International, 1968.

_____. *More Astral Projections.* Aquarian Press, 1964.

_____. *Casebook of Astral Projection.* University Books, 1972.

_____. *The Supreme Adventure.* James Clarke, 1961.

_____. *The Study and Practice of Astral Projection.* Aquarian Press, 1961.

Davis, Black. *Ekstacy: Out-of-the-Body Experiences.* Bobbs-Merrill, 1975.

Green, Celia. *Out-of-the-Body Experiences.* Hamish Hamilton, 1968.

Monroe, Robert A. *Far Journeys*. Doubleday, 1985.
_____. *Journeys Out of the Body*. Anchor Press, 1973.
Smith, Suzy. *The Enigma of Out-of-Body Travel*. New American Library, 1965.
Tart, Charles. "Out-of-the-Body Experiences," in *Psychic Exploration: A Challenge for Science* (E.D. Mitchell and J. White, eds). G.P. Putnam's Sons, 1974.

9. Obsessions and Possessions
Wickland, Carl A., M.D. *Thirty Years Among the Dead*. Newcastle, 1974.

10. Philosophic Speculations Regarding Life After Death
Bailey, Alice A. *Death, The Great Adventure*. Lucis, 1985.
Beard, Paul. *Living On*. George Allen & Unwin, 1980.
Cannon, Alexander, M.D. *The Invisible Influence*. Aquarian Press, 1969.
Croissant, Kay and Dees, Catherine. *Continuum: The Immortality Principle*. Continuum Foundation, 1982.
Fortune, Dion. *Through the Gates of Death*. Aquarian Press, 1968.
Fulton, Robert, et. al. *Death and Dying*. Addison Wesley, 1978.
Grof, Stanislav; Cayce, Hugh Lynn; and Johnson, Raynor C. *The Dimensions of Dying and Rebirth*. A.R.E. Press, 1976.
Grof, Stanislav and Halifax, Joan. *The Human Encounter with Death*. E.P. Dutton, 1975.
Hamilton, Margaret Lillian. *Is Survival A Fact?* Psychic Press, 1969.
Harlow, S. Ralph. *A Life After Death*. McFadden-Bartell, 1968.
Hick, John H. *Death and Eternal Life*. Harper and Row, 1976.
Hyslop, James H. *Life After Death*. E.P. Dutton, 1918.
Koestenbaum, Peter. *Is There an Answer to Death?* Prentice Hall, 1976.
Leichtman, Dr. Robert R. and Japikse, Carl. "The Role Death Plays in Life" in *The Life of Spirit*. Ariel Press, 1983.
Mitford, Jessica. *The American Way of Death*. Simon and Schuster, 1963.
Moody, Raymond A., Jr. *Life After Life*. Bantam, 1976.
Ring, Kenneth. *Life at Death*. Quill, 1980.
Rogo, D. Scott. *Life After Death: The Case for Survival of Bodily Death*. Aquarian Press, 1986.
_____. *Man Does Survive Death*. Citadel Press, 1973.
Shneidman, Edwin S., ed. *Death: Current Perspectives*. Mayfield Publishing, 1976.
Toynbee, A., et. al. *Man's Concern with Death*. McGraw Hill, 1968.
Weatherhead, Leslie D. *Life Begins at Death*. Abingdon Press, 1969.
White, John. *A Practical Guide to Death and Dying*. Theosophical Publishing House, 1980.

11. Reincarnation
Cerminara, Gina. *Many Lives, Many Loves*. Wm. Sloane, 1963.
_____. *Many Mansions*. New American Library, 1950.
Challoner, H.K. *The Wheels of Rebirth*. Theosophical Publishing House, 1969.
Ellis, Edith. *Incarnation: A Plea From the Masters*. C. & R. Anthony, 1936.
Endemann, Carl T. *Voyage Into the Past*. Alta Napa Press, 1981.
Head, Joseph and Cranston, S.L. *Reincarnation: The Phoenix Fire Mystery*. Julian Press, 1977.
Kelsey, Denys and Grant, Joan. *Many Lifetimes*. Pocket Books, 1968.
Leek, Sybil. *Reincarnation, The Second Change*. Bantam, 1975.
Montgomery, Ruth. *Here and Hereafter*. Fawcett, 1968.
Russell, Lao. *The Continuity of Life—Why You Cannot Die!* University of Science and Philosophy, 1972.
Shelley, Violet M., *Reincarnation Unnecessary*. A.R.E. Press, 1979.
Smith, Suzy. *Reincarnation for the Millions*. Dell, 1967.
Stearn, Jess. *The Search for the Girl with the Blue Eyes*. Doubleday, 1968.

Stevenson, Ian. *Twenty Cases Suggestive of Reincarnation*. University Press of Virginia, 1974.

_____. *Xenoglossy: A Review and Report of a Case*. University Press of Virginia, 1974.

Steiger, Brad. *You Will Live Again*. Dell, 1978.

Wambach, Helen. *Reliving Past Lives*. Harper & Row, 1978.

Woodward, Mary Ellen. *Scars of the Soul*. Brindabella Books, 1985.

12. Spirit Photography

Barbanell, Maurice. *He Walks in Two Worlds*. Herbert Jenkins, 1964.

Holzer, Hans. *Psychic Photography*. McGraw Hill, 1969.

13. Light

Leon, Dorothy. *Reality of the Light*. Anchor of Golden Light, 1984.

Ott, John N. *Health and Light*. Pocketbooks, 1974.

Russell, Walter. *Light*. University of Science and Philosophy, 1950.

Tibbs, Hardwin. *The Future of Light*. Watkins Pub., 1981.

14. Spirit Descriptions of Afterlife Experiences

Borgia, Anthony. *Life in the World Unseen*. Transworld.

Brandon, Wilfred. *Love in the Afterlife*. C. & R. Anthony, 1956.

_____. *Open the Door!* C. & R. Anthony, 1935.

_____. *We Knew These Men*. Alfred A. Knopf, 1942.

Burke, Jane R. *The Immutable Law*. E.P. Dutton, 1936.

Conacher, Douglas and Eira. *There is Life After Death*. Howard Baker, 1978.

Cooke, Ivan. *Thy Kingdom Come*. Wright and Brown.

_____. *The Return of Arthur Conan Doyle*. White Eagle, 1963.

Crookall, Robert. *The Supreme Adventure: Analyses of Psychic Communications*. James Clarke, 1961.

Darby and Joan. *Our Unseen Guest*. Borden, 1943.

Findlay, Arthur. *On the Edge of the Etheric*. Psychic Press, 1962.

_____. *Where Two Worlds Meet*. Psychic Press.

Hayes, Patricia and Smith, Marshall. *Extension of Life: Arthur Ford Speaks*. Dimensional Brotherhood Publishing House, 1986.

Homewood, Harry. *Thavis is Here*. Fawcett, 1978.

Leichtman, Dr. Robert R. *From Heaven to Earth*. Ariel Press, 1978-82.

Mandel, Henry A. *Banners of Light*. Vantage Press, 1973.

Randall, Edward C. *The Dead Have Never Died*. George Allen & Unwin, 1927.

Richelieu, Peter. *A Soul's Journey*. Turnstone Press, 1972.

Wetzl, Joseph. *The Bridge Over the River*. Anthroposophic Press, 1974.

White, Stewart Edward. *Across the Unknown*. Ariel Press, 1987.

_____. *The Betty Book*. Ariel Press, 1987.

INDEXES

BY NAME

BY SUBJECTS